from The BUSINESS GAME

BUSTING LOOSE

from The BUSINESS GAME

MIND-BLOWING STRATEGIES FOR
RECREATING YOURSELF, YOUR TEAM, YOUR
CUSTOMERS, YOUR BUSINESS, AND
EVERYTHING IN BETWEEN

ROBERT SCHEINFELD

WILEY

John Wiley & Sons, Inc.

Published by John Wiley & Sons, Inc., Hoboken, New Jersey.

Published simultaneously in Canada.

For general information on our other products and services or for technical support, please contact our Customer Care Department within the United States at (800) 762-2974, outside the United States at (317) 572-3993 or fax (317) 572-4002.

Wiley also publishes its books in a variety of electronic formats. Some content that appears in print may not be available in electronic books. For more information about Wiley products, visit our web site at www.wiley.com.

Library of Congress Cataloging-in-Publication Data

Scheinfeld, Robert.

    Busting loose from the business game : mind-blowing strategies for recreating yourself, your team, your customers, your business, and everything in between / Robert Scheinfeld.

      p. cm.

    Includes index.

    ISBN 978-0-470-45308-7 (cloth)

  1. Creative ability in business. 2. Success in business. 3. Industrial management. I. Title.

HD53.S355 2009

658.4'012–dc22

2009004153

Printed in the United States of America.

10 9 8 7 6 5 4 3 2

CONTENTS

FOREWORD

In the pages that follow, Robert Scheinfeld will be referring to business as a "game." I completely agree with that perspective. I've always found it to be extremely empowering—and freeing— to look at business that way, versus from the many more serious perspectives that are available.

I love playing The Business Game. I always have. In fact, I can remember the first time I became aware of my passion for it. I became a real estate agent when I was just 19, and the intense competition with other agents in my office drove me to learn and excel in sales and marketing. I also loved the fact that I could get paid in direct proportion to my own efforts and nobody could tell me what to do. Basically, I learned at a very young age in business that I must live or die by my own sword.

Much as I love playing The Business Game, I must acknowledge that it's a very difficult game to play well. There are so many moving pieces that must be chosen and aligned; so many forces affecting your bottom line that appear beyond your control; so many sales, marketing, management, and financial strategies that must be developed, refined, and optimized. You know the drill, I'm sure.

I know this from intimate personal experience starting and running four multimillion-dollar businesses myself over the past 22 years, and as the founder of OneCoach, through which I help thousands of small business owners increase their revenues and profits and sustain the growth of their businesses.

Do you love playing The Business Game, too? My guess is you do. Let me ask you these two questions, however:

1. Has your experience of playing The Business Game changed recently?
2. Has your desire (or need) to find a different way of playing reached a fever pitch?

Again, my guess is they have, or you wouldn't have found your way to *this* book.

Let's take a close look at the concept of playing games for a minute. The fascinating thing is that the same game can be played in very different ways.

Take the game of American football as an example. You can play touch football, flag football, arena football, or full-contact football. They're all the same basic game—football—but they're played very differently in each variation on the theme, and the actual experience for the player is quite different, too.

Take the game of baseball as another example. You can play T-ball, softball, or hardball. Again, they're the same basic game, but the rules vary and the actual experience for the player varies widely.

Consider the game of tennis. You can play singles or doubles, and the experience changes in significant ways with each option.

Finally, consider the game of basketball. You can play half-court, full-court, one-on-one, two-on-two, three-on-three, four-on-four, or five-on-five basketball. They're the same basic game again, but the rules are very different and the actual experience of playing is *very* different, too.

None of these games or variations on a theme are better than the others, although we may have our personal preferences for what we enjoy playing or watching. They're just different options, different possibilities we can choose from.

It's the same with The Business Game. The same basic game can be played according to very different rules. The same basic game can be played in very different ways. And the differences in the actual experience for the player can be huge. In this book, Robert Scheinfeld invites you to consider playing The Business Game in a radically different way.

The picture Robert paints for you in the pages that follow may surprise, delight, and excite you in what you instantly recognize as extremely positive ways. It may also shock you, disturb you, or seem unbelievable or even crazy to you. Regardless of what your reaction may be (initially and over time), this book will open your eyes to many new possibilities. It will stretch and challenge you in powerful ways and open new doors of opportunity for you.

If you choose to take action on what you discover here and apply Robert's model over time, you can absolutely experience the following five outcomes:

1. The fun you have playing The Business Game will soar.
2. Your stress level will drop through the floor.
3. You'll see a major transformation in every member of your team, in the vendors who support your efforts, and in their interactions with each other.
4. The "take it to the bank" results you ultimately produce will expand in dramatic and unexpected ways.
5. Your personal life will be affected and expand, too—relationships, energy level, health and wellness, and (perhaps most importantly) your general experience of joy, peace, and ease in your life.

I know Robert well. Prior to making the discoveries and breakthroughs he describes in this book, I considered him to be one of the brightest, most skilled, and most innovative entrepreneurs I've ever known. Beyond that, it has been extraordinary to watch how things have expanded and transformed for him since he busted loose from the traditional way of playing The Business Game and started playing what he calls "The New Business Game."

As you prepare to turn the page and read this book, I invite you to take a deep breath, buckle your seat belt, and get ready for a wild ride that will change you forever!

—John Assaraf
New York Times best-selling author of *The Answer*
www.OneCoach.com
www.JohnAssaraf.com

INTRODUCTION

First Series: To destroy, mercilessly, without any compromises whatsoever, in the mentation and feelings of the reader, the beliefs and views, by centuries rooted in him, about everything in the world.

Second Series: To acquaint the reader with the material required for a new creation and to prove the soundness and good quality of it.

Third Series: To assist the arising, in the mentation and in the feelings of the reader, of a veritable, nonfantastic representation not of that illusory world which he now perceives, but of the world existing in reality.[1]

—G. I. Gurdjieff, speaking of his intent for his "All and Everything" book series

When I was in my early thirties, living in a city whose name shall remain anonymous, I bought a house from a bank that had foreclosed on the owner. That owner had been a

---

[1]G. I. Gurdjieff, *Life Is Real Only Then, When "I Am"* (New York: Dutton, 1981), front matter.

famous, high-flying, big-money-earning quarterback for the professional football team in that city. He'd gone bankrupt. When I had moved into the house and gotten to know the neighbors, they told me stories about how the quarterback had been so physically beaten up by the game of football and in so much pain that on some mornings he couldn't walk down the stairs from his second-floor bedroom and had to stay in bed all day.

The quarterback played football—a game he loved—as a child, in high school, in college, then as a professional. He had lots of fun, won championships, received many honors, and earned a lot of money. But there was a *huge* price to pay later in his life in the form of physical pain and limitation. Perhaps he anticipated that consequence and it came as no surprise, but the odds are that as he played all those years he didn't consciously think about the price he might one day pay. He was just focused on playing!

If you're like me, you love playing The Business Game, whether you own your own business or you're an employee. It challenges, excites, and exhilarates you at a very deep level. Playing The Business Game may even be one of the things you enjoy most in life. But if you're like I used to be, and like the quarterback I just described, a big price will always be paid—a price you can see and feel—*if you play the way you were taught*. I call this "The Visible Price."

Maybe you're paying The Visible Price right now and you're already aware of it. Maybe you've been paying it for many years, also aware of it. Maybe you'll pay The Visible Price later on in a way that will come as a surprise to you. The Visible Price may be an emotional one, in the form of negative emotions like burnout, stress, fear, anger, or frustration. The Visible Price may be a physical one, in the form of exhaustion, pain in your body, illness, or disease. The Visible Price may be paid in the form of limited free time, troubled relationships, or constantly repeating up-and-down or success/failure patterns in your business affairs (which was a biggie for me before I busted loose).

The possibilities for when, where, and how you'll pay *your* Visible Price are unlimited, but The Visible Price *will be paid* and will continue to be paid, in some way, shape, or form, if you continue playing The Business Game in the way you were taught and the way you've been playing until now (which I call "The Big Lie" and discuss in Chapter 1).

What I just shared comes as no surprise to you, I'm sure. Numerous experts, authors, speakers, consultants, and coaches have discussed the most common prices being paid for playing The Business Game, the need for balance, reducing stress, and playing The Business Game differently. Many formulas, techniques, and strategies have been offered to remedy the situation, but few, if any, work in an ultimate sense—for reasons you'll soon see.

I must also share that there's a price to be paid for playing The Business Game the old way that you *can't* see or feel. I call it "The Invisible Price," and the impact of paying The Invisible Price in your life, as I'll explain in the pages that follow, is even larger than that of the Visible Price you can see and feel and may already be experiencing, yet it's rarely discussed.

You originally began playing The Business Game for specific reasons. You started with very specific goals. I divide those goals into two types that I'll discuss in greater detail in the pages that follow:

1. *True Goals*: These are the goals, generally beneath your conscious awareness and hidden from view, that if achieved would absolutely provide consistent and deep, deep, deep levels of satisfaction, fulfillment, joy, and pleasure for you. I refer to True Goals as what you *really* want. True Goals do not change as you and your circumstances change. They're a constant because they relate to who you *really* are, not who you think you are.

2. *Hypnotic Goals*: These are the goals, always conscious, that are very seductive and get a lot of your attention. You work very hard to achieve them, thinking that if you did, your life would change and improve in major ways. Common examples of Hypnotic Goals are increases in sales, profits, or personal income, and new homes or cars. I refer to Hypnotic Goals as

what you *think* you want. Hypnotic Goals often change as you and your circumstances change. True Goals occasionally find their way into your conscious awareness and *seem* like Hypnotic Goals, but from my experience it's rare for this to happen.

No matter what your personal story is, I can virtually guarantee that three things are True for you:

1. You haven't achieved *many* of your Hypnotic Goals yet, despite investing lots of time, money, and energy in pursuit of them.

2. When you have achieved Hypnotic Goals, some if not all of them didn't provide the ultimate satisfaction, joy, and pleasure you thought they would—or those feelings didn't last long if you did experience them.

3. You haven't achieved many (if any) of your True Goals.

In this Introduction and in Chapter 1 that follows, I'm intentionally going to be aggressive and heavy-handed in the way I paint a picture of the dark side of playing The Business Game. As I paint that picture, I'm aware that it might stimulate feelings of discomfort or resistance within you. I'm aware that you might say something like this to yourself in response: "Sure, The Business Game is tough, but my story doesn't match your picture. My picture isn't *that* bleak or depressing!" If I do trigger thoughts or feelings like that within you (and I may not), I ask your indulgence a while longer because I'll document and validate *all* my claims in the pages that follow.

This book is not designed to help you play the *old* Business Game better, faster, or more efficiently.

It's not designed to support you in proactively pursuing the Hypnotic Goals of growing your business, income, and wealth, living and working in more luxurious surroundings, boosting your ego or reputation, and so on.

I'm not going to offer you any advice in this book on sales, marketing, management, leadership, finance, or any of the subsets within those Business Game topics.

As the title suggests, this book is designed to support you in busting loose from the old Business Game—completely—and beginning to play an entirely new game that will amaze and delight you.

At this point, you might be wondering, "What does it mean to 'bust loose' from The Business Game?" I'll be discussing the answer to that question in great detail later in the book. For now, however, let me sketch out the following key points—some or all of which may be extremely difficult for you to accept as being possible at this point on our journey together. Busting loose from The Business Game means:

- Living in an inner space that's joyful, exciting, peaceful, and serene—no matter what's going on around you, what happens in your business or elsewhere in the world, or what anyone else says or does.

- Playing The Business Game for the sheer pleasure of playing, without any specific, conscious agenda, goals, or attachment to producing specific results—yet creating extraordinary results anyway, financial and otherwise.

- Having a strong, positive impact on your customers and the world at large through the distribution of your products and services—but again, without any effort, specific intent, goal, or agenda to do so.

- Doing *only* what you love to do, what *really* floats your boat—all day, every day—as part of playing The Business Game, and leaving everything else up to someone else (or eliminating the need for it entirely).

- Working only when you want to, and having more free time and freedom than you can possibly imagine right now, while still effectively playing your chosen role in your business—no matter how large or small the business may be.

- Playing The Business Game while being completely unaffected by and unconcerned about the economy, the stock market, the tax authority, gas prices, competitors, employee turnover, industry trends, technological innovations, lawsuits, or other factors that now make you feel vulnerable.
- Having support teams (employees, partners, board members, vendors, stockholders, investors, etc.) effortlessly and joyously unite, work together, motivate themselves, and hold themselves accountable for high levels of performance.
- Having amazing things come to you in joyful, fun, surprising, and effortless ways, instead of you having to go get them, work hard, or push, push, push to make things happen.
- And so much more, all of which I'll be sharing with you in the pages that follow.

An amazing journey led to me busting loose from The Business Game. That journey began with a conversation I had with my grandfather, Aaron Scheinfeld ("Gramps," as I called him) when I was a kid. Gramps was amazingly talented, a Renaissance man. Among his many extraordinary skills and accomplishments, two stand out most in my mind:

1. He turned a simple idea into one of the world's largest and most successful international businesses—Manpower, Inc.— now a Fortune 150 company and the world's largest temporary help service with sales in excess of $18 billion. That global success made possible levels of financial abundance and freedom most people (even extremely successful people) would drool over. I'll be telling you more about him in the pages that follow.
2. He was the happiest person I've ever known. I can still see and feel his joyfulness in my mind, especially when he played the piano or ukulele and sang or told silly stories.

Aaron Scheinfeld

When I was 12 years old, in response to my relentless nagging about the secret of his success, Gramps started chatting with me about a very unusual philosophy, a mind-set and set of strategies related to what he called "power in the invisible world" that he claimed were the true source of *all* his business success, happiness, and lifestyle. I discussed some of what he shared with me (and what I discovered in the search that followed) in my previous books, *The 11th Element* (John Wiley & Sons, 2003) and *Busting Loose from The Money Game* (John Wiley & Sons, 2006).

Gramps died shortly after our chats began, before he could complete mentoring me. What he shared ultimately amounted to a gigantic tease that created within me an obsession to find and map out the invisible power sources he told me about. I spent 34 years following that obsession, what I now call "The Treasure Hunt of the Century." As I searched for the treasure, finally found it, and busted loose from The Business Game myself, I metaphorically stumbled into quicksand, had flat tires, ran out of gas, saw my radiator overheat, drove down numerous dead ends, careened off cliffs, and got lost, confused, and extremely frustrated by the many twists and turns in the road.

Along the way, I had tremendous success playing the old Business Game, starting and building extremely profitable multimillion-dollar businesses on and off the Internet, for myself and others. One of my greatest achievements playing the old Business Game was building and operating a marketing machine that propelled Blue Ocean Software from $1 million to $44 million in sales in less than four years, resulting in the company being named three times to *Inc.* magazine's "Inc. 500" list. That tremendous growth, accompanied by outrageous profitability during the Internet boom and the "tech wreck" bust, led to Blue Ocean being acquired by software giant Intuit for $177 million in cash.

Prior to busting loose from The Business Game, I continually repeated an up-down, boom-bust cycle that caused me to feel a great deal of frustration and anger. When I crashed and burned the first few times, the numbers were smaller and I was single. Losing everything was excruciatingly painful, but I've always had a high threshold for pain. As I got older and the cycle continued, the numbers grew larger.

Eventually, the up-down cycle moved into millions of dollars, then multiple millions of dollars, and at that point, I had a wife and two kids. We'd created a home and lifestyle we all loved and thrived on. If I crashed and burned again under those circumstances, I knew the pain would be unbearable for me because I'd have to watch my family lose everything, too. Despite my historical high threshold for pain, I knew I couldn't survive that experience and I became desperate to find a way to avoid it.

By the way, as a brief aside, you may find it interesting to know that my father (Aaron's son) traveled a similar path. Despite tremendous early success with Manpower, he experienced many ups and downs in business and in life, including two volatile marriages that ended in divorce, and had so much repressed frustration that he struggled with cluster headaches, which are even worse than migraines. My bedroom shared a wall with his, and I was haunted for years by how it sounded—and felt—to hear him scream in pain when he got one of those headaches.

Several times, when I was in an up cycle, I thought I'd finally uncovered the last missing puzzle pieces that would enable me to tap the invisible sources of power Gramps told me about. At those times, I honestly thought I was seeing a clear and complete big picture about how to bust loose from The Business Game, but then the down cycle would come again and I'd have to go back to the drawing board, as the old saying goes.

As you'll discover in the pages that follow, and as you may already know from your own journey and studies, I've always had a knowing that we each have an expanded aspect of our Consciousness that partners with us to create our day-to-day life and experiences. I'll be discussing that part of you in great detail in the pages that follow. That expanded aspect is generally called "Higher Self" in the literature I'm familiar with, but there are numerous other labels. I now refer to it as "Expanded Self" or "The Real You," as you'll soon see.

When it felt like I might crash and burn again with my wife and family at the millions-of-dollars level, I got angrier than I'd ever been in my life—*at my Expanded Self*. "Look," I said to him, my eyes tilted up toward the sky, "I've been searching since I was a kid. I've worked my ass off to do the work you asked me to do in assembling the puzzle pieces you gave me. I've paid my dues. Obviously, there's something I'm still missing here. So, either you show it to me—*now*—or get me the hell out of here, because I won't run this up-down, up-down cycle anymore."

Now, before I continue, I must share that getting angry at expanded aspects of your Consciousness isn't a magic formula guaranteed to get results. I know that because I'd gotten angry plenty of times before along my journey and nothing moved as a result. But this time, there was tremendous movement. I began exploring again, absolutely committed to finding the missing pieces to the puzzle. And lo and behold, eight months later, I found them.

Despite all those challenges and the many times I felt like giving up, I persevered and ultimately busted loose from The Business Game myself. I'll be giving you a lot of detail on what that meant and how that looked for me, and others, in later chapters (and in the special downloadable bonus chapters described in Chapter 16). Because I felt it to be my mission in life and because of my passion for playing what I call "The Teaching Game," I used my personal experiences to create a map and tool kit others could use to bust loose from The Business Game themselves. In the pages of this book, I'll be sharing them with you.

I want to make two things crystal clear at this point:

1. I used the very same mind-set, map, tool kit, and navigation support you'll discover in this book to bust loose from The Business Game myself—over time. There was nothing else.

2. There's nothing special or unique about me. Anyone who uses the mind-set, map, tool kit, and navigation support offered in this book can bust loose from The Business Game.

I have a few more important thoughts to share, and then we'll officially begin our journey together. First, to support you in busting loose from The Business Game and beginning to play an entirely New Business Game, I have to support you in taking a quantum leap from where you are now and where you have been. I have to fry your circuits and dynamite the lies and illusions you've thought to be True most or all of your life, then support you in rebuilding everything in new ways. Therefore, as you read the pages that follow, especially parts of the first eight chapters, you may feel like you've entered *The Twilight Zone* or a science fiction movie.

Instead of discussing topics like sales, marketing, management, leadership, finance, team building, motivation, and productivity, I'm going to be discussing topics like Truth, Consciousness, power, abundance, quantum physics, lies, and illusions. If you want to bust loose from the old Business Game, that's where you *must* go. If you want to bust loose from the old Business Game, you must understand the True Source of everything that ultimately happens in your business (and your personal life, for that matter).

The popular saying "thinking outside the box" refers to thinking in creative and innovative ways. I'm fond of calling what you're about to discover "dynamiting the box." Why? Because it's that different from what is typically taught about business success—even the most creative and innovative of teachings. As a result, as you read, depending on your familiarity with such concepts, you may have thoughts like these:

- "This guy is nuts!"
- "What does this have to do with business?"
- "He can't be serious!"
- "This isn't what I expected when I bought this book!"
- "No way!"

Or my personal favorite:

- "Bullshit!"

You may chuckle, but please take these words seriously because in a few minutes (if you continue reading right now), thoughts like that *may* come up for you, and if they do, I don't want them to distract you or delay your progress.

You may feel at times overwhelmed, disoriented, skeptical, angry, or uncomfortable. That's to be expected. You can't bust loose from The Business Game without a radical shift in your perceptions about yourself, other people, the world, and the beliefs, ideas, and strategies you relied on previously (The Big Lie)—and radical shifts can be extremely uncomfortable!

However, if you're like most people I speak with about this work, no matter how much resistance you may feel from one part of yourself, another part will be whispering to you, "That's True . . . and somehow I've always known it." No matter how far out there what I'll be sharing may seem at first (or it may not, depending on your background), the journey we're going to take together and the ultimate destination you'll reach after taking it are very real—and you *can* "get there from here."

If you follow the action steps I give you at the end of the book and you still want or need proof, your own experiences will provide all the proof you want of the Truthfulness and validity of what I share. This is a key point I'll be discussing in great detail in later chapters.

Beyond this Introduction, the book has six primary sections with critical support material in between:

1. *The Big Lie*: A summary of what you were taught to be true about The Business Game—lies about rules, regulations, and how playing the game is supposed to work; lies about sales, marketing, management, leadership, and finance; lies about what it takes to succeed, and so on.

2. *The Big Truth*: To begin bursting the bubble of The Big Lie and open a gateway you can leap through to ultimately bust loose, there are several philosophical concepts you must have in your conscious awareness. I call those concepts "The Big Truth."

3. *Science*: Recent breakthroughs in science that document and validate even the wildest of The Big Truth philosophical concepts I share with you.

4. *Practical tools*: Four simple, easy-to-use tools you'll apply on a daily basis to bust yourself loose once you leap through the gateway I open for you.

5. *Navigation support*: Once you leap through the gateway, you'll find yourself in a world that feels alien to you. I therefore provide maps and other forms of support to help you get comfortable and navigate effectively in that new world.

6. *The invitation*: This is an invitation for you at the end of the book to apply what you discover here, prove its validity and power to yourself, and open up to a new and radically different way of life and playing The New Business Game.

As you'll soon see, I don't discuss the practical tools until Chapter 11. Why did I design the book that way? My goal is to support you in busting loose from The Business Game. The tools are what get you there. However, for the action steps within each of the tools to make sense to you, and for you to be truly empowered to use them with maximum effectiveness, a strong foundation must first be laid. I lay that foundation in Chapters 1 to 10.

You may feel impatient for me to get to the meat of the practical aspects of the book from time to time. If that happens, please remind yourself we're ultimately headed for extremely practical application in your life and business. I promise you that when we get there, you'll understand why I structured the book this way, and you'll be extremely appreciative of the foundation I laid for you in advance.

One more key point before we move on: When reading books, some people start at the beginning and read to the end, sequentially. Others skip ahead, jump around, skim parts, dip down, and read other parts. My intent is to support you in busting loose from The Business Game. To do that, I must give you specific puzzle pieces in a specific order and support you in assembling them in a specific way. If you follow my lead, a magnificent big picture will pop into view and you *will* bust loose. If you don't follow my lead, you may be left with a bunch of funny-looking pieces of cardboard sitting on a table—and you might short-circuit your ability to bust loose.

In short, please be patient, read the chapters sequentially at the pace you feel inspired to move, trust me, and follow my lead. I know how to support you in busting loose from The Business Game. I *can* help you do it, but only if you follow the precise map I'm in a unique position to share with you.

You must also understand from the start that I can't actually bust you loose through the pages of this book alone. I can only show you the way, open the gateway into a new world, help you jump through that gateway, and show you what to do in the new world you find on the other side.

To actually bust loose, there's work *you* must do. I'll show you exactly what to do, when, and how. I'll offer you tremendous support for your journey, but it is a journey and it will take time to reach the ultimate destination. It will also require tremendous commitment, patience, persistence, and discipline on your part to arrive there. But, man oh man, is it ever worth it, no matter how long it takes or how hard the work seems!

If you make the commitment and do the work, the rewards you'll receive are beyond anything you can possibly imagine right now. I can say that without the slightest doubt.

Before we continue, I want to share a few style and logistical details about the way I'm writing this book. First, everything I share in this book applies whether you own your own business or are an employee, although some of the dynamics and stories vary. To keep the writing simple, I will be using the term *your business* to refer to both situations.

Second, as you'll see, there is a lot of talk in the book about Truth and lies or illusions masquerading as Truth. To distinguish Truth from lies and illusions, I've chosen to capitalize certain words and phrases you may not be used to seeing capitalized. In addition, I will capitalize certain other phrases, like The Human Game or The Business Game or The New Business Game or Consciousness to highlight new names or labels I've created to describe aspects of The Truth as I see it. You'll get used to this, but I just wanted to make it clear from the beginning.

Third, throughout the book, I refer to the game of football. I want you to know in advance that each time I do, I'm referring to the game of American football, not soccer.

As I mentioned, this book goes beyond just "thinking outside the box" to support you in completely "dynamiting the box." Toward that goal, I've just lit the fuse and it's starting to burn. To begin your extraordinary journey and experience the "explosion" that busts you loose, simply turn the page to begin Chapter 1.

Note to readers who have already experienced the Busting Loose from The Money Game *book, a live Phase 2 event, a Phase 2 Home Transformational System, or another Phase 2 work: This book had to be written as a stand-alone creation. Therefore, in various sections, you'll see material that will be a review for you. It will be a very supportive and expansive review, with many delightful surprises. Then, in other sections, you'll find many new forms of support and inspiration that I'm certain you'll appreciate greatly.*

The Big Lie

I would sooner have you hate me for telling you the truth than adore me for telling you lies.[1]
—*Pietro Aretino, Italian Author, Playwright, Poet, and Satirist*

Right now, billions of people throughout the world are playing The Business Game and doing their best to win. Some play as employees, some as owners, and others at various levels in between. Every month, thousands of newbie entrepreneurs start their own small businesses—on and off the Internet—with dreams of success, abundance, and freedom flowing from their efforts. The odds are that you're one of those people.

As the players begin playing The Business Game, they're taught the official rules and regulations and do their best to follow them (more about this in a minute). They're then guided to huge

---

[1] Pietro Aretino, in *Bits & Pieces* (Chicago: Ragan Communications, 2004).

storehouses of advice, inside and outside of colleges and universities, within what I call "The Five Power Centers of Business"—sales, marketing, management, leadership, and finance—designed to help them succeed. Armed with the rules, regulations, and an always-expanding supply of theories, tools, techniques, and strategies, the players set off like warriors on the road to success and victory. The odds are that this describes you, too, either now or years ago when you first started playing The Business Game.

Yet despite the best of intentions, following the best of the best advice and investing tremendous amounts of time, energy, and money, every single player will ultimately fail to win The Business Game. Regardless of whether you're aware of it consciously, whether you want to admit it, or whether you've reached that place in playing The Business Game yet, this applies to you, too—as you'll soon see.

What do I mean by "fail to win The Business Game"? Here's a quick summary of the seven most common failure scenarios:

1. As owners, they fail in the traditional business sense, meaning closing their doors and going out of business.

2. As owners, they keep their doors open, but despite huge investments of time, energy, and effort, they experience tremendous struggle and stress and are barely able to squeeze out a decent living from the business, thus experiencing severe limits and restrictions.

3. As owners, they succeed in the traditional business sense, in a small, big, or *huge* way, meaning creating a profitable business, making a good living, building wealth, and having a comfortable or even opulent lifestyle, but paying a huge Visible Price for their success in the form of unhappiness, stress, anxiety, pain, disillusionment, health issues, relationship issues, lack of free time, and so on.

4. As employees, they're limited, restricted, and frustrated by job conditions controlled by others and never feel properly rewarded for their efforts or contributions to the company.

5. As employees, they give generously of their time, energy, and effort, perhaps over years or decades, only to be fired or demoted when new management steps in, downsized during tough times, passed over for promotions by people they feel are less qualified, and so on.

6. Both owners and employees may be compelled by internal or external forces to invest huge amounts of time doing things they don't like to do, tasks that aren't fun for them, activities that may even be painful, and so on.

7. As owners and employees, they'll work their butts off and create one degree of success or another, only to find it wiped out or compromised by fluctuations in the economy or stock market, shifts in industry trends, new technological innovations, a bold new assault from a competitor, and so on.

On and on it goes, with variations on the same basic themes of "It'll be different for me" or "It'll be different this time" being the familiar battle cry as such patterns repeat themselves endlessly through time. (I have tons of intimate experience with this myself).

Finally, as we'll be discussing in the chapters that follow, even if a player of The Business Game escapes one or more of the scenarios just listed, he or she will still pay a huge Invisible Price for playing it the old way.

I'm fond of using the metaphor of dog racing to describe the dynamics involved in playing The Business Game the old way. In each race, the dogs try as hard as they can to catch a mechanical rabbit, but they never catch it. It's always just out of reach. Why don't the dogs ever catch the rabbit at the track? Because the sport was designed, *intentionally*, so the dogs would forever be motivated to chase the rabbit but never actually catch it.

To continue the metaphor, the dogs may train hard, have the best diets in the world, get stronger and stronger, become faster and faster, win many races, earn lots of money for their owners (and for the people who place bets), live in fancier kennels, and wear fancier outfits on the track, but the bottom line is the dogs are still on the track and they're still racing to catch rabbits they'll *never* catch.

While it may shock and disturb you, and you may find it hard to accept—at first—the same thing is true for players of The Business Game. As we grow up, we're taught the rules and regulations for playing The Business Game. We're told we can win The Business Game. We're told about the many rabbits we can catch if we win. So, we get on the track and start chasing our rabbits, metaphorically, and once we do that, just like the dogs, we end up stuck on the track, going around and around in endless circles, running, running, running, but *never* catching our rabbits—no matter how fast, strong, rich, skilled, or powerful we get.

We get stuck in that endless chasing-but-not-catching-the-rabbit loop because The Business Game was designed with that specific outcome in mind—for reasons I'll be showing you in the pages that follow. That's a bold claim, I know, but it's a claim I'm prepared to fully document and validate.

Now I'd like to go into more detail about the rules and regulations you were given for playing The Business Game and the beliefs that naturally flowed out from them into your conscious awareness. I call that entire package "The Big Lie."

First, let's chat about games. If you're like most of the people I speak with, you may not currently look at business as a game. When I speak with people and ask them about it, many say something like this to me: "Business is definitely *not* a game. It's a serious endeavor, and the stakes are very high."

The first step in The Busting Loose Process is to really understand that everything within the business dynamic—sales, marketing, leadership, management, information technology (IT), human resources, expenses, invoices, accounts receivable, accounts payable, profits, competition, the economy, the stock market, and so on—is part of an amazing, elaborate, gigantic, unique, and complex game that was created with specific goals in mind. Some of The Truth of this you already get, but additional layers and insights will be added in the next chapter.

If you take a close look, most games have rules, regulations, and a clear structure. Everyone who chooses to play a game agrees to follow the rules and regulations and observe that game's structure. This is required to make the game work.

For example, American football is played with a leather ball that's shaped, sized, and constructed to meet rigid specifications. The playing field is 100 yards long. You play four quarters lasting 15 minutes each. A touchdown is worth six points, kicking the ball through the goalposts after a touchdown is worth one point, a field goal is worth three points, and a safety is worth two points. A first down is 10 yards. You may only have a certain number of players on the field at any given time, and they must each play a specific position. There are rules about what players can and cannot do on the field, and if those rules are broken, the offending team is penalized. The team with the most points at the end of the four quarters (or overtime if the score is tied at the end of regulation time) wins the game.

Baseball is another example. It is played on a field that is a certain shape and size that's called a diamond. Only nine players per team are allowed on the diamond during play, and, like football, each player has a specific position. The game is played with bats, balls, and gloves that meet precise specifications. There are nine innings during which each team is allowed three outs. Batters get four balls or three strikes. The pitcher stands on an elevated mound that is a specific distance from home plate where the batter stands. The bases are specific distances from each other. When a player touches home plate after touching each of the other bases, he scores a run worth one point. The team with the most runs at the end of nine innings (or extra innings if the teams are tied) wins the game.

Golf is our final example. The golfer plays on a course. There are a certain number of holes, greens, and fairways on the course, along with (typically) roughs, sand traps, and water hazards. The player uses clubs with L-shaped metal ends to hit precisely constructed balls into small holes. There are specific rules as to what players can and cannot do while playing, and if the rules are broken, the player is penalized. The player with the lowest number of strokes at the end of the round wins.

If you take a close and objective look at football, baseball, and golf, you see that the rules, regulations, and structures appear completely arbitrary and don't make much sense. Consider this:

- *Football.* Throw a piece of leather filled with air from one person to another or run while holding a piece of leather filled with air as you try to cross a white line and score points. Or try to kick the piece of leather filled with air through two metal posts to score points.

- *Baseball.* Use a wooden stick to try to hit a round piece of leather-wrapped rubber that's coming at you at high speed. Then, if you hit it and no other player catches it with a big piece of leather wrapped around his or her hand, you run around trying to touch three square pieces of cloth placed on the ground before touching a final piece of rubber to earn a run.

- *Golf.* Try to hit a small spherical piece of plastic-wrapped rubber with an L-shaped piece of metal to get the spherical piece into a tiny, shallow hole hundreds of yards away with the fewest possible hits or strokes.

You see what appears to be the same sort of arbitrariness if you look at the rules, regulations, and structures of other popular games—bridge, Monopoly, pool, chess, checkers, blackjack, and so on.

You could easily ask yourself, "How did anyone ever think up such weird games with such odd rules, regulations, and structures?" In fact, if aliens visiting from another planet were to watch our games purely objectively, without any education about them, they might think we were all crazy for playing them! Although the rules, regulations, and structures appear arbitrary on initial examination, hidden from view are the intelligence, plan, and intent used to create them—and the joy that comes from the playing.

Players rarely question the origins of the games they play, or the arbitrary nature of the rules, regulations, and structures. They begin playing games that were invented long ago, and do exactly what they're told by the powers that be.

The same is true of The Business Game. When examined closely and objectively, the rules, regulations, and structure of The Business Game appear arbitrary and don't make much sense either, as you'll soon see. However, in later chapters in this book, you'll see there's an intelligence, plan, and intent behind the design of The Business Game, too, and as I said, when you find out what it is, it'll rock your world. It will also open the door to busting loose from The Business Game.

As we pass a certain age growing up, we become players in a Business Game that was set into motion long ago. Like athletes and other game players, we never question what we're taught about playing The Business Game. We just accept the rules, regulations, and structure we're taught and play as if it were all etched in stone and nonnegotiable.

Here are five of the primary rules we've been taught are real and etched in stone for playing The Business Game. There are actually dozens of other rules, but the following are the ones we're most familiar with and the ones that do the most damage, as you'll soon see:

1. You have a limited supply of money to play with (capital).
2. You have income (money flowing in).
3. You have expenses (money flowing out).
4. Your income must exceed your expenses (resulting in profits) or you lose the game.
5. You must maximize, grow, and sustain profits to win.

These rules seem obvious, don't they? There's not much to challenge or disagree with, right?

Wrong, as you'll soon see!

There are numerous rules, regulations, and so-called magic formulas for success beneath the five basic rules in terms of how you're supposed to manage capital, generate income, reduce expenses, and grow profits. And there are boatloads of strategies for:

- Increasing sales.
- Improving marketing.
- Managing cash flow.
- Hiring, firing, motivating, and compensating employees.
- Minimizing employee turnover.
- Increasing employee morale, productivity, and efficiency.
- Effective time management.

In support of The Big Lie driving The Business Game, here are just a few common beliefs that have also been accepted as True:

- The tax authority is your enemy (to one degree or another).
- Your competition is your enemy (to one degree or another).
- You're vulnerable to the state of the international economy (boom times, recessions, and depressions).
- You're vulnerable to movements within the international stock and financial markets.
- Your freedom to make decisions and act is limited by bosses, stockholders, partners, board members, and investors.
- You're always vulnerable to new products, services, and technologies that can hurt your business (or job) or even make it obsolete in the blink of an eye.
- "Keep your friends close and your enemies closer."—Sun-tzu, *The Art of War*

All of these beliefs are what I call "power outside beliefs"—the significance of which you'll soon understand. Like the five basic rules, they all seem to be True and an accurate description of the way it is. I'm here to tell you, however, that *none* of the rules, regulations, or beliefs I just shared, and the many subset rules, regulations, and beliefs that flow from them, are True. Not one. They're all completely made up, as are the rules of all games. You just accepted them as True and accurate on blind faith. You now have the opportunity to change that. You now have the opportunity to bust loose from the old Business Game and begin playing a New Business Game.

Here are two important points I want to repeat and then discuss in greater detail:

1. You can't *win* The Business Game.
2. The Business Game was specifically designed to create utter and total failure.

You can't win The Business Game because:

- *There's no clear definition of winning.* How do you know if you've won The Business Game? Did you ever ask yourself that question? Do you win when your business turns profitable? When you surpass a specific sales or profit goal you set for yourself? When you cash out through selling some or all of the business or go public? From my experience, while many people have financial goals they've set for themselves, few people have clear definitions of what winning The Business Game actually means. They just play with some sort of vague "I'm winning if I'm making money" sort of thought process. If you don't know what winning means to you, how can you possibly win or know when you've won? You can't!

- *Your money and success are notoriously unstable and always at risk.* No matter how much money you pile up in your business accounts, or appear to pile up in the value of your stock or stock options at any specific moment in time, it is always at risk. You can lose all or huge chunks of it through poor management, overspending, a stock market crash, bad investments, failed marketing campaigns, embezzlement, lawsuits, tough times, outright business failure, and so on. No matter how strong sales or profits are, how motivated your team is, or how efficiently your organization is running, history shows it can change on a dime and often without advance warning.

The stronger the numbers and whatever other benchmarks you judge your efficiency by, the greater the illusion of security. But the reality is that the stability of your business and the safety of your cash and other assets are never truly certain, no matter how much you have or what you do with it. Again, history is filled with stories of individuals and businesses that were once riding high, once seemed invincible, but later crashed and burned.

- *There's no official ending point.* When does The Business Game end? When you reach some milestone you set for yourself? That doesn't work, because even though you may temporarily reach or pass such a milestone, your cash, assets, and stability are always at risk, so you could slip backward and lose what you've created or accumulated. Does The Business Game end when you retire or cash out? Maybe, but your retirement income, cash, and assets are still at risk, so it hasn't really ended. When you die? Well, maybe The Business Game ends at that point, but what good does winning do for you then?

  If there's no official ending point for the game, how can you possibly know if or when you've won? Can you say you've won a football game if you're ahead at the end of the third quarter? Can you say you've won a baseball game if you're ahead at the end of the seventh inning? Can you say you've won an 18-hole golf tournament if you have the fewest strokes after 12 holes? No!

- *You can't completely control the other people involved.* The Business Game is played with other people that we call customers and clients, partners, employees, stockholders, board members, vendors, accountants, bankers, and so on. In a perfect world, to ensure your long-term business success, you'd be able to get all these people to do exactly what you want them to do, when and how you want them to do it, but since they're separate from you and have independent decision-making ability, that will never happen—no matter how good you are at communicating, motivating, compensating, selling, marketing, and negotiating. Other people can always, therefore, be a wild card or fly in the ointment.

- *There's always another level of success or efficiency above yours.* With only a few exceptions, there's a trap built into The Business Game that many players fall into at one point or another. The trap gets sprung when a company or player at a specific level of success gets compared to another company or player that appears to be doing better, which diminishes their perception of their own achievements.

  For example, an owner, a partner, or an employee of a company with sales of X and profits of Y discovers that a competitor has sales of 2X and profits of 2Y. Or an owner, a partner, or an employee who was very happy earning X a year discovers that another employee at an equal level or his or her counterpart at a competitor is earning 2X, has more stock options, and so on. Or an executive who was traveling first class discovers that a friend or competitor just got a private jet. You get the idea. In these sorts of scenarios, even though you can say that a player is winning, in some respect, they won't feel like they are.

- *There's always a Visible Price and an Invisible Price to pay.* You also can't win The Business Game because, even if you seem to escape some or all of the "can't win" scenarios just described (or the many other variations on those themes I didn't mention), playing the game according to the traditional rules and regulations almost always leads to some form of stress, pressure, dissatisfaction, pain, or loss—especially when it comes to free time, health, and relationships. I'm sure you've experienced this yourself, or seen or known someone who succeeded in having a very successful company or career but ended up:

—Struggling with various illnesses, including serious ones.

—Lonely.

—Alienated from friends, family, and romantic partners.

—Dying young.

—Getting migraine headaches.

—An emotional basket case.

—Living in the lap of luxury but feeling empty inside and wondering, "Is this all there is?"

—On and on.

Imagine playing or watching any other game with rules, regulations, and a structure like I just described for The Business Game. Imagine playing or watching a game where there's no way to know who's winning, there's no official ending point, you can influence but never control your fellow players, no matter how good you get there are always other teams or players better than you, and you ultimately end up losing (due to the Visible and Invisible Prices you had to pay) even if you think you're winning.

Would anyone want to play or watch a game like that? No way! For the players, it would be an absolute nightmare. No one would volunteer to play a game like that. And no one would show up to watch, either. What would be the point?

Despite all of this, billions of people show up every day to play The Business Game, blinded to The Truth about what's really going on. Many of those people—perhaps you, too—believe they're winning The Business Game (or will one day), believe they've already won, or believe other people they see around them or in the media have won—but it's all an illusion. In Chapter 9, I reveal an even bigger reason why you can't win The Business Game. But first I have to provide you with a few more foundational pieces of the puzzle.

What you were never told is that The Business Game is very different from the other games we play. When it comes to The Business Game, nothing is etched in stone and absolutely *everything* is negotiable. You don't need to accept the traditional rules, regulations, structures, and beliefs associated with The Business Game. You don't need to be vulnerable to the forces and influences appearing to be outside of you and beyond your control. You actually have an alternative!

Since there's no way to win The Business Game, you have only two choices:

1. Continue playing according to the traditional rules, regulations, structures, and associated beliefs, knowing you'll lose and pay a big Visible and/or Invisible Price, no matter what you do.
2. Bust loose from the old Business Game entirely, create a New Business Game for yourself, choose your own rules and regulations, and transform your relationship with business *forever*.

However crazy or pie-in-the-sky this might sound to you, I guarantee that once you finish this book you'll be empowered to take the second option and bust loose from The Business Game entirely.

Returning to the dog racing metaphor, this book will support you in stopping the endless racing, getting off the track entirely, and playing a New Business Game that allows you to achieve all your True Goals (more about these later) and all the Hypnotic Goals you still want. However, you may be surprised to discover how few of your Hypnotic Goals you still want at that point!

To continue your journey, discover three questions that have haunted you your entire life, and learn how to answer them in a way that empowers you to bust loose from The Business Game, turn the page and continue on to Chapter 2.

CHAPTER

2

The Big Truth

The truth of the matter is that the timeless Essence of who you are is already awake within you now. The dust of the mind and ever more subtle layers of the intellect are merely brushed away to reveal it.[1]

—Katie Davis

Each person is born with an infinite power, against which no earthly force is of the slightest significance.[2]

—Neville Goddard (1905–1972), Philosopher

Traditionally, when you want to grow, change, fix, or improve some aspect of your business, you seek out experts and expertise in The Five Power Centers of Business—sales, marketing, management, leadership, and finance.

---

[1] Katie Davis, *Awake Joy* (Kihei, HI: Awake Spirit Publishing, 1993), p. 171.

[2] Neville Goddard, in *Bits & Pieces* (Chicago: Ragan Communications, 2004).

However, busting loose from The Business Game isn't a traditional activity. To bust loose, you must look in directions you don't normally look in, and seek out experts and expertise you don't normally consider. So that's exactly what we're going to start doing together in this chapter, beginning right now.

Throughout recorded history, three questions have haunted humanity:

1. Who am I?
2. Why am I here?
3. What's my purpose?

Ironically, as you'll see by the time you complete this book, the answers to those three questions hold the key to busting loose from The Business Game—*not* the strategies you can apply from within The Five Power Centers of Business.

My belief is there's no way to know the absolute Truth about the answers to those questions. Why? Because there are certain mysteries about the human experience that are so huge and complex they are beyond our understanding at our present level of Consciousness. Since we can't be absolutely certain about the answers to the three haunting questions, all we can do is create models that get us close enough to The Truth to give us practical benefit in our daily lives.

Therefore, what I'm going to share with you in the next few chapters is a working model that will empower you to bust loose from The Business Game. But it's just a model. Be clear on that. You can break it if you want to. You can argue with some or all of it if you want to. You can reject it as being too "woo-woo" or "out there" if you want to. Despite that, the model *does* get very, very close to The Truth, and it *will* empower you to receive practical and deeply transformative value in your business affairs and personal life. I say that from deep and consistent personal experience on my own journey, and from witnessing the journeys of thousands of others throughout the world who have traveled the same path you're about to discover.

The model has two components to it: philosophical and scientific. As I share the philosophical component with you, please keep two thoughts in mind:

1. These are critical puzzle pieces, no matter how they may seem at first glance. When you reach Chapter 11, you'll understand how important they really are—and when you turn the last page of the book, your understanding of their significance will have deepened further.
2. In Chapters 4 and 5, I share recent breakthroughs in science that document and validate the philosophical components of the model—including the wildest and most "out there" aspects of it. This will be valuable for you if believing or accepting any of the philosophy is challenging for you.

Let's take a look at the first haunting question.

Who Am I?

If you've been exposed to information about what's been called new age, metaphysical, esoteric, or spiritual thought, you've no doubt heard something like this: "We are spiritual beings having a physical experience." I agree with that statement, and it aligns perfectly with the model I'm presenting to you.

Who you *really are* is what I call an "Infinite Being." Who you *really are* is an infinitely powerful and magnificent Being. Snap your fingers, and boom, anything you want instantly manifests. No concept of power you're familiar with comes even close to the power and omnipotence of who you really are. All the forces of nature and man put together and multiplied a billion times are but a speck compared to the power The Real You has at its disposal every second.

Depending on your history and the beliefs you formed living through it, this is something that may sound or feel either familiar or alien to you. Regardless of how it feels to you, it's one of the things you'll be able to *prove to yourself and actually experience* if you choose to travel the path shared in this book.

Because The Real You has the power to create absolutely anything, your natural state is one of infinite abundance. In your natural state you don't lack anything. Nothing is missing. No desire ever goes unfulfilled. No plan ever fails. No goal goes unachieved.

As an Infinite Being, you're also in a constant state of what I call "True Joy." What is True Joy? If you created a container and put every positive emotion that's desirable to you in it—happiness, fun, peace, contentment, satisfaction, fulfillment, unconditional love, and so on—and then significantly amplified those feelings one thousand times, the contents of the container would still only be a pale imitation of True Joy. The Real You knows no other feeling but True Joy. Who you really are does not experience negative emotions such as anger, fear, worry, frustration, depression, sadness, or insecurity.

As an infinitely powerful, wise, abundant, and Truly Joyful Being, you have an unlimited desire to express yourself creatively and experience the fun and exhilaration that comes from that expression in all its shapes and forms. In fact, as you'll soon see, the entire human experience is essentially about creative expression, fun, and exploration, no matter what it looks like or what story could be told about it from a judgmental perspective.

Now let's take a look at the second haunting question.

Why Am I Here?

You came here to play a game!

In your daily life, you go about your daily routine. Then, from time to time, you step out of your routine to play games of various kinds. When I say games, I mean sports, board games, cards, mountain climbing, bike riding, bungee jumping, driving cars at high speeds, watching television or movies or plays, reading great novels, painting, singing, playing musical instruments, listening to music, or whatever else you really love to do. You choose to play games for fun, for enjoyment, for entertainment, to challenge yourself, to explore what-if scenarios, and so on.

The same is true when it comes to why you're here. As an Infinite Being living in what I humorously refer to as Infiniteland, at another level of Consciousness you decided to take time away from your daily routine to play a game, too. That game is called The Human Game, of which The Business Game is a major subset.

Does this surprise you? Does playing a game seem too trivial a reason to be here or to explain what we call the pain, hardship, and complexity of the human experience? If so, stick with me as more and more puzzle pieces are revealed. This is another concept that you will directly experience and ultimately prove to yourself if you follow the path outlined in this book.

Let's now look at the third haunting question.

What's My Purpose?

You have a general purpose and a specific purpose. The general purpose is to play The Human Game and receive the benefits people receive from playing *all* games: fun, enjoyment, entertainment, challenge, exploring what-if scenarios, and so on.

Your specific purpose is to play The Human Game in the unique and precise way you choose as a unique Infinite Being. We all play The Human Game, but we do it in completely different ways. Even when it looks like we're doing the same things, doing things the same way, or doing them for the same reasons, we're not. Everything is custom designed for us as unique Infinite Beings, as you'll clearly see after completing Chapters 4 and 5.

In *The Creating Cosmos*, Barbara Dewey says (using the term *Creating Cosmos* where I use the terms *Infinite Beings* and *The Human Game*):

> In the final analysis, I don't suppose the Creating Cosmos has a purpose greater than the joyful expression of creative possibility.

Solely in the service of that purpose it is a design of the most
sublime construction. It is breathtaking both in its simplicity and
[in] its opportunity. It grants total freedom within a context of
cooperation and partnership. There are no winners and losers in
the Creating Cosmos concept. Because each plays a game of his
own choosing there are only winners.[3]

As we discussed in Chapter 1, all games start out with a concept.
Then a playing field is built; then necessary tools and support
resources (like golf clubs, footballs, baseballs, tennis rackets) are
created; then rules, regulations, and structures are developed to
which all players must strictly adhere if they want to play. It's the
same with The Human Game.

Let's now discuss the concept that drives The Human Game. I'm
a big fan of the *Star Trek* television series. In that show, there's a
concept called the "Prime Directive." The Prime Directive is a core
principle that guides the actions of the crew of the starship *Enterprise*
as they explore space. The Human Game has a Prime Directive, too.
It's to fully explore what happens when you limit unlimited power,
when you limit the infinite ability to express creatively, when you
limit the infinite wisdom, abundance, joyfulness, and True Joy that is
your natural state. I'm going to introduce this concept from a
philosophical perspective in this chapter, continue the discussion
from a scientific perspective in later chapters, and conclude it from a
nuts-and-bolts, day-to-day, practical perspective in Chapter 9 after
you've received a few more important pieces of the puzzle.

All the games we play were originally invented by someone
who had a specific reason and motivation for creating them. The
Human Game is no exception. From an expanded and infinite
perspective, imagine that an Infinite Being thought, "Wouldn't it
be interesting to see what would happen if I limited myself,
restricted myself, hid all my power, wisdom, abundance, and

[3] Barbara Dewey, *The Creating Cosmos* (Inverness, CA: Bartholomew Books, 1985),
p. 92.

True Joy? Could I actually convince myself it was gone? Could I actually convince myself I'm the exact opposite of who I really am? What then? What would the whole journey and experience be like if I could pull it off? What kinds of cool games could be played within a context like that?"

Since you're an Infinite Being, if you want to play a game of limitation and restriction, you have to create an alternative Self to be the main player of that game. From this moment forward, I will refer to that part of you as the *Player*. You must then hide all awareness of who you really are and all your power, wisdom, abundance, and True Joy from that Player. You must then create a playing field on which to play, and other Players to play The Human Game with you. The Real You, your Infinite Being Self, then manages the entire experience from behind the scenes while you're blind to The Truth about who you really are and what's really going on. Going forward, I'll be referring to that part of you as your *Expanded Self*.

The Player who plays the Human Game is the part of you who is reading this book right now—the part you've always thought of as yourself. The other Players, as we'll discuss in detail in Chapter 7, are the people you see around you and interact with. The playing field is what we call the physical Universe, physical reality, or three-dimensional reality (which has visible and invisible components).

Words get tricky here, but it's important to understand that while the Player and Expanded Self aspects of you feel and appear separate, they're actually one and the same Infinite Being that is unified at a very deep and profound level. The apparent separation is a necessary part of the illusion created by an advanced form of sleight of hand we'll be discussing in the next three chapters.

From the moment you, the Player, are born, you actually begin hiding your tremendous power, wisdom, abundance, and True Joy from yourself and constructing an alternative reality (playing field) on which to play The Human Game. Before we continue our discussion of limitation, restriction, and The Human Game, allow me to plant the following seed in your expanding awareness, which also comes from Barbara Dewey:

> We mistakenly believe, therefore, that we are at the mercy of life rather than its creators. Such beliefs make us feel impotent and we have hastened to fill in for these perceived weaknesses with technological aids. We are not encouraged to use our natural telepathic capacities. We have phones. We do not need total recall. We have computers. We do not need our homing instincts. We have maps. We do not need to practice health. We have doctors.[4]

In addition to hiding your power and creating an alternative reality in which to play The Human Game, you also convince yourself the hiding places are so painful, dangerous, scary, and deadly that they should be avoided at all costs. We'll discuss this in later chapters.

Just as a baseball game has nine innings, football games have four quarters, and golf has 18 holes, the Human Game has two phases.

Phase 1

During Phase 1 of The Human Game, your Expanded Self uses all your power, creativity, and ingenuity to hide all awareness of who you really are and what your natural state is—and to keep you from finding it at any cost. Everything possible is done to convince you that the Player and the three-dimensional illusory playing field are real, and to limit and restrict you more and more until you're absolutely convinced you're the exact opposite of who you really are. In the popular success and self-help literature, this process is defined very differently and is generally called "programming" or "conditioning."

---

[4] Ibid., p. 86.

As you ponder this, ask yourself if you think it's an accident that The Human Game begins with us being born as helpless infants with no power, knowledge, or abundance of any kind! I have a name for examples of Truth staring us in the face that we ignore like this: Cosmic Jokes. There are many of them to be experienced!

It is because of the Phase 1 dynamics that Hypnotic Goals become so prominent and so seductive, why we rarely accomplish them (or can hold on to them if we do momentarily), and why we don't tend to find their achievement as fulfilling as we expected if we do achieve and hold on to them for a time.

Phase 2

After forgetting who you really are and deeply immersing yourself in severely limiting and restrictive experiences in Phase 1 of The Human Game, your Expanded Self starts nudging you into Phase 2. At that point, you begin to feel incomplete, like you're missing something, like nothing makes sense anymore, like there must be something else going on that you don't know about. You then start looking for answers and a higher purpose for your life.

At that point, you still don't fully get who you really are or how much power, wisdom, abundance, and True Joy you actually possess (even if you have belief systems that include similar concepts), but you begin seeking a direct experience of that Truth nevertheless. Your Expanded Self then flips roles, takes you on what I call "The Treasure Hunt of the Century," and supports you in reclaiming all the power, wisdom, abundance, and True Joy you hid in Phase 1.

Once you reclaim your power, wisdom, abundance, and True Joy, you can then start playing The Human Game without limits or restrictions of any kind. I call this crossing The Busting Loose Point. That's when things get very cool—especially in business! It is in Phase 2 that we shift our focus from Hypnotic Goals to True Goals. I'll have much more to share about this in the pages that follow.

By the way, it's no accident that you found your way to this book. This is not the sort of experience that you dabble with or dip your toe into. As you'll soon discover, if you haven't already, this is very intense stuff! You wouldn't be reading my words here unless:

- On some level, you wanted support in jumping into Phase 2 right now.
- You're getting ready to jump into Phase 2 and are using this book as basic training or warm-up.
- You're not ready to leap into Phase 2, but you wanted to know more about The Truth as you continue playing in Phase 1.

As you've been following along with me, this thought may have crossed your mind: "Why would anyone want to play a game like that? Have so much power, abundance, wisdom, and True Joy; hide it; then find it again. It sounds crazy." If thoughts like that did cross your mind, let me ask you three questions in response:

1. Why does anybody play *any* game?
2. If you take an honest and objective look, are the rules, regulations, and structure of The Human Game really any more arbitrary or crazy than those of golf, baseball, basketball, soccer, football, chess, checkers, or Monopoly?
3. What greater challenge could there be for an Infinite Being?

As we discussed earlier, people play games for the sheer fun, pleasure, challenge, and exhilaration of playing, no matter how crazy they may seem at first glance or how difficult playing gets at times. That's the point of it, not the literal details about how the game is played. People spend enormous amounts of time, energy, and money training for, playing, and watching games of all kinds and feel it's a perfectly legitimate activity. Why would it be any different for Infinite Beings with much more power, wisdom, abundance, and True Joy? It wouldn't, except that if Infinite Beings like that are going to play a game, it has to be one hell of a game or it wouldn't hold their interest.

Or think about this: Why would someone willingly leave a warm and comfortable home to experience pain, hardship, and risk of death to participate in activities like climbing Mount Everest or driving a racing car at high speeds?

Plus, consider this: Imagine you're an architect and you're hired to design an amazing building for a client. You visualize it in your imagination, then draw up the plans. That's a lot of fun and very rewarding, but it's even more exciting to see the building actually rise up in three dimensions and become real. The challenge, fun, and reward that come from embracing The Human Game idea, then seeing it manifest in three dimensions, then actually playing it are enormous. Just let this thought incubate for a while as I offer you more and more puzzle pieces.

The following may also have occurred to you: "Okay, maybe I can buy the idea of life being a game, but why, as part of playing that game, would someone willingly *choose* to experience such horrors as abuse, sickness, poverty, struggle, starvation, rape, murder, and death (in personal life)—or failure, bankruptcy, embezzlement, or being fired (in The Business Game)—as part of playing? Those things don't seem particularly fun or entertaining to me."

I'll be discussing this in more detail in the chapters that follow, but for now, let me share a few thoughts: Your Expanded Self sees no horror in any of those experiences and is actually having an absolute blast playing The Human Game, no matter what story is playing itself out on the illusory playing field. The Real You knows *none* of those experiences are real and it's all just a game.

Let me share a powerful metaphor with you to help you really get this idea. I call it "The Movie Theater Crutch." Imagine you're sitting in a theater watching a movie up on the screen that's making you feel extremely uncomfortable. Imagine there's a man, woman, and child in the scene you're watching.

Now, imagine that in the back of the same theater, leaning against the back wall, is the actor playing the man in the scene, the actress playing the woman, the actor playing the child, the director of the movie, the makeup artist, and the special effects engineer. Let's call this group the creative team.

While you're sitting in your seat squirming with discomfort, what is the creative team doing? Celebrating! They know it's not real. They know it's all made up. They know it's all just a story. They know no one *really* gets sick, hurt, or abused, lives, dies, or makes a million bucks. Since they don't take the action seriously or judge what's going on, they're free to simply celebrate their creative contribution to such an effective illusion.

The experience of the creative team is very similar to how your Expanded Self experiences everything taking place as you play The Human Game—and how *you* will experience it once you bust loose!

However, for reasons that will soon become clear to you, because you as the Player are so fully immersed within the illusion and judgment of it, and because everything seems too real to you, being able to live in that perspective will be nearly impossible— for now. That's why I call the metaphor I just shared The Movie Theater *Crutch*. We use crutches when we injure a leg to support us until the leg can function by itself again. Once you expand to the point that you have a direct experience of The Truth I just shared (which you will if you take this journey), you'll discard The Movie Theater Crutch, too. But for now, it can support you to one degree or another.

Your Expanded Self knows all experiences in The Human Game are simply made up to create a game and a playing field on which to play. Your Expanded Self knows all your experiences only *seem real* and horrible to the Players who are totally immersed within them and convinced they're real. And that's the whole point of The Human Game—to make it all seem real when it isn't.

Making the illusion appear real was the biggest challenge in the design of The Human Game. However, beyond appearing real, as I mentioned, The Human Game must be fascinating and hold our interest. Consider what Sol Stein, a master editor of some of the most successful writers of our time, wrote about the art of crafting truly compelling fiction:

> When the baseball, football, or basketball season is at its height, a considerable portion of the American male population and a not insignificant number of females deploy hours away from work watching their sport on television. What the baseball fan, for instance, hopes for, consciously or not, are the moments of tension and suspense when a ball is hit but not yet caught, when a runner is headed for a base and has not yet reached it. The same applies to other sports as well. The spectator rooting for his hero experiences tension, suspense, anxiety, and pleasure, all things the readers hope for when they turn to a novel. The reader is enjoying the anticipation and excitement that are often worrying in life but a pleasure when they are happening on the ball field or in a book.[5]

The same is true for us as Infinite Beings as we play The Human Game. We too want to experience tension, suspense, anxiety, and pleasure through our experiences. Stein continued by saying:

> But let us remember that when a team—even the team we are rooting for—is winning too easily, our enjoyment of the game decreases. What the sports spectator and the reader enjoy most is a contest of two strong teams, a game whose outcome hangs in the balance as long as possible.[6]

Stein's wise observations also shed light on why Phase 1 life isn't perfect and why we therefore create ups and downs, challenges, and the illusion of conflict and resistance in our daily experience—including within The Business Game as we chase our rabbits!

If you start out as an Infinite Being, and in Phase 1 of The Human Game the goal is to limit yourself and convince yourself you're the opposite of who you really are, things can't work perfectly.

---

[5] Sol Stein, *How to Grow a Novel* (New York: St. Martin's Press, 1999), p. 8.

[6] Ibid., p. 10.

You must have problems. Things can't make sense if examined closely and objectively. You *must* be uncomfortable a lot of the time.

As we'll discuss in detail in the next chapter, blocks and resistance to achieving your goals, executing your plans and strategies, and fulfilling your deepest desires for your business must be common in Phase 1. The feeling there's something missing or something wrong must nag at you, loudly or quietly. Why? Because that's the whole point of Phase 1—to convince you, the Player, that you're the opposite of who you really are. If the goal is to limit, you don't expand. If the goal is to restrict, you don't open up. That's the way it works.

Key Point

To make Phase 1 of The Human Game work, all Truth must be hidden, distorted, or skewed to keep you away from it—and away from your power, wisdom, abundance, and True Joy.

As we discussed, the goal of Phase 1 of The Human Game is to convince yourself you're the exact opposite of who you really are. Therefore, whenever a teaching attempts to explain what The Human Game is all about or how to play it to maximum advantage *in Phase 1*, that teaching must be skewed or distorted, or something important must be left out.

In addition, to keep you away from your power, wisdom, abundance, True Joy, and The Truth about who you really are, the techniques offered in association with those skewed and distorted teachings must be sabotaged so they don't work—either consistently or at all.

If you accept the challenge offered at the end of this book and leap through the gateway I open for you into Phase 2, you'll see this everywhere—in the self-help literature, success literature, sales and marketing training, human resources training, money management techniques, metaphysics, mysticism, science, religion, and so on. You'll look at what's being taught, track it, and say, "That's True, that's True, that's True, oh. . . . " And you'll see exactly where it got skewed, distorted, or sabotaged, or something was left out. It's actually quite fascinating and entertaining.

Many business owners and employees apply self-help techniques to change, fix, or improve their businesses, so let's take one of them as an example to illustrate the point I just made. When studying the popular self-help technique called visualization, you're taught that you have unlimited power and can create any result you want if you just repetitively see a vivid picture of the result in your mind's eye.

It's True that you have unlimited power in your natural state. However, by design, access to that power is blocked in Phase 1 of The Human Game. It's also true that your Expanded Self can create anything he or she wants. However, that process doesn't take place in *your* mind's eye as the Player. It takes place in the mind's eye of your Expanded Self, using a magical creative process described in Chapters 5 and 6.

Self-help tools like visualization, affirmations, manifestation techniques, the law of attraction, and other popular self-help techniques are brilliant Phase 1 creations. Why? Because we create them, we convince ourselves they're real, and we apply them, but they don't work consistently (or at all), and that creates confusion, frustration, and limitations that perfectly reinforce the goals of Phase 1.

As I mentioned in the Introduction, I created a similar dynamic with my own earlier self-help work when I was in Phase 1. I had a clear perspective on a lot of The Truth, but to play in Phase 1 of The Human Game, I had to skew it so my success system would be unreliable and ultimately fail—keeping me locked in limitation and restriction—until I was ready to enter Phase 2.

Phase 1 of The Human Game is designed to take you to the point where you feel:

- Enormous frustration and pain with the old game.
- Incomplete, like something's wrong, that there must be more to life, that something else must be going on that you don't know about.
- An intense desire to know and experience The Truth.

Reaching that point at a high level of intensity is one of the signals you may be ready to move into Phase 2 (or at least expand your view of what's possible for yourself on the road to going there).

Key Point

Part of the Phase 1 strategy involves teasing yourself into believing you can change things, fix things, improve things, get things running smoothly, get all your ducks in a row (and keep them there), get everything you want, and become wealthy, successful, and happy. By design, however, that can *never* happen while you're playing in Phase 1 of The Human Game. This is why it never actually happens, despite illusions to the contrary and what all the business, self-help, success, personal growth, and spiritual gurus claim. This is a subtle but very important distinction to grasp.

This is the reason there's always an Invisible Price to pay, on top of the Visible Price to pay, when you play The Business Game according to the rules and regulations you were taught while playing the Phase 1 game. Why? Because everything you do in Phase 1, no matter how it looks or what story you could tell about it, ultimately reinforces and locks in the Phase 1 dynamics of limitation, restriction, belief that the illusion is real, and you're being the opposite of who you really are within it. It's kind of like quicksand, where the more you struggle, the stronger its hold on you becomes.

Let me share a story with you to hammer this point home. When the sale of Blue Ocean Software to software giant Intuit was actually completed (meaning all the money was transferred and distributed), I wanted to celebrate with my wife, so I went to the local liquor store and asked, "What's the most expensive bottle of champagne you have?" I was taken to a special room that had to be unlocked with a key, and shown a bottle of Louis Roederer *Cristal* from an excellent year. The price tag? $850.

I bought the bottle, carefully carried it to my car, kept my right hand on it to stop it from rolling off the front passenger seat as I drove the short distance home, and, after pulling into my driveway, carefully lifted it off the seat to remove it from the car. Then, as I started to exit the car, it slipped out of my hands, fell to the concrete driveway, and smashed! Why do I share this story? Because in Phase 1, I could not even allow myself to fully enjoy and savor a gigantic victory like selling Blue Ocean Software for $177 million!

Remember, whenever you decide to play a game—whether it's chess, checkers, football, basketball, auto racing, mountain climbing, or whatever—you have to play by the rules, follow the regulations, and respect the structure, or you can't play.

When playing The Human Game, the experience of True Power, True Abundance, True Wisdom, and True Joy doesn't return until you've been playing in Phase 2 for a while, which I'm going to show you how to do. It's in Phase 2 that a gateway opens, allowing you to bust loose from The Business Game. This is described in detail in later chapters after I've laid a solid foundation for you.

When you're ready to discover more of The Truth about Phase 1 of The Human Game and how it has been shaping your business affairs to date, turn the page to begin Chapter 3.

CHAPTER

3

The Fantasy Factory

Surely someday . . . we will grasp the central idea of it all as so simple, so beautiful, so compelling that we will all say to each other, "Oh, how could it have been otherwise!"[1]

—*John Wheeler, Physicist*

The distinction between what is real and what is imaginary is not one that can be finely maintained . . . all existing things are . . . imaginary.[2]

—*John Mackenzie, Philosopher and Poet*

---

[1] John Wheeler, as quoted by John Horgan, *The End of Science: Facing the Limits of Knowledge in the Twilight of the Scientific Age* (London: Abacus, 1998). Web site: http://suif.stanford.edu/~jeffop/WWW/wheeler.txt.

[2] Neville Goddard, *The Law and the Promise* (Marina Del Rey, CA: DeVorss, 1961), p. 44.

I'd now like to describe three additional metaphors that will support you in understanding the true nature of The Human Game, The Business Game, the field on which we play those games, and prepare you for the scientific documentation that will follow in Chapters 5 and 6. The first two metaphors link together and revolve around amusement parks and movies.

An amusement park is a place that was specifically designed to offer rides and attractions to entertain you. Using Disney World as an example, it includes Epcot Center and Animal Kingdom, so there are also opportunities for deep study and exploration of a variety of educational topics.

You go to an amusement park by choice. Nobody drags you or forces you to go. You generally go with people you know. You experience the rides and attractions that appeal to you and ignore the ones that don't. You arrive and leave as you prefer. You go once or you might return multiple times. I now invite you to look at the world or what has been called the physical Universe or three-dimensional reality as if it were a gigantic amusement park.

As I mentioned, if you're an Infinite Being and you're going to play a game, you can't just play *any* game. You'd be bored out of your mind. It would be like a professional basketball team playing an eighth-grade basketball team. There would be no challenge, no point, no fun, no real game. If you, as an Infinite Being, are going to play a game, it must be the ultimate game. It must be extremely sophisticated and complex, and cleverly designed to keep you riveted, challenged, and on the edge of your seat at all times. That's no simple task!

Therefore, continuing this metaphor, to play The Human Game, a gigantic amusement park had to be created that would offer a wide variety of extremely complex rides and attractions (games). One of the most popular attractions in that amusement park is The Business Game. However, unlike familiar amusement parks such as Disney World, the amusement park in which The Human Game and The Business Game are played was designed to offer a rare breed of rides and attractions that I call "total-immersion movie experiences."

Let's take a look at Hollywood movies for a moment. In Hollywood movies, nothing is as it appears. Every scene is carefully scripted and planned before it is filmed. Nothing ends up in the final cut of a movie unless it perfectly supports the telling of the story exactly as the creators of the movie envisioned. Nothing is random or accidental in the final cut of a movie you see on the screen. Every aspect is carefully crafted so it will have a specific impact on you—make you laugh, cry, be angry, open your heart, feel a sense of wonder or awe, and so on.

Everything in a Hollywood movie looks real and substantial, but it isn't. It's all made up. It's all an illusion, and special effects extend the illusion to an incredible degree. You know it's an illusion as you sit in the movie theater, but you temporarily suspend that knowledge so you can be entertained. If you went behind the scenes to see how a movie is really made, what the sets actually look like, how the special effects are created, and what happens in the editing room, and you then looked at the final cut you saw on the screen and compared them, you'd be amazed by the complexity and the time, energy, and effort that are involved. As you know, Hollywood illusions are absolutely convincing and must be. If they weren't, we'd walk out of the theater or refuse to spend our hard-earned money to see the movies in the first place.

All of this is true for your business and The Human Game as well. In your movie, nothing is as it appears. Every scene is carefully scripted and planned before you experience it. Nothing ends up in your movie unless it perfectly supports you in having the precise Human Game experience you want to have. Nothing is random or accidental in your movie, either. Everything has been created *exactly the way it is* to support you in playing The Human Game exactly the way you want to play it, no matter how you might label or judge it at the moment. It has all been carefully crafted to have a specific impact on you (especially The Business Game)—to limit you, restrict you, convince you you're the opposite of who you really are, and persuade you that the total-immersion movie experience is real.

Just like in a Hollywood movie, everything in your world looks real and substantial, but it isn't. It's all made up. Everything you perceive with your five senses is an illusion—all props and special effects designed to create an alternative reality that allows you to play The Human Game—and your own special effects extend the illusion to an incredible degree, too.

When I take you behind the scenes to show you how total-immersion movies are made in The Human Game amusement park, you'll be amazed by the complexity, time, energy, and effort that are involved there, too. It must be that way. The illusions created to support you in playing The Human Game must be absolutely convincing, or The Human Game would end abruptly, the equivalent of you walking out of the theater during a boring or poorly crafted movie.

As you'll see after turning more and more pages in this book, to make The Human Game and The Business Game appear real, the required special effects put every Hollywood effects and animation studio to shame.

With Hollywood movies, millions of dollars are spent, hundreds or even thousands of people are involved, and extremely intricate and expensive equipment and computers are used. It sometimes takes months or even years to move from the start of a project to the moment it appears on the screen. Why is all that time, energy, effort, and money invested? "To make money," you might say. That's true, but what must happen before Hollywood can make money? You must be entertained, right? And for you to be entertained, what must happen? You must *feel* something.

Just about everyone I know loves movies. If for some reason you don't, follow along with me and you'll still get the big-picture point I want to make. Why do so many people love movies? When I ask people, most of them respond with one or more of these five comments:

1. They're fun and entertaining.
2. They provide a diversion from the daily routine.
3. They enable you to see different points of view.

4. They enable you to have unique and vicarious experiences beyond your norm.

5. They're interesting.

This makes sense, doesn't it—especially in light of what we've been discussing in this chapter? However, under the surface of these insights is a secret few people ever uncover or fully understand. The secret is *feelings*. We love movies because of the feelings they stimulate within us. The truth is, we don't really care about the specific details of the action on the screen. We just care about how the action on the screen makes us feel!

By the way, that's also why we enjoy reading books, playing and watching sports, listening to music, going to the theater, playing video games, riding roller coasters, going skydiving, climbing mountains, bungee jumping, making money or achieving goals or solving problems in business, and so on. It's *always* about feelings. The external experiences matter only to the extent that they trigger the inner feelings we love so much.

Think of something you really love to do—a game you love to play or watch, a task you enjoy doing in your business, an experience you love having in your business, something you find extremely enjoyable. Then ask yourself, "Why do I love it so much? What's the *real* appeal?" You'll see that what you really love is what's going on inside of you, the feelings, and what's going on *outside* is just the trigger for those feelings.

It's the same with The Human Game. At its core, The Human Game is all about feelings, and everything that happens on the screen of your total-immersion movie is also just a trigger to set specific feelings into motion that support you in playing in The Human Game amusement park the way you choose to as a unique Infinite Being.

Key Point

At their core, movies, The Human Game, and The Business Game are all about *feelings*, not thinking, logic, or intellect. Infinite Beings are feeling Beings, not thinking Beings.

Let me give you an additional illustration to deepen your understanding of this key point. I've never been a big fan of baseball, but I once spoke with a friend who was fanatical about baseball. I said, "I prefer football. There's more action and a faster pace. To me, baseball is slow and boring. Why do you love it so much?"

"Baseball is primarily a mental game," he explained. "The fun comes from watching the possibilities. Whenever something happens—there's a strike, a ball, an out, a bunt, a single, double, triple, or home run, whatever it is—it creates a whole new set of possibilities. Watching the possibilities and the movement of 'what would happen if . . . ' scenarios is where the fun comes from."

The Human Game was designed to operate in a similar way. It, too, is about exploring "what would happen if . . . " scenarios, because every time one thing happens in your life, in your business, or anywhere in the world, everything changes and there's a whole new set of possibilities to explore and play with—across all kinds of Human Game experiences. That's part of what's required to keep us interested and wanting to continue playing The Human Game.

In fact, if you look at history, you'll see that whenever we begin to focus on a new game, we explore an infinite variety of "what would happen if . . . " scenarios as a powerful microscope is taken to the possibilities available through that game. As an example, I just watched a movie called *Riding Giants* about the history of big wave surfing. It's a powerful and fascinating example of how our exploration and play of games expands and evolves over time.

Now, here's the really interesting part. When you're in a movie theater, you're just watching the movie. You may get very involved with the story and closely identify with the characters, but you still know you're you. You still know you're sitting in a theater. You know the movie isn't real. You know the action is taking place outside of you. And while you can get an idea of what the experiences of the characters are like, you're not them and you can't have their actual experiences. In short, there's a distance between you and the experiences taking place in the movie.

When playing The Human Game, however, you don't just watch, *you totally immerse yourself* in the story. Imagine sitting in a theater, seeing a movie scene start to play on the screen, stepping through the screen into the scene, forgetting who you really are, and actually becoming one of the characters for a while, actually believing you're that character and everyone and everything else in the movie is real. That's what I mean by "total immersion" and what happens when you play The Human Game.

Let's now take a look at how a Hollywood movie is made. Then we'll bring it back to how your total-immersion Human Game movie is made. Before a Hollywood movie can be made, a subject of interest must be chosen. The movie must be *about* something. There must be a story someone wants to explore or tell. A script is written that contains the details of how the story will unfold. Then a director, cast, and crew are hired and filming starts. When the whole story has been completed, filming stops.

It's the same thing with The Human Game. You have to pick specific rides or attractions in The Human Game amusement park to write stories about and have total-immersion movie experiences with. I call this a mission or life purpose. What do I mean by rides and attractions? Everything you experience in the physical universe, whether visible or invisible, is a ride or an attraction within the model we're describing here.

If you're playing the role of being a parent, that's a ride in the amusement park. If you're the owner or employee of a company, the job and the company are attractions. If you enjoy playing or watching a sport like football, golf, tennis, or basketball, playing and watching are rides. As I explained earlier, The Business Game, in all its complexity and splendor, is just one of the rides and attractions. On and on it goes through everything you see happening in what you call "the world"—for you and everyone else.

After you choose specific rides and attractions to play with for your total-immersion movie experience, metaphorically, a script is written that details how your experience will unfold as you play in

The Human Game amusement park. Just like in Hollywood movies, a director, in the form of your Expanded Self, is then hired to oversee your total-immersion movie experience from behind the scenes. A cast is then hired to be the other people playing small or large roles in your Human Game adventure with you. Filming starts, which is the equivalent of you being born; and filming ultimately ends, which is the equivalent of you dying.

As a quick but important review, everything you see on the screen in a movie is a combination of the writer's intent, the producer's decision to make it real, the director's vision and sensitivity to the overall purpose of the proposed project, and the various performers' abilities to support the entire effort. In other words, what you see on the screen is the final expression of a great deal of creative activity you do *not* see. Yet, it's the unseen creative activity that is the true cause and source of the story you see unfolding. It's this unseen creative activity my grandfather opened my eyes to when I was 12, the unseen creative activity I spent decades understanding and learning to fully tap, and the unseen creative activity I'll be sharing with you in the pages that follow.

The final metaphor I'd like to share with you in this chapter is that of the sun and clouds. As we've discussed, who you really are is an infinitely powerful, infinitely wise, infinitely abundant, and Truly Joyful Being. Compare that to the sun. When you think of the sun, you think of enormous amounts of energy, power, light, and heat, right? It's a good fit.

When you play The Human Game, however, you must create illusions that convince you you're the opposite of who you really are—that is, convince you that you're a severely limited, restricted, vulnerable, fragile, poor, weak, and powerless creature (to one degree or another, in one or more areas of your life) who gets tossed about by people, places, and things you have no control over (including the tax service, the economy, the stock market, competitors, employees, etc.). All the things you do to convince yourself you're the opposite of who you really are are the equivalent of creating a bunch of clouds, putting them in front of the sun, and convincing yourself that there's no sun, the clouds are real, and the clouds are all there is.

The accompanying image visually illustrates this concept for you.

The sun of who you really are, the cloud cover you created to hide that knowledge and experience from yourself, and the limited and restricted world you live in as a result (shown darker for effect).

To extend the metaphor, if it's cloudy out, is the sun still shining? Yes. When there's a hurricane blowing, is the sun still shining? Yes. If it's raining, is the sun still shining? Yes. If it is night where you are, is the sun still shining somewhere else? Yes. No matter what happens on our planet, the sun is always shining.

It's the same with you. No matter what's going on in your life or business, no matter what the circumstances look like, who you *really* are doesn't change—the sun of who you really are is always shining. You're still an Infinite Being who is infinitely powerful, abundant, wise, and Truly Joyful. You can't make your Infiniteness go away. All you can do is create the illusion of it being gone (the cloud cover) and convince yourself that illusion is real. I'll explain exactly how you did that in Chapters 4, 5, and 6. We'll return to the sun and clouds metaphor in later chapters, as it is key to the path you'll travel to bust loose from The Business Game.

When you're ready to discover more of The Truth about The Human Game, The Business Game, illusions, and the true nature of the playing field we designed to play The Human Game on, turn the page to begin Chapter 4.

4

Dropping Anchors

One of the saddest lessons of history is this: If we've been bamboo-zled long enough, we tend to reject any evidence of the bamboozle.[1]

—*Carl Sagan*

Man seeks to escape himself in myth, and does so by any means at his disposal. Drugs, alcohol, or lies. Unable to withdraw into himself, he disguises himself. Lies and inaccuracy give him a few moments of comfort.[2]

—*Jean Cocteau*

If you have a boat, whether it's a sailboat, motorboat, yacht, or gigantic cruise ship, and you want to keep it in a specific location, you use one or more anchors. The anchor keeps the boat where you want it, no matter how hard you or forces of

[1] Carl Sagan, in "Wisdom Quotes," www.wisdomquotes.com/003041.html.

[2] Jean Cocteau, in "Wisdom Quotes," www.wisdomquotes.com/003017.html.

nature may try to move it. Similarly, to keep you locked into Phase 1 of The Human Game, you create and use your own anchors. In this chapter, I'm going to discuss the core nature of those anchors, which are really lies and illusions that appear to be True.

In Chapter 2, I explained that there are two goals for Phase 1 of The Human Game:

1. To convince you that the illusory playing field for The Human Game, the so-called physical Universe (your total-immersion movie experience) is real.

2. To convince you you're the opposite of who you really are within that illusion—that is, to one degree or another, small, weak, powerless, poor (in one or more ways), vulnerable, and at the mercy of outside forces beyond your control.

When the two goals are achieved, I call it pulling off The Phase 1 Miracle. Why do I call it a miracle? Because it is! To convince yourself the illusion is real and you're the opposite of who you really are within it is an off-the-charts amazing accomplishment, as you'll see and experience for yourself one day if you take this journey and bust loose.

To pull off The Phase 1 Miracle, you must start early. From a scientific, psychological, and metaphysical perspective, there are differing opinions of when The Human Game actually begins for the Player. Some say it begins when we exit the womb as infants and take our first breath. Others say it begins at the moment of conception. Others say it begins once the fetus within the mother's womb reaches a certain level of development and awareness.

To me, all such options (and variations between them) are possible and can be used as raw material by our Expanded Selves in scripting our total-immersion movie experiences and pulling off The Phase 1 Miracle. Whenever the starting point is, and it always takes place in childhood, from that moment forward, here is what we do:

- We create illusions (I'll explain how we do that in Chapter 6).

- We pop ourselves into the middle of them and totally immerse ourselves within them.

- We look at the illusions, interact with them, and lie to ourselves about them (we tell ourselves a story that reinforces the Phase 1 dynamics of us being the opposite of who we really are).

- We do this over and over with every resource at our disposal from within our own personal perspective and experience, and from what appears to be outside of us (parents, siblings, coaches, teachers, friends, associates, bosses, employees, partners, police, the media, the forces of nature, the economy, the stock market, the tax authority, etc.).

- We repeat the process until we're absolutely convinced the illusion is real and we *are* the opposite of who we really are within it.

Key Point

The True purpose of childhood and growing up is to support pulling off The Phase 1 Miracle!

Here are some brief and simple examples to flesh out what I just shared. As part of The Phase 1 Miracle, we create the following types of scenes in our total-immersion movie experiences:

- Hurricanes, tornadoes, earthquakes, fires, tsunamis, and so on, to make us (and our possessions) seem small, powerless, and physically vulnerable.

- Colds, flus, germs, viruses, cancer, heart disease, AIDS, venereal disease, and other illnesses to make us feel vulnerable, at risk, and powerless as we play The Body Game (another subset game of The Human Game).

- Recessions, depressions, embezzlement, theft, corporate espion- age, employee defections to competitors, blocks or resistance to the achievement of our goals, ineffective or lazy or dishonest employees, new technologies, aggressive competitor actions, and so on, to make us feel small, powerless, worried, stressed out, and vulnerable as we play The Business Game.

- Stock market crashes, real estate bubble bursts, bank failures, insurance company failures, credit crunches, foreclosures, and so on, to make us feel small, powerless, worried, stressed out, and vulnerable as we play The Money Game.

- Other people lying to us, hurting our feelings, abusing us, leaving us, divorcing us, quitting their jobs, cheating on us sexually, being mean or cruel to us, treating us unfairly, and so on, to make us feel small, powerless, and vulnerable as we play The Relationships Game.

- Wars and other national and international conflicts, many of which are surprise attacks (like Pearl Harbor and 9/11), to make us feel small, powerless, and vulnerable.

On and on it goes as The Phase 1 Miracle illusion machine whirls and whirls!

Now I'll share some more detailed examples of how we pull off The Phase 1 Miracle. In the Introduction, I discussed my grandfather, Aaron Scheinfeld. In the early days of his career, long before he founded Manpower, Inc. (which happened when he was 58), Gramps was a prosperous attorney. However, like so many others, he got caught up in the wild stock market speculation preceding the Crash of 1929 in the United States. During that time, he overextended himself financially while trading on borrowed money (margin debt).

When the stock market crashed, he lost everything and went deeply into debt. Gramps was unwilling to declare bankruptcy like many others did and insisted on repaying all his debts with interest, no matter how long it took. However, as an attorney operating during the Great Depression when most of his clients couldn't pay his fees, he had to barter with them, extend them credit toward a better day, do pro bono work hoping for a return favor one day, and so on. In short, Gramps and his family experienced great struggles and hardships throughout the Depression, exacerbated by his decision to repay his debts with interest.

Gramps ultimately got through that experience, repaid all his debts with interest, built great wealth, and ultimately busted loose from The Business Game. He did all of that without a lot of scars from the experience. However, for his wife, my grandmother Sylvia, and for my father, it was a different story. For them, like so many who went through the Great Depression as children or adults, there were lasting scars (Phase 1 Miracles).

Decades after the Great Depression ended, even after my grandmother had access to great wealth, she was extremely frugal, would rarely allow herself to spend much money on luxuries, and felt guilty whenever she did. Why? Because the idea that you could be wiped out and lose everything in an instant never weakened or left her.

Decades after the Great Depression, after he'd built great wealth for himself and up until the day he died at age 81, my father never felt safe financially. He always worried and was driven to pile up more and more wealth so he could feel safer. Why? For the same reason as my grandmother!

Let me share another story with you to illustrate how we pull off The Phase 1 Miracle in other ways. In the Introduction, I mentioned my experience with Blue Ocean Software, the most successful business experience I created in Phase 1. To fuel our next level of business growth and success, we made the decision to take the company public. We made the decision that if we were going to do that, we wanted to partner with the best of the best for each aspect of going public.

Because we'd been growing so quickly with such high profits, potential allies were drooling over working with us, and we had the luxury of picking and choosing our partners. As a result, we partnered with one of the most highly respected and prestigious venture capital firms. That firm then aligned us with one of the best investment bankers. We formed a board of directors composed of some of the brightest lights from the executive ranks of the software business. Our finances were audited by one of the most highly respected accounting firms.

Everything seemed perfectly lined up as we marched ever closer to the magic date of going public with an extremely high valuation. But then we witnessed what has been called the "tech wreck" or the bursting of the Internet bubble. We continued to prosper, but our partners, not wanting us to sell shares of our company at a discount under such conditions, advised us to delay the public offering until the markets recovered. We didn't need the money, so we postponed the public offering and went about our business until our venture capital partner linked us up with Intuit and we sold the company for $177 million in cash.

This example of the best-laid plans not leading to the desired result, and a disaster coming out of nowhere to block it, is a common experience as part of pulling off The Phase 1 Miracle. Now, in this example, you could say there was still a happy ending because we sold the company at a good price, but most times, when a Phase 1 Miracle illusion is being pulled off, there's an *unhappy* ending. And even in this case, everyone who owned stock or had stock options would (or could) have made a lot more money had we gone public. A lot of people also would have stayed with the company, but they ultimately left or were let go after it was sold due to incompatibilities with the Intuit management team.

Here's another example. In Phase 1, through many of my business experiences as an employee before going off on my own as an entrepreneur, numerous times I produced extraordinary results as a salesperson, sales manager, corporate communications manager, regional manager, and vice president of marketing, but later, under extraordinary circumstances, I was then fired, laid off, demoted, reprimanded for what appeared to an insecure boss to be bypassing the chain of command, improperly compensated with stock options for my contributions (which was later admitted and rectified), and so on—as my Expanded Self brilliantly locked in my own personal Phase 1 Miracle.

As I'm writing this chapter in November 2008, a *huge* wave of Phase 1 Miracle illusion is rolling through the fabric of The Business Game. Six weeks ago, the U.S. stock market crashed, followed by similar crashes in other international markets. Since then, stock prices have continued to fall. Real estate values have dropped through the floor. Credit has dried up, and loans for just about everything, especially real estate, have become extremely difficult to get. People are being laid off and fired. Businesses and individuals, filled with fear, have tightened their belts and stopped or slowed their spending, which gives the waves of fear more strength. There is "doom and gloom" talk everywhere, especially in the media, and there's even talk about another depression being possible in the United States.

Did stories and experiences from your own business and personal lives come to mind as you considered what I just shared about how The Phase 1 Miracle is pulled off? If so, the wheels are already turning for you to prove to yourself what I've been sharing. If not, I suspect such experiences will come to mind as you continue reading the book and after you set it down—if your Expanded Self is planning to launch you into The Phase 2 Game now or in the near future.

We create these sorts of illusions, and repeat them over and over with different people, in different situations, and in different places; then we reinforce them through relentless discussion through the media (books, newspapers, magazines, television, music lyrics, and movies) and our discussions with friends, family, and associates, until—boom!—The Phase 1 Miracle is locked into place, alive and well.

To hammer this key point home, imagine you're the curator of a museum that has an ancient and precious jewel on display. You want to protect the jewel from being stolen, so you install an elaborate security system with many layers and levels to it. You may have seen something like this in a movie like *Entrapment* with Sean Connery and Catherine Zeta-Jones.

First, there's protection around the windows, doors, and skylights. Next, there are motion detectors inside specific rooms. Then there are invisible laser beams crisscrossing other rooms. Then there are heat sensors that set off alarms if they sense body heat. Then, finally, under the jewel itself, there's a weight sensor that sets off the alarm if the jewel is removed from its stand.

Continuing the security system metaphor and merging it with the sun-and-clouds metaphor I shared in the previous chapter, you keep yourself away from The Truth, your infinite power, wisdom, abundance, and True Joy in Phase 1 by making those clouds, those lies, the equivalent of an elaborate, multilayered security system. One of the layers of that system is denying The Truth when it's staring you straight in the face, finding it too weird, strange, "out there" or "woo-woo" for you. This, by the way, is the True explanation for any feelings of discomfort, doubt, or disbelief you may be feeling now, or that you have been feeling as you've been reading, or that you may feel later about the content of the model I'm sharing with you.

What I just described may have stirred up feelings of discomfort within you. Perhaps it didn't. Either way, there *is* good news here for you. What is it? The Phase 1 Miracle illusions, the solid and dense cloud cover blocking out the sun of who you really are, the lies, were all put into place simply to lock you into Phase 1.

However, when you move into Phase 2, all of that changes. When you move into Phase 2, you have the opportunity to reverse all those dynamics, and, over time, expand into a place where none of the illusions limit you, restrict you, or affect you adversely in any way. You also get to disable the metaphorical security system you installed in Phase 1.

When you expand to that point, as it relates to The Business Game, you'll simply create whatever total-immersion movie business experiences you choose to play with for the sheer fun of playing—and what *appears* to be happening outside of you in the economy, stock market, industry trends, technologies, or with competitors will be irrelevant to you—or used as raw material to support you in having even more fun. For example, if you had chosen to play a stock-trading game at that point and you had sold short right before a stock market crash, would the crash have been bad news for *you*? No, it would have been great news and a fun experience! If you aren't playing a stock-trading game, do stock prices affect you? No. If oil prices rise and you're playing an oil business game, is the price increase bad for you? No! You get the idea.

This is how and where I live now—playing the New Business Games that interest me and are fun for me without any concern about what *appears* to be going on outside of me. During a time when so many Players of The Business Game are experiencing the illusion of struggle, my businesses are all thriving (as are the businesses of many other Phase 2 Players I know)! It's an extraordinary place to be and to live. You, too, can live there if you choose to follow the path outlined in this book. I'll be sharing lots more about this in the chapters to come.

When you're ready to discover The Truth about the unseen activity that is the True Source of everything you experience, the unseen activity that at present keeps you locked into the limitations of The Business Game, and the unseen activity that can ultimately bust you loose from The Business Game, turn the page and continue with Chapter 5.

The Physics of Fiction

Reality is merely an illusion, albeit a persistent one.[1]

—Albert Einstein

There's no out there out there.[2]

—John Wheeler, Physicist

I shared a lot of philosophy with you in the past few chapters. Maybe you resonated with some or all of it. Maybe some or all of it sounded "woo-woo" to you, or you're having trouble seeing how it could relate to your business or busting loose from The Business Game in a practical way. As you'll soon see if you haven't already, the philosophy is a critical part of The Busting Loose

---

[1] Albert Einstein, in "Wisdom Quotes," www.wisdomquotes.com/003090.html.

[2] John Wheeler, speech at the Santa Fe Institute, April 16, 1990, as reported in Tor Nørretranders's *The User Illusion* (New York: Penguin Group, 1998), p. 10.

Model. Your awareness of it lays a beautiful foundation for the discussion of cutting-edge scientific research in this chapter and the one that follows.

Thousands of books, articles, briefs, and other documents have been written about the scientific research I'll be summarizing and interpreting for you here. Most of it isn't necessary or relevant for our busting loose purposes. Therefore, I'm going to summarize the key points briefly and move on. If you want to dive more deeply into the research on your own, I recommend a book called *The Field: The Quest for the Secret Force of the Universe* by my friend Lynne McTaggart. Other scientific resources you can consult will be described in the Appendix of this book.

To play games, including The Human Game and The Business Game, we must have tools, support resources, and a playing field on which to play. Take baseball as an example. After the inventor of the game first thought it up, he or others then had to physically create a diamond, bats, balls, and gloves before people could actually play the game.

The same thing is true for The Human Game. It's one thing for an Infinite Being to consider creating a gigantic amusement park where total-immersion movies could be created and experienced, but quite another to actually build the amusement park and make it fun and exhilarating to play there. So what we're going to discuss now is how the amusement park (three-dimensional reality) is created to support us in playing The Human Game.

Throughout history, scientists have been trying to figure out how our physical universe is structured, how it really works, and the laws that supposedly govern it. To solve such mysteries, scientists attempt to break the physical universe into smaller and smaller pieces to understand what the core building blocks are and how they interact with each other.

As scientists looked more deeply into this mystery throughout history, they discovered smaller and smaller particles that were given names like cells, molecules, atoms, protons, and electrons. When they penetrated more deeply into the subatomic world, however, scientists began to notice even smaller particles that didn't seem to behave according to the known laws of physics. Those discoveries led to a series of breakthroughs that are now called *quantum physics*.

When I was first introduced to quantum physics, I couldn't understand much of it. It fried my brain! The subject was very dense to read and wade through. But I had a sense there were important puzzle pieces for me there, so I persisted. Finally, the light began to dawn, I clearly saw the puzzle pieces that were there for me, and I added them to my collection. I'm now going to share them with you.

One scientist, David Bohm, was at the forefront of the first breakthroughs in quantum physics. Bohm concluded that the only way to explain the strange behavior scientists were seeing with subatomic particles was that the tangible reality of our everyday lives is an illusion. Bohm asserted that underlying what we call reality was a deeper order of existence, a vast and more primary level of reality that gave birth to all the objects and appearances of our physical universe. Michael Talbot summarized this in his book *The Holographic Universe*:

> Put another way, there is evidence to suggest that our world and everything in it—from snowflakes to maple trees to falling stars and spinning electrons—are also only ghostly images, projections from a level of reality so beyond our own it is literally beyond both space and time.[3]

Inspired by Bohm, numerous scientists kept looking for the deeper order he asserted was there. They ultimately found it in the form of a gigantic field of "intelligent energy" that has many names but is most often called *The Zero Point Field* (hereafter referred to as simply "The Field") within the scientific community.

Scientists discovered that The Field exists as energy with infinite potential that hasn't been formed into anything yet. However, from that infinite potential, literally anything *can* be created. Using a

---

[3] Michael Talbot, *The Holographic Universe* (New York: HarperCollins, 1991), p. 1.

somewhat crude but instantly understandable metaphor, imagine The Field as a magical form of clay from which anything can be molded—anything!

As scientists continued researching The Field, they developed a theory to explain how the physical universe is constructed from it. The theory involves four components:

1. The Field
2. Particles
3. The physical universe
4. Consciousness

I've already defined The Field and particles for you. You know about the physical universe. Consciousness is what physicists call *energy*, and what others have called "Mind," "Source," "Brahma," "God," and a host of other names throughout history and across cultures. Consciousness is not physical, but it's the creative force behind everything that appears to be physical—all people, all places, and all things. For the purposes of the model we're working with here, I'm going to define Consciousness as The Real You, you as an Infinite Being, your Expanded Self. In other words: You *are* Consciousness.

Depending on the beliefs you currently hold, you may be able to accept this easily. If you have a strong belief in God or some other form of Supreme Being, however, you may need to slightly modify this concept to say that God or a Supreme Being endowed *you* with Consciousness and the power to play The Human Game independently of Him/Her/It. There isn't really any conflict or problem here that can't be resolved in a practical way. It just depends on how you choose to look at it. Really getting that *your Consciousness* is creating everything you experience, down to the smallest detail, is absolutely critical to busting loose from The Business Game.

Here's how the scientific theory flows. The Field exists in a state of infinite possibility, which means anything is possible and anything can be created from it. There are no limits, no restrictions of any kind. However, when Consciousness focuses on The Field with a specific intent to create something, that state of infinite possibility collapses into a single so-called reality (or what we now know is an illusion) determined by that intent. In quantum physics terms, it's called "collapsing the wave form."

To make this very simple, if Consciousness focuses on The Field with the intent to create a chair, mountain, hand, or house, infinite possibility collapses into a single illusion called chair, mountain, hand, or house.

Once a collapse from infinite to finite takes place, the illusion of the physical universe begins to be created. What seem to be physical particles appear in that illusion and combine in specific ways to build the intended objects and living things we interact with in our daily lives—and the laws by which they appear to operate. The entire process is shaped and guided every step of the way by the original intention of the Consciousness that focused on The Field. And, it's all an illusion!

Key Point

Dive into anything in the physical world, and if you go deep enough, you end up at The Field.

At my live events and in the multimedia Home Transformational Systems I offer, I show an amazing video called "Powers of 10"[4] that visually illustrates this key point. It's extremely powerful for hammering home all the points I make about so-called reality being an illusion.

Barbara Dewey, writing in *Consciousness and Quantum Behavior*, said,

---

[4] www.powersof10.com/.

It's as if God said, "If I'm going to become physical, then I have to carry with me all the laws that make a physical world work. I will do this by inventing a tiny particle which, through its design, will, first, create the universe and then dictate all behavior like gravity, magnetism, the strong force, and the like throughout that universe because of the way I have constructed it. At the same time— and to make things easier for Me—I will invent senses that make the possessors of those senses think they see and touch and hear real things, think they witness space and feel time pass, when in fact all that realness will just be an illusion."[5]

In short, scientists are documenting that you can't see anything, hear anything, feel anything, experience anything (including sales, profits, products, services, employees, financial ups and downs, or anything related to your business) unless *your* Consciousness *creates it* by focusing on The Field with a specific intent to create exactly that. For example, you can't see my words on this page unless *your* Consciousness focuses on The Field with the intent to create them and then actually constructs the illusion of paper, ink, words, and pages, particle by particle, piece by piece, for you to see. This book has no independent existence or power of its own. Your Consciousness has the only real power and existence in the equation.

Key Point

If you are aware of it, you are creating it, down to the smallest detail. As wild as this may seem, you'll prove it to yourself through direct experience if you take this journey and bust loose.

As another example, you can't see your checking account, a financial statement, a profit and loss statement, or any numbers anywhere unless *your* Consciousness focuses on The Field with the intent

[5] Barbara Dewey, *Consciousness and Quantum Behavior* (Inverness, CA: Bartholomew Books, 1993), p. 9.

to create them and then actually constructs them, piece by piece, particle by particle, for you to see. The numbers don't have independent existence or power of their own. Your Consciousness is the only power and existence in that equation, too. Does that seem hard to believe at this point? Possibly. Is it true nevertheless? Absolutely.

Key Point

Real = "Infiniteland" (the term I use to describe where you really come from) and you as an Infinite Being. *Everything else is an illusion.*

Speaking about this phenomenon in the movie *What the Bleep Do We Know!?* Amit Goswami, Ph.D., a brilliant scientist on the cutting edge of quantum physics and Consciousness research, said:

We all have the habit of thinking that everything around us is already a thing existing without my input, without my choice. You have to banish that kind of thinking.

Instead, you really have to recognize that even the material world around us, the chairs, the tables, the rooms, the carpet, time included, all of these are nothing but possible movements of Consciousness. And I'm choosing, moment to moment, out of those movements, to bring my actual experience into manifestation.

This is the only radical thinking that you need to do. But it is so radical—so difficult—because we tend to believe that the world is already out there, independent of our experience.

It is not. Quantum physics is so clear about this. Heisenberg himself, co-discoverer of quantum physics, said, "Atoms are not things; they're only tendencies."

So instead of thinking of things, you have to think of possibilities. They're all possibilities of Consciousness.[6]

---

[6] Amit Goswami, Ph.D., speaking in the movie *What the Bleep Do We Know!?* (Twentieth Century Fox, 2005).

This concept—the observer is creating the observed and you cannot separate them—is the reason the scientific community insists on running double-blind experiments. Why? Because scientists know if they go into an experiment with an agenda or desired outcome, they'll bias the results of the experiment. They know that by the sheer act of observing something, the observer changes it.

Barbara Dewey went on to say,

> The law of cause and effect works backward for consciousness. We place cause *before* effect. We see the results building in a one-two-three process. First we have the ovum and the sperm, then the cellular division which will eventually form a foetus, and so on. We say the ovum and the sperm are the cause of all the effects which eventually lead to the birth of a baby. However, in terms of consciousness, the *idea* of a human is the *cause* of this entire process. The intermediary steps are the *effect* of the creating and causal idea of *human*. In other words, consciousness reverses cause and effect. Cause, for consciousness, is the end result. The *effect* of this cause is a physical beginning.[7]

To continue that thought, let's take the human body as an example. As scientists view it, the body is composed of subatomic particles that combine to form atoms, that combine to form molecules, that combine to form cells, that combine to form organs, that combine to form systems (respiratory, circulatory), that all ultimately combine to form a human body. Once assembled, each of those parts and particles has specific and very complex tasks to perform so the body can function. However, the true source of *all of it* is The Field/Consciousness.

Think about that for a minute. That's a lot of particles that must somehow be:

1. Combined in specific ways.
2. Glued together once they combine into various shapes and forms so they stay in those shapes and forms.

---

[7] Dewey, *Consciousness and Quantum Behavior*, p. 24.

3. Taught how to perform their various tasks.

4. Able to communicate with each other to facilitate the performance of those tasks.

As you experience your own Human Game total-immersion movie experience, it is your Consciousness that creates the particles from The Field, glues them together, tells them how to combine, teaches them how to perform their tasks, gives them ongoing guidance as things change, and allows them to communicate with each other as needed.

When other games are played—such as baseball, football, soccer, softball, volleyball, or golf—you physically go to the field, court, or course to play. With The Human Game, however, you don't go anywhere. You're creating the whole Human Game and the entire amusement park out of *your* Consciousness, and that's where the whole Human Game is played.

We're going to get more into detail on this in the chapters that follow, but for now, I want to plant that seed because it's The Truth and it's the key to busting you loose from The Business Game. Plus, the really cool thing is if you accept the invitation I extend at the end of the book, you'll have very real, very direct, and absolutely mind-blowing experiences of yourself as the Consciousness that's creating everything you experience—including The Business Game and all the stories of what your experience with The Business Game is like now and has been like to date.

Let's now return to the philosophy I shared previously and take a fresh look based on what you have learned. As you now know, who you really are is an Infinite Being with infinite power and creative ability. Do you see how that aligns perfectly with the concept of infinite potential that scientists attribute to The Field?

I suggested that The Human Game is all about exploring what happens and what you can play with when you limit and restrict unlimited power. Do you see how that aligns perfectly with what scientists say happens when Consciousness focuses on The Field and collapses infinite possibility into the one illusion we call the physical universe—objects and living things—that we then explore and play with? That whole collapse process, by its very nature, is a limiting and restricting process!

I suggested that to play The Human Game, we must create a playing field on which to play and then convince ourselves the playing field is real. Do you see how that aligns beautifully with the theory of how the physical universe is constructed by Consciousness? You already know how real it appears.

In the next chapter, I'll take this one step further and show you how the illusion of the playing field and everything in it (including us as Players) is actually created, but for now there are three key points to review and lock into your awareness.

Key Points

1. Consciousness creates everything you experience, down to the smallest detail (including money and every aspect of The Business Game).

2. You and your Expanded Self *are* Consciousness, so *you* are creating everything you experience, down to the smallest detail (including money and every aspect of The Business Game).

3. The Human Game is being played entirely *in* Consciousness, and every detail is custom designed by your Expanded Self to support you in playing The Human Game and The Business Game the precise way you want to play it.

Do you find it hard to believe that *you* (the Expanded Self aspect of yourself, to be absolutely accurate) could be creating everything you experience? Consider your dreams at night. You lie down, close your eyes, fall asleep, and have experiences. In those dreams, your Consciousness creates entire worlds—people, places, things—and they appear absolutely real and solid, yet they're not. They're all made up, all creations of *your* Consciousness. The same thing is true when you have daydreams or visualize experiences in your imagination.

Think about it for a minute. When you dream, you appear to see out of the eyes of the person you are in the dream, right? Yet where are the eyes? There aren't any. Where are *you*, the Player of The Human Game, while all of this is going on? You're *not* just inside the person you appear to be. You are actually everything in the dream—everything. It's all *you*! *You* are all the people, all the objects, and all the living things you interact with while dreaming. *You* are even the very space and environment the dream appears to take place in (buildings, forest, homes, cities, etc.). It's *all* you . . . all *your* Consciousness.

Really think about that. In fact, if you have a vivid dream tonight, even if you perceive it to be only a few minutes long, observe this phenomenon. You'll see people who appear real who aren't really there. You'll see objects that appear real that aren't really there. You'll see other living things (animals, plants, trees) that appear real but aren't really there, either. Again, all of it is *your* Consciousness.

Do you still find all this hard to believe? Ask yourself the following seven questions, be brutally honest with yourself about the answers, and see where that exercise takes you:

1. Is your hometown there before you get there?
2. Is your hometown still there after you leave?
3. If you take an airplane flight from point A to point B, how do you know you actually went anywhere?
4. If you see a report on the news about a war, earthquake, hurricane, tsunami, or other event taking place somewhere else, how do you know it actually happened?
5. How do you know that anything we call "history" actually happened?

6. If you remember something from your own past, how do you know it actually happened?

7. What time is it?

If you're honest with yourself, you'll discover there's no proof that anyplace is actually there; no proof that you ever went anywhere by plane; no proof that anything you think happened in the so-called history of our planet or your own past actually happened; no proof that time exists or that the supposed correct time is correct. As part of the brilliant Phase 1 design, we just mentally connect the many illusory dots in what we experience (even though there are so many gaps we ignore as we do that); we assume it's all real, true, and accurate; and we act as if it's all real, true, and accurate—just like we do with the illusions we see at the movies.

To discover the nuts and bolts of how Consciousness creates the playing field for The Human Game, how those nuts and bolts hold the key to playing The New Business Game, and how you can turn that key in a lock to bust yourself loose from The Business Game, turn the page to begin Chapter 6.

6

The Two Ps

The universe may be nothing more than a giant hologram created by the mind.[1]

—David Bohm (1917–1992), Physicist

To bust loose from The Business Game, it's important to deepen your understanding of how the playing field of The Human Game is created and how your Expanded Self (Consciousness) creates all the experiences you have as a Player—including the balances in your financial accounts, the apparent flow of money in and out of your business, interactions between employees and vendors, and so on. To do that, I want to share another metaphor with you. The metaphor is that of a hologram.

---

[1] David Bohm, as quoted by Gregg Braden, *The Spontaneous Healing of Belief* (New York: Hay House, 2008), p. 37.

As I was struggling to understand quantum physics and how the puzzle pieces I extracted from it could be assembled into my expanding Busting Loose Model, I noticed several references to holograms. As I dove into the research and studied the true nature of holograms, I realized it was a perfect metaphor and puzzle piece.

A hologram is an image of a three-dimensional object or scene that appears to be real but isn't. Many scientists on the cutting edge of quantum physics and related research believe the hologram is an ideal metaphor to illustrate how the illusion of the physical universe is made to appear real. I agree with them. In their use of the metaphor, scientists go deeply into many facets of holograms that support their work, but in this chapter I'll be focusing on only two key facets. In the Appendix, I'll show you how to find additional information if you want it.

If you've seen what you thought was a hologram in the *Star Wars* movies, on a credit card, or in some other place, you saw something that had a three-dimensional look and feel, but didn't look real. Those examples are just imitations of the true power of a real hologram. However, if you saw the movies *The Matrix* or *The 13th Floor*, or a *Star Trek* movie or television show where the characters used what's called the "holodeck," you've seen what's really possible with holograms. In fact, at my live events, I show video clips from movies and television shows to give participants a strong visual image of what's possible with holograms. You'll find a link to a website page with a list of the movies I took the clips from in the Appendix.

In *The Holographic Universe*, Michael Talbot said,

> Physicist William Tiller, head of the Department of Materials Science at Stanford University and another supporter of the holographic idea, agrees. Tiller thinks reality is similar to the "holodeck" on the television show *Star Trek: The Next Generation*. In the series, the holodeck is an environment in which occupants can call up a holographic simulation of literally any reality they desire, a lush forest, a bustling city. They can also change each simulation in any way they want, such as cause a lamp to

materialize or make an unwanted table disappear. Tiller thinks the universe is also a kind of holodeck created by the "integration" of all living things. "We've created it as a vehicle of experience, and we've created the laws that govern it," he asserts. "And when we get to the frontiers of our understanding, we can in fact shift the laws so that we're also creating the physics as we go along."[2]

To explain how beautiful a metaphor the hologram is, I'm going to get technical for a minute, then bring it back to a simpler explanation. A hologram is created through a very specific process. Suppose you wanted to make a hologram of an apple. To do that, you'd first bathe the apple in the light of a laser beam. Then a second laser beam is bounced off the reflected light of the first beam and the resulting interference pattern (the area where the two laser beams commingle) is captured on film or a holographic plate, as shown in the first diagram.

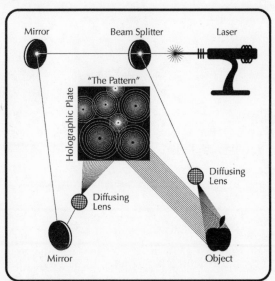

How a holographic pattern is created.

[2] Michael Talbot, *The Holographic Universe* (New York: HarperCollins, 1991), p. 158.

In this case, the pattern imprinted on the film would contain very specific information about the apple—its exact red color and other details of its skin; its height, width, and depth; the size, length, location, and color of the stem; perhaps the size and location of a small dent in the skin created when someone dropped it; and so on.

When the film is developed, it looks like a meaningless swirl of light and dark lines. But as soon as the developed film is illuminated (energized) by another laser beam, a three-dimensional image of the apple appears in space looking absolutely real and accurately depicting all the information stored in the pattern, as illustrated in the next diagram.

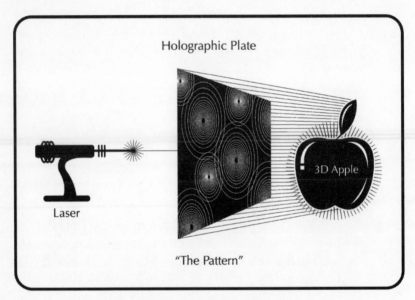

How an actual hologram is created.

With very sophisticated holograms, like in *The Matrix* and *The 13th Floor* or on the *Star Trek* holodeck, like present-day engineers and scientists are experimenting with, and like the Hollywood special effects and animation studios are playing with, the holographic illusion is created through computers, software programs, and complex mathematical algorithms.

The two important points to focus on within the hologram metaphor are:

1. To create a hologram, which is the *illusion* of something physical, you must first create a *pattern* that holds all the details of the illusion you want to create.
2. To actually see the hologram, you must then add tremendous amounts of *power* to the pattern, which then pops out the illusion that appears to be absolutely real.

In other words:

$$\text{Pattern} + \text{Power} = \text{Illusion}$$

Here, then, are the components of my Model for how *your Consciousness* creates the illusion of the physical universe and everything in it—and makes it appear so real that it completely fools you and allows you to play in Phase 1 of The Human Game:

- Your Consciousness approaches The Field of infinite possibility with an intention to create something and make it appear physical or real in The Human Game amusement park (a body, environment, object, animal, plant, checking account statement, cash, employee, stock certificate, etc.).

- Your Consciousness then creates a pattern in The Field with all the necessary detail about what it wants to make physical— including all the details about you (the Player) and all the other Players of The Human Game you create to join you (body size, shape, hair color and length, personality, aching back, and so on). Another name for these detailed patterns in popular culture is "beliefs," which we'll be discussing in detail later in the book.

- Your Consciousness then applies power (from your infinite supply) to the pattern, and the desired creation then pops out as a holographic illusion, with you, the Player, in the middle of it.

- Because the pattern is so detailed and so much power was applied to pop it into reality, it appears absolutely real and totally convincing. The manifestation diagram illustrates this concept.

Manifestation: How Consciousness creates the illusion of the three-dimensional world.

As you move from birth through infancy and childhood to adulthood (all just a series of complex holographic creations and illusions, by the way), the number of patterns in The Field (beliefs) grows exponentially to form the complex playing field you call reality and your life. Your Expanded Self controls what goes into the pattern and therefore what appears in your holographic illusion—all driven by a brilliant plan that flows out of your life purpose and mission—to perfectly support you in playing The Human Game the way that you want to play it.

Key Point

You aren't watching your Human Game hologram like you'd watch a movie, play, or sporting event. Your Expanded Self is simultaneously creating the hologram and popping you right smack into the middle of it as the Player of The Human Game.

As I mentioned earlier, Phase 1 of The Human Game is about totally immersing yourself in the illusion of the three-dimensional world and convincing yourself it's real. Your Consciousness and your Expanded Self are real. The Field is real. The patterns your Expanded Self creates in The Field are real. The power your Expanded Self applies to the patterns in The Field is real. But everything else you see and experience in your hologram in Phase 1 of The Human Game is just a holographic illusion. You may be able to accept this now, or you may not. But if you want to bust loose from The Business Game, you must get to the point where that Truth becomes very real for you. I'll show you how to do this in the chapters that follow.

One of the keys to the illusion creation process is the amount of detail stored in the pattern in The Field, and that's where your true power as an Infinite Being really shines through. Remember, The Human Game is designed to be an ultimate game that tricks you into believing that an illusion is real. Therefore, the amount of detail that must be stored in the patterns in The Field and the amount of power needed to pop them into your hologram are unimaginable from your current perspective.

Key Point

If any detail in the holographic illusion misses the mark or appears fake, the illusion instantly collapses and The Human Game ends. That can't be allowed to happen, so tremendous effort is invested to make everything appear absolutely real and convincing.

Let me give you a mind-blowing illustration of this that was related to me by my friend Bill McDonough.[3] In *The Lord of the Rings* movie trilogy, there's a character named Gollum. Whereas all the human characters in the movie were played by real people, Gollum

---

[3] www.mcdonough.com.

was primarily computer generated. In making the final movie in the trilogy, *The Lord of the Rings: The Return of the King*, the creators produced an artificial world they wanted you to accept as real. Since Gollum was in so many scenes with other humans in that artificial world (which looked absolutely real), they didn't want him to stand out as looking fake, because if he did, the illusion would be blown and your movie experience would suffer. Therefore, they needed Gollum to appear as real as the people.

Although Gollum was primarily computer generated, his movements and expressions were directly animated by an actor using a technique called *motion capture*.[4] The motions of the actor were digitally recorded in three dimensions and transferred to Gollum.

Within the special effects and animation industries in Hollywood and the video gaming industry, gigantic strides have been made to create animated people, animals, monsters, creatures, settings, and objects that look real. Interestingly enough, when it comes to people, one of the most challenging features to model and animate is hair, which, it turns out, is a very complicated creation. It has so many layers and facets to it. It changes dramatically as people move, when it's blown by the wind, when it's wet or dry, and so on. Therefore, simulating hair realistically is an enormously complex software challenge that had not yet been fully overcome by animators.

With each film Hollywood releases, studios invest in an aspect of computer animation to push the envelope, tell their story better, and differentiate themselves in an effort to compel audiences to see their films. Most audiences today are visually sophisticated and expect to see a new set of special effects—like realistic hair, dinosaurs, giant apes, or superheroes.

Since the special effects and animation experts were committed to making Gollum's hair look absolutely real (even though he didn't have much hair), they teamed up with several of the biggest movie studios and spent months and millions of dollars having brilliant

---

[4] www.bustingloose.com/motion.

programmers finally develop computer algorithms and software that could do it. Does this sound crazy or like overkill to you—all that money and effort just for hair? If so, remember what's at stake. If the illusion collapses, so does the project—and millions of dollars in profits.

The same thing is true for The Human Game and the holographic illusions you call reality. You can't see or experience anything unless your Expanded Self creates a pattern in The Field and adds power to pop out the illusion of it—and whatever is in the pattern is what you see and experience (including money, bank balances, and financial statements). Like Hollywood, Consciousness is constantly pushing the envelope on making the patterns more and more sophisticated and the illusions appear more and more real.

If you look down at the floor in front of you right now and see a carpet with a stain on it, or a wooden floor with a scratch on it, they're the result of details in patterns in The Field. There's no carpet there, no stain, no wood, no scratch. It's all made up—all just an illusion. But the illusion must be complex, detailed, and incredibly refined or it won't fool you, and if it doesn't fool you, if even the tiniest detail is out of place, "Game Over."

You might be interested to know that within today's scientific and business community, the technology required to make very real-appearing holograms has been accelerating at a rapid pace. Two technologies that appear to be at the forefront at the time of this writing are Cisco's Telepresence[5] technology and the Teleportec[6] technology.

My friend Bill McDonough is a visionary and a pioneer in the green movement and the recycling movement, and in the architectural and product design possibilities flowing from them. In August 2006, he made a presentation using the Teleportec technology I just mentioned. During that presentation, he was standing behind a podium live in Charlottesville, Virginia, and was seen standing

---

[5] www.cisco.com/en/US/products/ps7060/.

[6] http://teleportec.com/technology.html.

behind the same podium as a holographic projection at the Castle Theater of the Maui Arts & Cultural Center in Maui, Hawaii—thousands of miles away. The degree to which he seemed real to the Hawaiian audience was extraordinary. And bear in mind that holographic technology of this kind is still in its infancy!

As time passes, you'll see those holographic technologies evolve and get more and more real-appearing. You'll also see the entertainment and video game industries move more and more into what is being called virtual reality as our appetites for a more total immersion experience rise as a mirror of what The Human Game is all about.

Key Point

Our ability to actually pull off the illusions of the playing field, the amusement park for The Human Game, and to make everyone and everything appear absolutely real is an enormous accomplishment—one of the most amazing aspects of who we really are and how much power we really have.

But it goes beyond that. If you're going to create illusions as part of playing The Human Game, you must do three things:

1. Make those illusions appear absolutely real.
2. Have those illusions reinforce the Phase 1 dynamics when you're playing the Phase 1 Game.
3. Have those illusions become amazing rides and attractions Players can experience and have fun playing with and exploring in the amusement park, in Phase 1 and Phase 2.

For example, if you're going to create the illusion of a human body in your hologram, that body must not only appear real, but it must also provide excellent raw material for playing subset games within The Human Game. You can't create the illusion of a body and have it be empty inside. There must appear to be something inside the body that people can play with and study (through biology and medicine). That's why the body was created to appear to be assembled out of subatomic particles, atoms, molecules, cells, organs, and systems. That's why the body appears to have veins, arteries, blood, other fluids, a heart, a brain, and so on.

As another example, if you create an ocean in your hologram, it can't stop at the surface. You must also create a world beneath it so Players can dive into it, play in it, and study it (through swimming, snorkeling, scuba diving, and oceanography).

If you're going to create space in your hologram, you must create something in that space—stars, planets, comets, galaxies, and black holes—so Players can look up, wonder about it, explore it, and even fly through it (astronomy and spacecraft).

If you create billions of people, they can't have just appeared out of nowhere, so you must create a story line to explain them and make them believable, and again, to give Players something to study (history, evolution, and archaeology). On and on it goes for all the sciences and other creations in The Human Game amusement park.

As we discussed, in Phase 1 of The Human Game, the goal is to create patterns in The Field and pop illusions into your hologram to limit you; restrict you; hide your power, wisdom, abundance, and True Joy—and convince you that you're the opposite of who you *really* are. Therefore, it should come as no surprise that so many of the experiences you've had in your life up until now—including in business—have been frustrating, annoying, difficult, and different from what you might have preferred. However, that's the way the patterns were designed, that's what power was applied to, and that's what *had* to pop into your hologram as a result.

All of us could create long lists of complaints about our businesses and personal lives—past and present. I'm sure you can think of many things you'd love to eliminate, change, or improve if you could. As Phase 1 Players, by design, we become absolute masters at harshly judging our holographic creations. We'll discuss this in detail in later chapters.

However, as you now know, The Truth is we're all brilliant and amazing Creators—quantum special effects animators, you might say. Nothing you see in your hologram is real. It's all illusions, all stories you made up, told yourself in Consciousness, and convinced yourself were real. It's all smoke and mirrors and always was—whether you judge it good or bad or better or worse.

The fact that we can make holographic illusions seem so real is an absolute miracle. The fact that we can actually look at an absolute miracle and judge it as bad, lousy, terrible, awful, and in need of change, fixing, and improvement, or want to make it go away is even more of a miracle. And the fact that we can actually use our make-believe creations to convince ourselves we're the exact opposite of who we really are is even more of a miracle. Your Expanded Self, The Real You, is an absolute genius at creating illusions. David Copperfield and Hollywood beware!

By the way, if the thought hasn't already crossed your mind, it will, so I want to address it now. Scientists have been studying the hologram. Therefore, although they think it's real, they've actually been studying an illusion. However, within the illusion, and particularly within quantum physics and related scientific fields, our Expanded Selves left clues to The Truth for us; and it's those clues I've drawn from and shared with you in this and the preceding chapter.

I'd like to summarize some of the key points made in this chapter before we continue:

Key Points

- You + Your Expanded Self = Consciousness.
- You're not just *watching* a hologram; you're actually creating everything in it—including yourself.

- *Nothing* you experience is real.
- It's all completely made up.

- It's all a creation of *your* Consciousness.
- Your Expanded Self has direct access to The Field.
- Your Expanded Self designs the patterns.
- Your Expanded Self manages the application of power to the patterns.
- Your Expanded Self controls what pops into your holographic illusion as guided by the life purpose and mission you chose when you decided to play The Human Game.

As we conclude this chapter, please remember what I said in the Introduction: You don't need to take my word on anything I just shared with you, whether it makes logical sense and feels right to you or not. If you accept my invitation at the end of the book and make the leap into Phase 2, you'll have experiences that will prove to you, beyond the shadow of any doubt, that everything I just shared is True.

To discover who all the other people in your hologram *really* are and how they *really* interact with you to support you in playing The Human Game, turn the page to begin Chapter 7 and continue your journey into busting loose from The Business Game.

CHAPTER

7

The Many Faces of Power

A loving person lives in a loving world. A hostile person lives in a hostile world. Everyone you meet is your mirror.[1]

—Ken Keyes Jr., Writer

T here are some games we prefer to play alone. But most games are played with other players for maximum enjoyment and fun. The same is True of The Human Game. If you created an elaborate playing field for a game and no one else was there to play with you, it wouldn't be much fun, would it? Plus, there's no way you could pull off The Phase 1 Miracle. To convince yourself the illusion is real—and that you're the opposite of who you really are—other people are required.

Therefore, as part of playing The Human Game, you create other Players in your hologram to lock in the Phase 1 dynamics, to assist you

---

[1] Ken Keyes Jr., in *Bits & Pieces* (Chicago: Ragan Communications, October 2004).

in playing and having fun, and to allow for the kind of complexity that's needed to keep your challenge, interest, and enjoyment levels high. Just like in a dream, these other Players, these "other people" (as you once called them), aren't actually separate from you, although they certainly appear to be. They're *you*. They're other aspects of *your Consciousness*. They're 100 percent created by *your* power, which is why I call this chapter "The Many Faces of Power."

You can compare the roles other people play in your hologram to the roles actors play in Hollywood movies, television shows, and plays, although there are some important differences we'll discuss. Actors appear in movies, television shows, and plays by choice and agreement. They enter and exit the stage when they're told to. If they agree to play a particular role, they're given a script that gives them specific lines to say and actions to take, and they say and do what they're told.

There are actors who play large parts we call starring roles. Others play smaller parts we call supporting roles. Still other actors who remain in the background and never speak to or impact the central characters are called extras. Extras are just there to make the scenes appear real or to hammer home another point important to the unfolding story.

The same thing is true for your Human Game holographic total-immersion movie experience, and interestingly enough, most of the people you see in your hologram are extras. If you really think about it, even though you're told there are billions of people in The Human Game amusement park, throughout your entire life you see only a small fraction of them *in person*, and only a small number of those actually interact with you and have any impact on you.

Key Point

As hard as it may be to believe, when other Players appear in *your* hologram, they're 100 percent *your* creation. No one has any power or independent decision-making authority *in your hologram* beyond what your Expanded Self gives them through the script details to support you in playing The Human Game.

Here's a question and comment I hear often at this point in laying out The Busting Loose Model: "You're saying my spouse, kids, parents, sister, friends, brother, employees, customers, and boss aren't real? They're just holographic illusions? No way. I can't accept that, and I don't like how it devalues them in my mind."

If thoughts like that have crossed your mind, let me share the following for now; then we'll come back to this discussion later. First, it's not just other people who aren't real. Nothing in your hologram is real as I previously defined the term for you—including you and me. We're all just part of a holographic illusion created by Consciousness to allow us to play The Human Game.

Second, as I explained in the preceding chapter (and we'll delve more deeply into this in later chapters), the entire Human Game is a miracle, an amazing accomplishment, a brilliant creation that you can—and will—be in absolute awe of at every moment. There's not the slightest trace of devaluing anyone or anything in the Model. It's quite the opposite.

Finally, if you choose to play the Phase 2 game and take the action steps I share in the final chapters of the book, I absolutely guarantee, beyond the shadow of any doubt, you'll prove the validity of my claims about others through the Phase 2 experiences you'll create *with the other Players* you create to play the Phase 2 Game with you.

When I share that everyone else is just your creation, an aspect of your Consciousness, *you in disguise*, it's quite natural to wonder how I could be creating you and you could be creating me simultaneously, or how you could be creating your partner or boss and he or she could be creating you simultaneously, or wonder the same thing about any individual or group of people who appear separate from you. It can get very confusing.

I must now make one key point very clear before we continue. There's a concept in quantum physics called *tangled hierarchy*. As I choose to interpret it, it means that trying to resolve certain mysteries or riddles from a logical or analytical perspective results in an endless loop that gets you nowhere.

For example, suppose I say to you, "All writers are liars." Am I telling the truth or lying? Try to resolve it logically. You can't. If I say all writers are liars and I'm a writer, then I must be lying. So if I'm lying, then the opposite must be true—all writers must tell the truth. But then I'm lying when I say all writers are liars. So writers can't all tell the truth because they can lie, and on and on it goes in an endless loop. The only way out of the loop is to jump out of it completely— or never go there in the first place.

The same thing is true for trying to figure out if someone else has their own hologram, what's going on in someone else's hologram, or what role you are playing in someone else's hologram. You can't do it. Trying to figure it out creates an endless loop that gets you nowhere. For the purposes of the Model I'm sharing here, and to support yourself in busting loose from The Business Game, I invite you to keep the focus on yourself at all times. From your perspective, it's *your* hologram, *your* total-immersion experience, *your* game in the three-dimensional amusement park, a creation of *your* Consciousness.

Key Point

If you are aware of it, you are creating it, down to the smallest detail. So, when playing the Phase 2 Game, you keep the focus on yourself and your hologram.

To repeat another key point for emphasis, in your hologram, others have absolutely no power, independent existence, or independent decision-making authority. In your hologram, they're 100 percent *your* creation, and that's all you concern yourself with. You leave all thought about *their* holograms, including your role in them, alone. If you'd like to learn a bit more about this, I have a special gift for you—an audio recording of a brief lecture I gave on the subject. Just visit this page on my web site to hear or download it: www .bustingloose.com/others.html.

By the way, a corollary of this that applies to your personal and business lives is that you're always absolutely safe and protected in your hologram. No one else can intrude into your hologram and hurt or damage you, your company, your team, your sales, your profits, your cash flow, or anyone you care about, in any way. The only way someone could *appear* to hurt or damage you, your company, your team, your sales, your profits, your cash flow, or anyone you care about is if your Expanded Self creates a pattern with those details in The Field, energizes it, pops it into your hologram, and convinces you it's real. And the only reason he or she would do that is if having such an experience would provide perfect support for you in playing The Human Game—no matter how you might judge it from your limited perspective as the Player and star of your total-immersion movie. And in that case, it could be accurately said that there is no hurt or damage taking place, even if it seems like there is.

Key Point

There's no power outside of you in your hologram—not in anyone, not in anything. *You* have all the power in your hologram.

Everyone else who appears in your hologram was created from a pattern in The Field that was put there and energized by your Expanded Self. Remember, you can't see or experience *anything or anyone* in your hologram that isn't created *by you* in that way. All the patterns in The Field relating to other people are created to allow them to play one or more of these three roles in your hologram:

1. Reflect something back you're thinking or feeling about yourself or a belief you have about yourself or the hologram.
2. Share supportive knowledge, wisdom, or insight with you.
3. Set something in motion to support you on your journey.

We now look at each of these three possibilities separately.

Reflection

In her book *As You Believe*, Barbara Dewey wrote,

> The illusion of separation not only symbolizes our self-doubt and
> alienation, it gives us a chance to work through the interior distress
> of various dichotomies by externalizing them. We see ourselves in
> others, hating in them what we hate in ourselves, loving in them
> what we love in ourselves. We contend with others because we are
> contending within ourselves. We punish and reward others as we
> would ourselves. The illusion of separation offers us the chance to
> resolve the interior inhibitions to unqualified love in a state of true
> union. Without this illusion and our reactions to other people, we
> might never even know such stresses existed.[2]

Note Dewey's use of such words as *self-doubt*, *alienation*, *distress*, *hate*,
punish, and *inhibitions*. Do you see how beautifully it all ties into the goal
of Phase 1, which is to create the illusion of limitation and restriction
and to convince yourself you're the opposite of who you really are?

As Barbara expressed so beautifully in the preceding quote, you
pop many people into your hologram—in and out of your business—
to reflect back what you're thinking or feeling about yourself to
support you on your journey (which takes on added significance in
Phase 2, as we'll discuss in later chapters), or to display a belief you
have about the illusion.

For example, if you create an employee or associate who is
constantly saying, "If I don't do it myself, it won't get done
correctly," the odds are that's a belief *you* hold, whether you're
consciously aware of it or not, and you're reflecting it back through
the other aspect of yourself. If you know you have a belief like that,
or you create another aspect to reflect that sort of belief back, the
odds are also strong you'll pop many people into your hologram who
will act in such a way as to support the validity of the belief. Then

---

[2] Barbara Dewey, *As You Believe* (Inverness, CA: Bartholomew Books, 1990), p. 82.

you'll say, "You see, that *is* how people are!" and the belief gets reinforced. That's how powerful you are.

Similarly, if you believe, "I'm always underappreciated and underpaid at work," or "Friends and family borrow money from me and never pay it back," or "People will take every opportunity to overcharge and rip you off," you'll create other aspects to pop into your hologram that appear to prove and provide evidence that those beliefs are all real!

As another example, if you create people who come into your hologram and treat you shabbily or ignore you (like I did when I was younger and deeply immersed in Phase 1), it's a reflection of the fact that you're treating yourself shabbily and ignoring yourself—in one way or another.

At a time when I was angry at the world and lashing out at everyone around me, I created a dog in my hologram who barked at people and noises with such intensity that I often thought she'd rupture a kidney or have a heart attack if she kept barking like that. When I moved through that phase and calmed down, she suddenly passed away. This whole reflection thing will absolutely amaze you when you begin to see it clearly!

From my experience in the laboratory of my own life and working with thousands of clients worldwide, reflections can become quite detailed and complex, just like the very nature of The Human Game. We'll discuss them in more detail in later chapters.

Knowledge, Wisdom, and Insight

To play The Human Game, there are times when it's supportive to give yourself specific nuggets of knowledge, wisdom, and insight. As a result, you'll pop teachers, speakers, experts, friends, associates, and complete strangers into your hologram to enlighten you directly—or enlighten yourself indirectly through books, magazines, newspapers, audiotapes, or videotapes you create. This is the role you've created for me to play in your hologram, for example.

As an Infinite Being, you have instant access to *all* knowledge, wisdom, and insight, but while playing The Human Game, you can create knowledge, wisdom, and insight *appearing* to flow to you, with any storyline attached, by simply creating patterns in The Field, energizing them, and popping them into your hologram—just as you did with this book.

Setting Things into Motion

In Chapter 3, I gave the example of baseball and explained how The Human Game was designed to allow you to explore what-if scenarios so you could have fun tracking the possibilities and watching how everything moves when the variables change.

As a result, you frequently create other aspects of yourself and pop them into your hologram to set things in motion to support you in playing The Human Game the way you want to play it. For example, you might create someone to pop into your hologram and offer you a job, fire you from a job, give you a lucrative contract for your business, introduce you to an influential contact, give you an investment tip, lend you money, say or do something to offend or upset you, give you a speeding ticket, or run a red light and crash into your car. In each case, such creations open doors, nudge you through them, and set powerful events in motion in your total-immersion movie experience that support you perfectly in playing The Human Game exactly as you want to play it.

If you accept the invitation at the end of this book and choose to play the Phase 2 Game, you'll create many other aspects of your own Consciousness popping into your hologram to say and do things that support you in reclaiming power from the limited Phase 1 patterns in The Field, collapsing them, and appearing to assist you in busting loose from The Business Game. Again, you created me to support you in doing this.

You can probably already guess some of what I'm about to share with you on this subject, but when you're ready to pop another myth and discover The Truth about the so-called law of cause and effect, turn the page and begin Chapter 8.

The Myth of Cause and Effect

The will is not free—it is a phenomenon bound by cause and effect—but there is something behind the will which is free.[1]

—*Swami Vivekananda*

In Phase 1 of The Human Game, and particularly within the context of The Business Game, you were taught that the law of cause and effect is real and true. You were taught that if you want to create success in business, solve problems, and so on, you must take specific actions (causes) that will lead to desirable outcomes (effects) and that there's an inextricable link between the two. You're

---

[1] Swami Vivekananda, in "ThinkExist.com," http://thinkexist.com/quotes/with/keyword/cause_and_effect/.

also taught that if you aren't getting the desirable outcomes you prefer, you need to find better actions (causes) to set into motion.

Let me now redefine the term *cause and effect* from the perspective of the Model we're working with here. I would do that by saying that cause and effect means there is an inextricable link between the actions a Player takes *in the hologram* and the results or outcomes he or she produces from those actions taken *in the hologram*.

Before we continue, please take another look at the manifestation illustration that I introduced in Chapter 6.

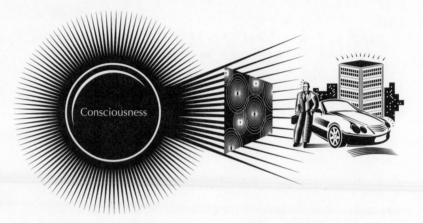

Manifestation: How Consciousness creates the illusion of the
three-dimensional world.

On the far right of the illustration is the visual depiction of the hologram. On the far left and in the center are the visual depictions of the creative process the hologram rises out of. From what you now know, and after taking a close look at the illustration, let me ask you a question:

Is there any real power or any real cause and effect *within* the hologram?

The answer is . . .

No!

Why? Because the hologram doesn't exist. It's an illusion. It can't be there unless a creative process put it there, so the True power, cause, and effect are within the creative process that put the illusion there, not the illusion itself.

Think of it this way: When you're sitting in a theater watching a movie, you're seeing images on the screen. They're illusions. The people and objects aren't really there. But a creative process put them there. Without the creative process, the screen is blank. If an actor in a Hollywood movie appears to hit another person and the other person appears to get a black eye, is there Truly any power, Truly any cause-and-effect relationship *on the screen* between the two illusory actions: movement of fist and blackened eye? No, it just looks like there is. Why? There are two reasons:

1. The whole thing is an illusion, so nothing really happened. The person wasn't really hit, and there wasn't really any black eye. An actor participated in the illusion of a fist hitting another actor, and the illusion of a black eye was created by a makeup artist.

2. If we give the illusion on the screen some "realness" for purposes of discussion, then, since the action on the screen is an illusion, the Hollywood script is the true cause of the scene and everything that happens in it. The actors, the makeup artist, and the whole creative team follow the script to produce the true effect, the illusion that appears on the screen.

The same thing would be True, of course, for the illusion of cause and effect in a television show, play, novel, video game, and so on.

Before you consider the words I'm about to share with you, please take another look at the manifestation illustration. Done? Okay. Whenever there appears to be cause and effect within the hologram, it's because details were inserted into patterns in The Field by your Expanded Self to create the illusion of cause and effect. In essence, your Expanded Self creates a pattern that says, "Make it look like X action caused Y event." It's really that simple.

Key Point

There is no cause and effect *within* the hologram. Your Consciousness, your Expanded Self, is always the cause and the hologram is always the effect.

Okay. Let's go deeper now. I'd like to tie this back to your business by asking and answering a series of questions. If we were actually together, I'd ask a question, then pause and wait for you to answer. We can't do that here, but despite that, I invite you to do your best to mimic an in-person interaction by reading the question, pausing to consider it, and answering it yourself before reading my answer (if you feel so moved). Here we go:

Q: What are sales, profits, income, and expenses?
A: Holographic illusions, like everything else in The Human Game total-immersion movie experience.

Q: What are products, services, and their costs or prices?
A: Amazing and brilliant holographic illusions!

Q: What are employees, partners, stockholders, board members, vendors, customers, clients, sales trainers, consultants, accountants, and bankers?
A: They are holographic illusions, aspects of *your* Consciousness, you in disguise, playing the roles *you* created them to play, saying and doing only what your Consciousness created them to say and do.

Q: What are recessions, depressions, stock market crashes, real estate bubble bursts, currency values, oil prices, and credit crunches?
A: Stories appearing to be true. Holographic illusions created by *your* Consciousness, which, in Phase 1, are all used to reinforce

the Phase 1 goals of convincing you the illusion is real and you're the opposite of who you really are within it.

Q: What are balance sheets, profit and loss statements, quarterly earnings, tax returns, and the other numbers you see as part of playing The Business Game?

A: Holographic illusions created by an amazing creative process!

Q: What are salaries, bonuses, commissions, stock options, and distributions?

A: All forms of money are just holographic illusions appearing to be real!

Q: Where do sales, profits, income, expenses, products, services, costs, prices, employees, partners, stockholders, board members, vendors, customers, clients, sales trainers, consultants, accountants, bankers, recessions, depressions, stock market crashes, real estate bubble bursts, currency values, oil prices, credit crunches, balance sheets, profit and loss statements, quarterly earnings, tax returns, and all forms of money *really* come from?

A: Patterns with specific details within them inserted into The Field by *your* Consciousness.

Okay, now here come two big questions that are important keys to your opportunity to bust loose from The Business Game:

Q: Do the actions you as the Player are taking now, the actions you took in the past, and the actions you'll take in the future—in and of themselves—have any real power or cause-and-effect ability to produce results of any kind in your business within the hologram?

A: No!

Q: Can you, as the Player, *really* do anything, on your own, to grow
   sales and profits; reduce expenses; manage, motivate, and train
   employees; outfox competitors; plan for or protect yourself
   against outside forces you seem vulnerable to; and solve
   problems?

A: No!

Key Point

Everything that happens as you play The Business Game is
coming from patterns in The Field, shaped and determined by
your Expanded Self to support you in playing The Human Game
the way you really *want* to—in Phase 1 and Phase 2.

Key Point

Your Expanded Self writes the script for what happens in your
business and for all the people, places, things, and events that
appear to affect or influence it. You're just an actor playing your
part!

Does this bother you? Does it make you feel uncomfortable?
Does it make you feel small, powerless, or like some sort of puppet? If
you have thoughts or feelings like that, they'll pass. The Truth is the
exact opposite. Does an actor feel diminished for playing a role when
someone else wrote the script? No. He or she relishes the opportunity to play the role and loves every minute on stage or on camera.
It'll be the same with you once this realization settles in. You're an
amazing part of an amazing creative process, illusion, and experience. Plus, as I mentioned earlier, you and your Expanded Self are
one unified Infinite Being. The apparent split into two parts—
Expanded Self and Player—is an illusion.

In Phase 1, all the script details, all the details your Expanded Self inserted into patterns in The Field, all the illusions you experienced to date as you played The Business Game—all of it—was designed to limit you, restrict you, convince you the illusion was real and you were the opposite of who you really are.

Therefore, no matter what struggles you've had historically with sales, profits, bosses, employees, salespeople failing to meet quotas, partners, board members, stockholders, morale, vendors, customers, equipment, competitors, and so on—they were all your creation, down to the smallest detail. They were all part of the story you were writing and unfolding through time to support you beautifully in playing The Human Game in Phase 1. They were all part of a total-immersion movie experience designed to reinforce the Phase 1 dynamics and lock in The Phase 1 Miracle.

In Phase 2, after you go through a period of what I call "expansion" (the length of which will be determined by your unique script), you will get to the point where your Expanded Self starts writing different stories, starts inserting different patterns into The Field, energizing them, and popping you into total-immersion movie experiences of playing a New Business Game that you'll play without limits or restrictions of any kind; that you'll play without vulnerability to any person, place, force, or thing appearing to be outside of you; and that you'll play for the sheer pleasure of playing. We'll be chatting much more about what this means in the chapters to come.

You've almost completed the foundational segment of the book, and you're almost ready to move into the practical segment. Before doing that, however, we need to take another look at The Business Game from your now substantially expanded perspective. To do that, please turn the page and continue on to Chapter 9.

Redefining the Nature of Business

In a simulated reality, the simulators determine the laws, and can change the laws, that govern their worlds.[1]
—John Barrow, Astrophysicist and 2006 Templeton Prize Winner

I n the preceding chapter, I began the process of inviting you to rewrite your perspective on what's really going on now, and what has always been going as you've played The Business Game. In this chapter, I want to continue that process, deepen your awareness of The Truth, and start sketching out new possibilities that now exist

[1] John Barrow, *Living in a Simulated Universe*, Department of Applied Mathematics and Theoretical Physics (DAMTP), Centre for Mathematical Sciences, Cambridge University. Abstract: www.simulation-argument.com/barrowsim.pdf.

for you as a prelude to moving into the practical "what to do" and "how to do it" aspects of busting loose from The Business Game.

There will be some repetition between what I covered at the end of the previous chapter and what I cover in this chapter. That's intentional and is designed to really hammer home important points that may still feel strange, weird, or alien to you. As you'll see clearly if you start playing the Phase 2 Game, there's a *huge* difference between having an intellectual awareness of something and having a direct experience of it. To move from intellectual awareness to direct experience, repetition is very supportive, especially with some of the aspects of The Busting Loose Model that are more challenging to accept or believe.

I grew up reading Superman comics in which the Superman character's X-ray vision enabled him to see what was hidden from view, what others couldn't see. Now that you understand the True nature of The Human Game, The Business Game as a subset of that larger game, The Field, Consciousness, holograms, and the creative process that creates all holographic illusions, you have access to your own form of X-ray vision.

In short, *you* now have the ability to see what's hidden from view and what others can't see. It's now time to fully awaken and enhance that skill by using it. If you stay with me and then accept my invitation to make the quantum leap into Phase 2, your X-ray vision will get stronger and stronger and more and more penetrating as you use it.

The Business Game was an absolutely brilliant creation—a stroke of true genius. It was created as one of the cornerstones in Phase 1 of The Human Game (as was the creation of Hypnotic Goals and their role as the rabbits we can't catch or hold onto). The Business Game was created specifically to limit and restrict you. It's important for you to fully appreciate just how brilliant a creation it was, so let's review the five core rules and regulations of The Business Game using your X-ray vision. In Chapter 1, we discussed these five primary rules of The Business Game:

1. You have a limited supply of money to play with (capital).
2. You have income (money flowing in).

3. You have expenses (money flowing out).

4. Your income must exceed your expenses (resulting in profits) or you lose the game.

5. You must maximize, grow, and sustain profits to win.

Let's take a fresh look at each of the five rules individually.

Rule 1: You have a limited supply of money to play with (capital).

Based on what you now know (or from within the Model if you're still not sure you accept it fully), is that true? Do you really have a limited supply of capital to work with as you play The Business Game?

No!

Where does money come from? It comes from patterns in The Field with specific details in them. If the details specify a larger or smaller amount of money for a business in any aspect of operations, that's what will be seen and experienced in the hologram. If the details change, the changes will then be seen and experienced, too.

Is there any limit to the number of patterns your Expanded Self can insert into The Field or what details can be included in them?

No!

Is there any limit to the amount of power your Expanded Self can apply to those patterns to pop them into your hologram appearing to be real?

No!

As an Infinite Being, there's no limit to your power, and your supply doesn't rise or fall as you use it. You're always at full power no matter what you do. It's not like a battery that can be drained and needs to be recharged, or a car's gas tank that needs to be refilled.

The logical conclusion to draw, then, is that the supply of money (capital) available to you and your business, along with the strength of your cash flow, is unlimited. The only limit that is ever set on capital and cash flow are the limits specified in the script your Expanded Self writes for your total-immersion movie experience.

And the entire Phase 2 game is about expanding to the point where you can play without any limits or restrictions.

As we'll discuss later in more detail, that doesn't necessarily mean you'll create billions of dollars in capital or millions of dollars in cash flow, although you certainly could. What it means is that whatever amount of capital and cash flow you need in order to play The New Business Game the way you really want to play it will be there, instantly, effortlessly, joyfully. That amount could be what you'd call large or small. In my case, for example, to play The New Business Game the way I choose to right now, the way that's most fun for me (it could change down the line), I don't need multiple millions or billions in sales, profits, or cash flow, so I don't create the illusion of numbers appearing that big.

Let's now discuss the other four rules, the apparent movement of money, together.

Rules 2 to 5: You have income; you have expenses; your income must exceed your expenses (resulting in profits) or you lose the game; and you must maximize, grow, and sustain profits to win.

Here are several points that summarize the specifics of those rules:

1. Money flows in and out of your business.
2. Money is *out there*, separate from you, and you must go get it and bring it into your business (income).
3. As you spend money (expenses), it moves away from you to others; you have less and they have more.
4. You must make sure your income exceeds your expenses, resulting in profits.
5. If you want to win The Business Game, increase your personal income and net worth, improve your lifestyle, or play The Business Game in expanded ways, you must raise your *profits*.

Let's now turn on your X-ray vision again. If the real source of money is your Consciousness and The Field, not the hologram, does money really flow in and out of your business? Is money *out there*? Do you need to find ways to bring it into your business? Does it really flow away or go anywhere when you spend it?

No!

You've created the illusion of money moving in your hologram, but it's not real. You just convinced yourself the movement was real.

Is there any "out there" where you can go to get money and bring it into your business?

No!

The Human Game is a game created by and played entirely in Consciousness. There is no "out there" out there.

When you spend money, do you really have less, and does another person, company, or entity really have more?

No!

All that really happens is a few details change in a pattern in The Field—and you create the illusion of money moving from one aspect of yourself to another aspect of yourself. It doesn't go anywhere or to anyone!

To reinforce an important point I made in the preceding chapter: Is income real? Are expenses real? Are profits real? Do you really need to increase profits if you want to increase your personal income and net worth, improve your lifestyle, or play The Business Game on an expanded playing field?

No to all four questions!

Let's also return to movies as a metaphor for the True nature of The Human Game to hammer these points home. Does money really move in a film? If a scene in a film shows a company earning a million dollars in the fourth quarter, a CEO earning a salary of $500,000 a year, an entrepreneur having a net worth of $50 million, a business owner selling a company for $100 million, or a CFO embezzling $250,000 from the company, did any of it *really* happen? Nope. It's all illusions, all stories appearing real—just like the illusion of money moving in your hologram.

In summary, the supply of money available to you is infinite. You can't run out. You can't lose it. You, as the Player, don't have to do anything to create money or increase its flow to you (although you can certainly play a role of appearing to do something if playing that way would be fun for you). Prudent management is *not* required. Why? Because there's nothing there that needs managing (although you can create something and create the illusion of managing it if that would be fun for you), and you can't do it wrong or mess it up!

Debts, loans, and interest don't exist. Those concepts are completely made-up Human Game, Phase 1 constructs—as are the concepts of net worth, stock price, and corporate valuation. And there aren't any assets (including patents, trademarks, proprietary technologies, etc.) that need to be managed or protected.

As the Creator of everything in your hologram, when you spend, you're really paying yourself since the money doesn't actually go anywhere else. Your supply of money does *not* decrease once you've knocked out enough cloud cover (as you'll soon see). When anything else appears to be True, it's a holographic illusion you've accepted as real.

In Chapter 1, we also talked about the following common beliefs that are generally accepted as True in Phase 1 (you may have different beliefs on one or more of them). Let's look at them with your X-ray vision:

Phase 1 belief: The tax authority is your enemy (to one degree or another).

In Phase 1, we look at the tax authority as our enemy because they're taking our money, money we worked hard for, and since our supply of money is limited and there's never enough, we'd prefer to keep it. Plus, our interactions with the tax authority (audits and other interactions about tax returns) don't tend to be a lot of fun.

But what is The Truth about the tax authority, as you now know it (or from within the Model if you're not fully convinced yet)? The tax authority and any representative of it you have contact with is you, is *your* Consciousness in disguise. Whatever happened in the past in your interactions with the tax authority was your creation and was designed to reinforce Phase 1 dynamics. In Phase 2, all the stories can be rewritten, and they *will* be rewritten as you knock out cloud cover and expand through it!

Phase 1 belief: Your competition is your enemy (to one degree or another).

Who is your competition? Your competition, all the companies and individuals involved, is you: *your* Consciousness in disguise. Whatever happened in the past in your interactions with them was your creation and was designed to reinforce Phase 1 dynamics. In Phase 2, all the stories can be rewritten and *will* be as you knock out cloud cover and expand through it!

Phase 1 belief: You're vulnerable to the state of the international economy (boom times, recessions, and depressions).

Who creates the illusion of the world economy, boom times, recessions, and depressions, and who writes all the stories of what supposedly happens within them? You! And in Phase 1, all those stories were written specifically to reinforce Phase 1 dynamics. In Phase 2, however, all the stories can be rewritten and will be as you knock out cloud cover and expand through it!

🔑 Key Point

Numbers were created specifically to give you an experience of limitation and restriction, and that is their True purpose.

Phase 1 belief: You're vulnerable to movements within the international stock and financial markets.

Who creates the illusion of the stock exchanges, and who writes all the stories of what supposedly happens within them? You! And in Phase 1, all those stories were written specifically to reinforce Phase 1 dynamics. In Phase 2, however, all the stories can be rewritten and will be as you knock out cloud cover and expand through it!

Phase 1 belief: Your freedom to make decisions and act is limited by bosses, stockholders, partners, board members, and investors.

Who are bosses, stockholders, partners, board members, and investors? They're all you: *your* Consciousness in disguise. Whatever happened in the past in your interactions with them (and whatever is happening now) is your creation and was designed to reinforce Phase 1 dynamics. In Phase 2, again, all the stories can be rewritten and will be as you knock out cloud cover and expand through it!

Phase 1 belief: You're always vulnerable to new products, services, and technologies that can hurt your business (or job) or even make it obsolete in the blink of an eye.

What are new products, services, and technologies? Holographic illusions. Stories appearing real. Who creates those illusions and writes those stories? You! In Phase 1, everything that happened with them (yours and those of your competition) was all designed to reinforce Phase 1 dynamics. In Phase 2, however, like everything else, these sorts of stories can be rewritten and will be as you knock out cloud cover and expand through it!

Phase 1 belief: "Keep your friends close and your enemies closer."—Sun-tzu, *The Art of War*.

There are no such things as friends and enemies. They're all you, *your* Consciousness in disguise. And it doesn't matter where you keep them. Everything that happened with the illusion of friends and enemies in Phase 1 was designed to reinforce Phase 1 dynamics. In Phase 2, all those stories can be rewritten and will be as you knock out cloud cover and expand through it!

By the way, in answering the questions I just posed, if you aren't absolutely convinced about the philosophical model I shared with you in previous chapters (who you really are, Phase 1, Phase 2, etc.), consider the questions from a scientific perspective. If you look at them from the perspective of quantum physics alone, you still see that the fundamental rules, regulations, and structure of The Business Game go directly against The Truth and how things *really* work.

 Key Point

Abundance Just Is!

Abundance is who you really are. It's your natural state. Remember what the quantum physicists say:

The Field = Unlimited power and infinite possibility

Sales, profits, and strong positive cash flow are *easily created* in *any amount* and can appear to come from *any source*—by simply creating a pattern in The Field, energizing it, and popping it into your hologram. Rich, poor, struggle, ease, profits, losses, and strong or weak cash flow are all *equal holographic creations* from different patterns in the Field—just as sales, profits, and cash flow are magically and easily created out of thin air in a novel, play, or video game by the writer, playwright, or computer programmer. It's *all* just stories!

Key Point

It takes the same amount of power and effort to create *any* illusion in the hologram—no matter how you'd choose to judge, label, or describe it.

Further, consider the following, which we'll discuss in more detail in later chapters:

- Increased sales, profits, and cash flow in your hologram aren't good.
- Weak sales, profits, and cash flow in your hologram aren't bad.
- The sales, profits, and cash flow you're experiencing now and experienced in the past were designed—in every moment—to perfectly support you in playing The Human Game and The Business Game exactly as you wanted to.
- The same thing is True for any other aspect of your business or career that you'd say you've had problems with or struggled with.

I could go on and on here, but for now, let me just ask you this: Do you see how beautifully and brilliantly the five primary rules and the common beliefs that flow from them limit, restrict, and devalue you? Do you see how alien they are to The Truth of who you *really* are? Do you see how alien they are to The Truth of how things *really* work? Do you see how brilliant this was as a strategy to support the goal of Phase 1 in The Human Game—which is to convince yourself that you're the opposite of who you really are and that the illusion is real?

In truth, you have the power and ability to create any amount of money in your hologram *appearing* to flow through your business or show up in any way. You have the power to write any story about any business-related experience of sales and profit growth, success, problem solving, public offering, business sale, industry domination, innovation, employee-related illusion, and so on, and pop yourself into the middle of it to play and explore.

The limitations you experienced in the past and the restrictions you're experiencing now while playing The Business Game were created from *limited* patterns your Expanded Self created in The Field. That's it. It says nothing about who you really are or what you're really capable of creating in Phase 2, except the degree to which you've been able to fool yourself.

As I noted earlier, it is amazingly cool that you can:

- Reclaim the power that has been propping up those limiting patterns, illusions, and stories.
- Collapse them out of your hologram.
- Claim your infinite abundance and open fully into it.
- Bust loose from The Business Game—completely and permanently.
- Rewrite every aspect of your current Business Game story— including every detail about what happens with sales and profits; marketing; cash flow; hiring, firing, motivating, and compensating employees; minimizing employee turnover; increasing

employee morale, productivity, and efficiency; time management; vendors and suppliers; taxes; your levels of stress, joy, and fun; your personal life; and so on.

This is what I call "Redefining the Nature of Business" (hence the title of this chapter), and I'll show you exactly how to do this in the chapters that follow.

In Chapter 1, I explained that you can't win The Business Game. Before we continue, let's take a fresh look at that idea using your X-ray vision. As you now know, as an Infinite Being, you started in the fullness of infinite abundance, which is your natural state. The Business Game was created to give you the exact opposite experience—an experience of limitation, restriction, and finiteness.

Therefore, as long as you continue playing The Business Game from a Phase 1 perspective, you *must* continue to experience limitation, restriction, instability, vulnerability (with sales, profits, cash flow, investments, industry trends, competitors, the economy, stock market, employee issues, etc.)—in one way, shape, or form.

Plus—and pay close attention here—no matter how much money you *appear* to pile up as profits, assets, personal income, or net worth in the hologram, it's not real. It's a holographic illusion. It's still severely limited in comparison to how much you really have as an Infinite Being, it's still fragile and vulnerable to attack and loss, and there will still be a Visible Price or an Invisible Price to pay for you as a Player of The Business Game. So, which do you really want?

- An artificial state of abundance or success that is fragile and designed to limit and restrict you—no matter how big the numbers appear to get from time to time.
- Your natural state of infinite abundance, access to an unlimited supply of money, and the ability to play The Business Game without any limits or restrictions of any kind, for the sheer pleasure of playing.

I chose the second option and made the commitment to do whatever it took to expand to the point where I could *directly experience* who I really am and my natural state of infinite abundance—in my business affairs and the rest of my life. That's what ultimately led me to bust loose from The Business Game.

You're now ready to discover the practical nuts-and-bolts steps for actually busting loose from The Business Game. To make that leap, turn the page and begin Chapter 10.

10

The Sun and Clouds Effect

The sun . . . passeth through pollutions and itself remains as pure as before.[1]

—*Francis Bacon, Philosopher*

The sun does not shine for a few trees and flowers, but for the wide world's joy.[2]

—*Henry Ward Beecher*

I n Chapter 3, I introduced the metaphor of the sun and the clouds. I explained that who you really are is an infinitely powerful, infinitely wise, infinitely abundant, and Truly

---

[1] Francis Bacon, in "GIGA Quotes," www.giga-usa.com/quotes/topics/sun_t001.htm.

[2] Henry Ward Beecher, in "GIGA Quotes," www.giga-usa.com/quotes/topics/sun_t001.htm.

Joyful Being whom I compared to the sun. Then, to pull off The Phase 1 Miracle, you created a complex set of illusions and convinced yourself they were real and you were the opposite of who you really are. I compared that Phase 1 Miracle to creating clouds, putting them in front of the sun, and convincing yourself that there is no sun, the clouds are real, and the clouds are all there is.

To make the sun–clouds metaphor more useful for our purposes here, imagine the cloud layer as being solid and dense, like concrete, steel, or diamonds: very difficult to penetrate. Phase 1 clouds are not wispy or smoky; you can't put your hand right through them like the clouds that appear in the sky of the illusion.

In this chapter, I use the sun-clouds metaphor to shift gears and begin moving into the practical aspects of this book. If the sun of who you really are is still there, has always been there, and has just been hidden and blocked by the cloud cover you created in Phase 1, and you want to see and feel the sun shining (reexperience your natural state of infinite power, wisdom, abundance, and True Joy, including in your business), what do you need to do? Knock out the cloud cover, right? If the sun is just blocked from view and you remove the block, the sun must automatically shine in, right?

So that's what you do as you play in the early stages of the Phase 2 game. You combine a specific set of tools to form a drill bit that you use to drill tunnels through the solid cloud cover, poke holes through it, and allow more and more of the sun of who you really are to shine in. You then continue using the drill to widen the tunnels and holes and allow more and more of the sun of who you really are to shine through. Then you repeat that process until you knock out chunks of the cloud cover so huge amounts of the sun of who you really are can shine in. Each time you poke a hole through the cloud cover and some of the sun of who you really are shines through, your hologram transforms in dramatic ways. The illustration presented here will give you a visual idea of what I mean.

As you poke holes in the cloud cover in Phase 2, your hologram
transforms in dramatic ways.

The assembly of the drill bit and the actual drilling operation
begin with a simple shift in focus. In The Busting Loose Model I've
shared with you, there are three components to everything you
experience as you play The Human Game:

1. The Creator (Consciousness = you + your Expanded Self).
2. The True Creative Process (patterns and power in The Field).
3. The creations (everything you see and experience in your
   hologram: people, places, things, your body, etc.).

By design, until now, if you're like I was and like most people I
speak with, you've focused primarily on your creations—the illusions
and the stories. You convinced yourself they were real. You gave
your power to them. And they acted as if they were real and had
power as a result. You never saw *your* Consciousness as the Creator of
everything you experience, and you ignored The True Creative
Process, which you knew nothing about consciously.

If you've studied manifestation techniques, the law of attraction,
or the metaphysical idea that you create your own reality, you may

The three spheres of creation.

feel tempted to disagree with what I just shared. You may feel you did see yourself as Creator of your human experience and you did understand something of The True Creative Process. That may be partially accurate. However, as I explained in Chapter 2, the majority of the "you create your own reality" teachings out there are Phase 1 creations designed, ultimately, to reinforce the Phase 1 dynamics, even if they contained seeds of The Truth within them. As a result, they had to be skewed, distorted, incomplete, or sabotaged to keep you limited and away from The Truth—or you had to create having an intellectual understanding of The Truth that didn't translate into True Transformation in your hologram. You are now working with Phase 2 teachings that have no such limitations.

> **Key Point**
>
> To bust loose from The Business Game, you must first shift your focus away from your creations and place it squarely on The True Creative Process and yourself as the Creator.

Let's review your role as the Creator of everything you experience as you play The Human Game. You are an infinitely powerful being. Your natural state is one of infinite power, wisdom, abundance, and True Joy. That's the sun of who you really are. Therefore, when you experience *anything else*, you know:

- A Big Lie is at work.
- An illusion is in motion, appearing real.
- Your Expanded Self created it by applying tremendous power to a detailed pattern in The Field.
- That pattern can be drained of power and collapsed or rewritten (transformed), thus changing your experience in the hologram.

How You Drain, Collapse, and Rewrite Patterns

To pull off The Phase 1 Miracle, billions of patterns had to be inserted into The Field, energized, and popped out as illusions with you in the middle of them. To bust loose from The Business Game, you don't need to transform or rewrite *all* those patterns, just some of them.

In Phase 2 of The Human Game, your Expanded Self takes you on a special journey that I call "The Treasure Hunt of the Century." On that journey, your Expanded Self takes you to the key patterns in

The Field where you invested the greatest amounts of power to limit and restrict yourself in Phase 1. You then work with your Expanded Self to transform the contents of those patterns, the patterns then collapse or get rewritten, and so does the limitation and restriction you were experiencing in your hologram as a result of them. That's what ultimately pokes the holes in the cloud cover and opens you back up to your natural state of infinite abundance.

Key Point

You don't have to create wealth, financial abundance, prosperity, or business success. They are already yours. They always were. You just hid them from yourself. In Phase 2, you simply "unhide," rediscover, and reexperience them.

To understand how you drill through the solid, dense cloud cover, let's take a closer look at how patterns in The Field are created. You must understand exactly what is inside the patterns before you can fully collapse or rewrite them and bust loose from The Business Game. I'm going to explain what's inside the patterns in this chapter, but the explanation won't reach full significance until we discuss how to live day to day in Phase 2 in later chapters.

In Chapter 6, we chatted about Hollywood movies, special effects, and the commitment of Hollywood filmmakers to make their illusions appear as real and convincing as possible—no matter how sophisticated their special effects must be to do it. We also discussed that the patterns in The Field from which the illusion of The Human Game rises must be extremely complex and absolutely convincing, or the game ends. The complex patterns we create in The Field are built on a foundation of what the popular self-help and psychological literature calls "beliefs." A belief is an idea or concept we make up and accept as true. The Business Game, as you've seen, is a giant collection of beliefs we made up and then invested enormous amounts of power convincing ourselves were true.

Key Point

A belief is nothing but an idea or concept we make up and accept as true. All beliefs are lies, Phase 1 Miracle illusions. There is no such thing as empowering beliefs. In Phase 2, we don't *change* beliefs; we exchange them for The Truth.

However, just accepting an idea or concept as True and creating a belief about it isn't enough to make it appear absolutely real and *persist* in your hologram. For example, suppose you create a pattern in The Field and energize it to create the illusion of a business checking account with $50,000 in it and accounts payable totaling $75,000. "I have $50,000 in my checking account and $75,000 in bills" is therefore a belief, an illusion appearing real, that you create. However, that belief alone doesn't have much stability or staying power. You could easily forget about the account or the $50,000 in it or the $75,000 in bills, or you could forget to track how the numbers change over time.

Therefore, you can't just create a pattern in The Field, put some power in it, pop it into your hologram, and expect the illusion to fool you and remain in place. You have to reinforce the pattern to keep the power in it and keep the holographic illusion continuing to regenerate itself and limit you. Judgment does this. This is so important, and your understanding of it is absolutely key to busting loose from The Business Game and stepping back into a direct experience of who you really are.

Critical Key Point

Judgment is the glue that keeps illusions locked into place and appearing real in your hologram.

For example, let's say you create a belief/illusion that you have a checking account with $50,000 in it and $75,000 in bills. Let's say you then go beyond just having that belief and say to yourself, "I can't pay my bills. That's bad. I don't like that." What are you *really* saying when you judge it that way?

It's real!

When you judge an illusion as being negative by saying, "I don't like it" or "That's bad" or "I want that to go away" or "I want to change that," or in some cases, even if you judge it as being positive by saying, "I like that" or "I want more of that" or however else you judge and describe the experience, you reinforce the illusion that it's real, you keep your power in it (or add more to it), and it stays in your hologram.

However, judgment isn't always enough to keep an illusion locked into your hologram, either. Why? Because in many cases, the judgment is weak and doesn't have enough glue in it. Therefore, you must create consequences to strengthen the glue and further reinforce the pattern in The Field. Continuing with the example of a business checking account and bills, what happens if you pay a bill late? You get charged a *late fee*, and if you do it often enough, the vendor stops providing its product or service to you, which damages your business. What happens if you don't pay a bill at all? Your credit is shut off and your account gets sent to a *collection agency*. What happens if you *bounce* a check? The bank charges an *insufficient funds fee*, and if you do it enough times, the bank closes your account and terminates its relationship with you, which would be really *bad* for business!

Let's take a look at the positive side of this scenario. Suppose you create a belief/illusion/lie that you have a business checking account with $100,000 or $1,000,000 in it. You look at that account and judge it by saying, "That's good. I like that." The consequence you create is the illusion of feeling temporarily prosperous and temporarily having the freedom to buy or do many things that please you and support the operation of your business.

By applying your X-ray vision to these scenarios, what's the true significance of the consequences? They add more detail to the patterns in The Field and further reinforce the illusion that money, checking accounts, bills, creditors, banks, collection agencies, and things you can buy or do (or can't buy or can't do) are real. It's kind of like going the extra mile to make Gollum's hair and movements appear absolutely real in *The Lord of the Rings*! Do you see how tricky, brilliant, and effective this whole process is? Whether or not it's clear at this point, I promise you, if you leap into Phase 2 and start playing the Phase 2 game, you'll have mind-blowing realizations about how judgments and consequences locked you into your Phase 1 illusion.

Here are some of the other negative consequences we install within our patterns in The Field to make illusions appear even more real:

- Imprisonment.
- Time-outs for young kids or being grounded for teens.
- Being expelled from school.
- Loss of prestige or status.
- Injury.
- Death.
- Being fired or demoted.
- Damaged reputation.
- Losing a coveted year-end financial bonus.
- Bankruptcy.
- Financial penalty.

Here are some positive consequences we install within our patterns in The Field to make illusions appear even more real:

- Financial rewards of all shapes and sizes.
- Temporary feelings of pride, self-confidence, satisfaction, or being loved and appreciated.
- Job promotions.
- Popularity.
- Efficiency and productivity.
- Fame.

Since you create your own playing field, rules, and regulations as you play The Human Game and The Business Game, you also create your own consequences—*rewards and punishments*—to enhance the illusions you create. You then reward and punish yourself by putting reward and punishment patterns in The Field, adding power to them, and popping them into your hologram so they appear real. Then you strengthen those illusions—especially the illusion of cause and effect—within the hologram. It's really quite a brilliant and extraordinary creation.

Creating beliefs, judging them, adding consequences, then applying tremendous power to make the now-enhanced pattern pop into your hologram and appear unquestionably real is the creative cycle that locks you into limitation and restriction in Phase 1 of The Human Game—and it applies to absolutely everything you see and experience in your business and throughout your hologram. The other interesting thing to note is that once an enhanced pattern is created in this way, and the experience recurs in your hologram, each successive time you look at it you say to yourself, "You see, that *is* how it works; it *is* real!" and the apparent evidence of its reality locks it even more deeply into your hologram.

Key Point

There isn't "real" and "unreal" in your hologram. *Everything* in your hologram is unreal. *Everything* is just a belief, an illusion, a lie.

This is also the explanation for why the law of attraction, positive thinking, visualization, goal setting, manifestation techniques, affirmations, and other popular self-help strategies and techniques don't work consistently. You can seek to attract, think positive thoughts, visualize, set goals, attempt to manifest, and affirm all day long, but if your Expanded Self doesn't create a pattern in The Field that matches what you *appear* to be attracting, thinking, visualizing, setting a goal for, seeking to manifest, or affirming, and add enormous power to it, it can't pop into your hologram.

It doesn't matter how hard you try, how focused you keep the illusion of *your thoughts*, how many times you think positively about it, how many times you visualize the outcome manifesting or you review the goals you set, or how many times you repeat an affirmation to yourself or hear it on tape. It's going to fall flat without a corresponding change in a pattern in The Field that must be initiated by your Expanded Self. Conversely, if you remove all your power from a pattern, the pattern collapses, and whatever that pattern was creating in your hologram disappears from your hologram.

> ### Key Point
>
> There's no power in the hologram or in the Player as he or she plays within the hologram. All the power is behind the scenes within The True Creative Process and your Expanded Self.

Have you ever seen a video of a building being demolished—where the entire structure collapses in a matter of seconds? The initial construction of a building must be done piece by piece, brick by brick, beam by beam, and it takes months or years. But collapsing it is accomplished in seconds or minutes. Why? Because the demolition workers put explosive charges in strategic places within the building to undermine the core foundation of the building. When those charges are detonated, the building collapses rapidly. If you've never seen a video like that, visit the following page on my web site to see an example. It's a very powerful visual image to have in your mind as you work toward busting loose from The Business Game: www.bustingloose.com/dynamite2.html.

It works the same way in Phase 2 of The Human Game. Your Expanded Self knows where the patterns with the most power in them are hidden in The Field, what's in them, which ones are limiting you the most, and so on. In Phase 2, your Expanded Self guides you to those foundational patterns and supports you in reclaiming the power from them, dissolving the judgment and consequences, collapsing the patterns, and therefore removing the limitations they contained from your hologram.

Again, just like with demolishing a building, you don't need to collapse *all* the patterns you created in Phase 1—just the key foundational ones. To bust loose from The Business Game, you'll do exactly that with the patterns you created to most limit the natural flow of abundance to you. That's why I call it The Treasure Hunt of the Century. What more valuable treasure could you ever find than opening up fully into a direct experience of the infinite abundance and unlimited raw creative power that's your natural state?

Key Point

It takes much *less* time to knock out the cloud cover in Phase 2 than it took to create it in Phase 1, but it does take time, generally a lot of it.

I'm going to emphasize the point I just made, then come back to it repeatedly in later chapters. Why? Because it's very important and often becomes a temporary source of frustration for Phase 2 Players. The Phase 2 game was designed—*was designed*—to unfold over time, not to happen with a snap of the fingers or overnight. It was designed that way so your ultimate appreciation of the expansion process would soar off the charts, and that kind of appreciation can't be felt when something happens very quickly, no matter how badly part of you may want it to happen "yesterday."

When oil companies drill for oil, on land or under water, they use unique drilling equipment. As we discussed, you too must use unique drilling equipment to knock out the cloud cover and bust loose from The Business Game. To discover more about your Phase 2 drilling equipment, turn the page and begin Chapter 11.

CHAPTER

11

Assembling the Drill – Part 1

When you want something other than these attachments and relationships, they naturally fall off by themselves. You are not to break them, but they themselves will fall like a wall of sound.[1]
　　—Papaji, Yogi-saint of the Advaita Vedanta and Bhakti traditions

T here are four tools you'll combine to create a highly effective drill bit that will be used to drill tunnels through the solid, dense Phase 1 Miracle cloud cover. I'm going to introduce all four tools in this chapter, discuss the first tool in detail, and then

---

[1] Papaji, as quoted by Katie Davis, *Awake Joy* (Kihei, HI: Awake Spirit Publishing, 1993), p. 41.

we'll discuss the other three tools in Chapter 12. Here are the names of the four tools:

1. Appreciation
2. The Process
3. The Mini-Process
4. Transformational Vocabulary

All four tools are extremely powerful and necessary parts of The Busting Loose Model. However, of the four, The Process, which we'll discuss in the next chapter, is the crown jewel—the one you'll use the most for quite some time, and the one with the most transformative power. But before you can apply The Process, you must first discover the magic of Appreciation, so that's where we'll begin our discussion.

Appreciation, Tool 1

If you're like most people, you were taught that the purpose of money is to provide an efficient means of exchange for goods and services. You were taught civilizations once bartered for goods and services, but that became awkward and inefficient so money was created to simplify the process. You were also taught that the process of exchanging money became easier and more efficient as we moved from coins to bills to credit cards to electronic funds transfers. However, like everything else in Phase 1 of The Human Game, what you were taught was just a smoke screen, a cloud, an illusion designed to trick you and lock you into limitation and restriction.

When somebody does something nice or helpful for you, or you receive something of value from another person, how do you respond? You say "Thank you," right? You express appreciation for the value you received, value that you see and feel within yourself. If you go into a store, restaurant, or other place of business and *pay* for something, aren't you also receiving something of value?

Don't you also feel appreciative and say thank you in such circumstances—if you're a well-mannered person?

If money disappeared from the planet tomorrow, what would change? Would all the businesses close? Would all the books disappear from the shelves in bookstores? Would restaurants and shops close? Would cars stop rolling off the assembly lines? Would doctors' offices, gas stations, dry cleaners, and copy shops close their doors? Would *any* good or service that you now enjoy or benefit from suddenly become unavailable?

No!

So, if money disappeared but you could still obtain goods and services, what would still be there in the *transaction*?

The expression of appreciation!

You'd still feel appreciative for what you received, and you'd still want to say thank you to the people who provided the good or service for you. You'd receive something valuable and you'd want to express appreciation for it. If you went into a restaurant and had a great time, you'd say thank you to the server who waited on you. If you went into a dress shop and chose a beautiful gown, you'd say thank you to the clerk or owner. If you went into an electronics store for a computer or cell phone, you'd say thank you after receiving it.

Every bill you pay is for something valuable you received. You may not like paying your rent or mortgage, or other accounts payable items, but having a place to live is valuable, isn't it? You may not like paying back a loan, but the money lent to you allowed you to buy or do something valuable. For each line item on your accounts payable, or each bill piled on your desk, you received something of value that genuinely supported your business activities beautifully, didn't you?

You may not like the total you see, but if your credit card bill has 10 items on it, you received value when you originally had each of those 10 experiences, didn't you? If you look closely with your Phase 2 X-ray vision, whenever you pay for anything, all you're *really* doing is saying, "Thank you, I appreciate what I've received." As you'll see, however, when we use the Appreciation tool in Phase 2, we go way beyond simply saying thank you or being grateful.

Key Point

Whenever you create and experience the illusion of receiving a good or service in your hologram, there are three aspects of the creation to Appreciate:

1. Yourself for how amazing you had to be create that illusion and make it appear so real.

2. Your creation—be it person, place, or thing—for how amazingly real it seems; for how perfectly he, she, or it is supporting you in playing The Human Game and The Business Game; and for the specific benefit you received from it (the enjoyment of the contributions of an employee, a meal, printing, advertising, accounting services, raw material for an inventory item, and so on).

3. The True Creative Process that made 1 and 2 possible.

Based on what you now know about The Human Game and The Business Game, if you entertain a valued client at dinner in a restaurant and pay with cash, check, or credit card, who are you paying? Yourself, right? There's no one else out there to pay. Everything and everyone is a creation of *your Consciousness*. So, who is ultimately providing the value and who is really being thanked?

You!

As you now know (or from within the Model if you're not convinced yet), in the restaurant example I've been using, there's no restaurant. Your Consciousness is creating the illusion of it—the room, tables, chairs, art on the walls, music playing in the background, kitchen, food, plates, glasses, waitstaff, bus person, chef, the other people who appear to be eating there with you (extras, if we use the movie analogy), everyone and everything else you experience while you're there. None of it is really there, yet you convinced yourself it was all there and was all real. That's an incredible accomplishment, so you have a tremendous opportunity to fully feel—and express—your Appreciation for it. And each time you do, as you'll see in the chapters that follow, a tunnel gets dug slightly deeper through The Phase 1 Miracle cloud cover!

> ### Key Point
>
> The real purpose of money is to express Appreciation for the magnificence of yourself as the Creator of everything you experience, for the magnificence of all the illusions that appear so real, and for The True Creative Process that is responsible for them.

If you're like many of the people I speak with, a thought like the following may have flashed through your awareness (or will later): "I can't go around patting myself on the back like that or calling myself or what I do magnificent. That would be egotistical and self-centered." Even if you didn't just have a thought like that, follow along with me for a moment because it's likely to come up later. Do you remember that I said one of the key goals of Phase 1 in The Human Game is to convince yourself you're the opposite of who you really are? This is a perfect example of that.

Look at how brilliant and tricky we are as Creators. Who you really are is a magnificent, Infinite Being. In your natural state, your Appreciation for every aspect of yourself and everything you do and experience is off the charts. But that experience of Appreciation can't be allowed in Phase 1.

So, what happens in Phase 1? First, we don't allow ourselves to Appreciate *ourselves* or what we do very much, if at all. What's that experience typically called? Insecurity or low self-esteem, and we all have *huge* amounts of it buried deep within us. Even if we'd say we feel pretty good about certain aspects of ourselves or our achievements, deep down we don't—and we *can't* after The Phase 1 Miracle has been locked in.

But we don't stop with not Appreciating ourselves. We won't allow others to Appreciate us much, either (with few, but some, exceptions). What do most people do when someone who appears to be outside of them Appreciates them? Deflect it, right? "Oh, it was nothing," we'll say, or "It was a team effort," or some other form of what I call "deflection language." And how do we generally *feel* when someone Appreciates or compliments us? Uncomfortable and awkward, right? What a brilliant Phase 1 creation!

Let's go more deeply into expressing Appreciation now. Do you ever run out of love? If you love your child, brother, sister, friend, or significant other, and you express that love verbally or through a kiss, a touch, or a gesture of some kind, do you have less love afterward? Does the amount of love you have, or your capacity to express it, diminish? No!

In fact, if you look closely, you have an endless supply of love, and every time you express it, your capacity to express—and receive—love actually expands. It works the same way with Appreciation and expressing Appreciation, *including in the form of money*. You have an endless supply of Appreciation, and every time you express it, your capacity to express—and receive—Appreciation expands, too. Therefore (we'll discuss the mechanics of this in later chapters), as you increase your expression and feelings of Appreciation for yourself as Creator, for your creations (the illusions), and for The True Creative Process, the flow of Appreciation that reflects back to you must expand, too, *including in the form of money*—and that's exactly what happens when you play in Phase 2 of The Human Game!

Key Point

Your supply of money does *not* decrease as you send it outward and spend it. It actually loops back to you and increases.

Now that you understand the concept of Appreciation and the transformative and expansive power it holds, let's take a brief look at its practical application. Then we'll further enhance it when I show you how Appreciation ties in to the crown jewel tool called *The Process* in the next chapter.

What's it like now for you when you pay bills—individually or through your business? When I ask that question at my live events and with coaching, consulting, and *Business School of Consciousness* clients, here's what I hear most often:

- "It's scary because I don't always have enough in my checking account, and if I don't pay or my check bounces, I'm in trouble."
- "When I pay a bill for one thing, it means I might not have money to do something else I'd like to do. It often seems like an either-or deal and I don't like that."
- "I just feel resigned to the fact that what I have is going to be depleted by the amount I have to pay."
- "For me, it's a gigantic hassle. I could be doing something else. I don't like spending time writing out checks, putting them in envelopes, putting stamps on them, and putting them in the mail."
- "I feel powerless when I pay bills, and I don't like feeling that way so I compensate by putting off paying, which leads to late fees, which leads to anger at myself for being so stupid."
- "I don't mind paying bills, but paying taxes drives me nuts. It just doesn't seem right. It seems unjust. It's my money. I made it. Why does the government get to take so much of it whether I like it or not?"

If you have similar thoughts and feelings or other *negative* thoughts and feelings when you pay bills or spend money, what's being reinforced when you think and feel that way? Three things:

1. Your beliefs about the limits on your power and abundance.
2. Your judgment of those beliefs.
3. The reality of the consequences you have associated with them.

In effect, you're making your financial limitation patterns stronger and stronger, and when you do that, the financial limitation must persist in your hologram. If you'd describe your feelings as neutral or flat when you pay bills or spend money, you may not be reinforcing limitation, but you are missing the opportunity to drain power from the patterns, dissolve the judgment glue within them, transform lies into Truth, and pop more holes in The Phase 1 Miracle cloud cover.

The opportunity you give yourself in Phase 2 of The Human Game with the illusion of money (and all other illusions that make you feel uncomfortable or limited) is to shift your focus from *spending money* and *paying bills* (and whatever other lies you're telling yourself) to expressing Appreciation. Doing that takes practice, self-discipline, and persistence in the beginning because it feels alien to you, but it ultimately becomes natural and old hat to you. Starting now, every time you spend money, pay bills, write checks, hand someone cash, or sign a credit card slip, you want to take a moment to Appreciate your creation (the illusion), yourself as the Creator of it, and the value you received.

In addition, in your business, besides the illusory flow of money, there are other illusions you'd describe as problems, challenges, bad news, fires that need to be put out, crises, and so on. In each case, as you'll see, you have the opportunity in Phase 2 to appreciate your creation (the illusion), yourself as the Creator of it, how well those illusions supported you in pulling off The Phase 1 Miracle, how well they're supporting you in the moment to knock out the cloud cover, and the sheer magnificence of The True Creative Process that made it all possible.

How to Express Appreciation instead of *Spending Money* and *Paying Bills*

Ninety percent of the time I express Appreciation in the form of money with a credit card. So when I sign credit card slips or write checks when I receive credit card *bills* in the mail (which I now call "requests for Appreciation"—this is a preview of the Transformative

Vocabulary tool), I look at the bill or go down every line item on the statement and express Appreciation for the creations they represent.

At this point on my journey, feelings and expressions of Appreciation flow naturally and continually expand and I don't have to push myself to express and feel them. However, when my Phase 2 journey began, it was a very different story, as it may be for you when you begin your Phase 2 journey.

In the earlier stages of Phase 2, here's how I expressed Appreciation. For example, suppose I was looking at a credit card slip for dinner at one of my favorite sushi restaurants after finishing a fine meal. I expressed Appreciation by saying words like this to myself *and feeling the genuine feelings that accompanied them*: "Wow! What an amazing creation. I created this whole thing—the restaurant, the waiter, the sushi, the sushi chef, the sake I drank, the table where I sat, and the other people in the restaurant. It was all a creation of my Consciousness. It all seemed so real and tasted so good! Amazing. I'm one hell of a Creator!" As I added a tip, totaled it, and signed the credit card slip, I then concluded by saying something like this to myself: "I express this Appreciation from the infinite abundance that's my natural state, knowing that as I do it, this expression will just expand and reflect right back to me."

If you've had experience using the self-help technique called affirmations, you may be thinking something like this: "That sounds just like using affirmations. I thought you said affirmations have no power." In Phase 1, without a corresponding pattern in The Field that gets energized, affirmations have no power. Plus, most people affirm for things they don't really believe are true or possible for them. However, when you affirm The Truth in Phase 2 as part of drilling through the clouds with your Expanded Self at your side, it *does* have power because your Expanded Self is helping you knock out cloud cover and expand so new patterns *do get created* in The Field to support the effort. I'll discuss this in greater detail in later chapters.

I'd do the same thing if I created what could be judged a bad experience in the restaurant from a Phase 1 perspective. Why? Because, as we discussed, there's no power in the hologram—not in anything, not in anyone. The other people are other aspects of me, saying and doing what I asked them to say and do. The food is entirely a creation of my Consciousness, so if I experienced what could be called poor service or lousy food, I created that miraculous illusion from a pattern in The Field, convinced myself it was real, and judged it as bad—which is a colossal achievement and definitely something to Appreciate. As I mentioned, this same idea has wide application in your business for all the people, places, and things illusions you're currently judging as bad.

I gave you examples of the words I use when expressing Appreciation. I change them all the time. There isn't any rule or magic formula for expressing Appreciation. There's no right way, wrong way, better way, or best way. None of that exists in Phase 2. There's just what you choose to do, and what generates truly Appreciative *feelings*. You can always trust yourself and your Expanded Self and just say and do what you feel motivated to say and do.

Key Point

The words you say to yourself to express Appreciation don't matter. The feelings the words help you create within yourself are what count. Phase 2 is *all* about feelings!

What happens when you express Appreciation like this instead of spending money or paying bills like you do now? Two things:

1. The expression of Appreciation supports you beautifully in drilling through the cloud cover.
2. It ultimately sets into motion the circular flow of increased Appreciation to you that means increased Appreciation flowing back to you in the form of money.

Here's another way to look at this. Suppose you went to Las Vegas and played the slot machines. Suppose you found a slot machine that immediately returned three dollars for every dollar you put into it. How many dollars would you put into that machine? As many as you could, right? How would you feel every time you put a dollar in the machine? Excited, right? Because you knew three dollars would be coming back. It's ultimately the same thing when you bust loose and can fully express Appreciation instead of spending money or paying bills.

When you expand to that point during your Phase 2 journey (which you *will* if you play the Phase 2 game), you will *know* that each time you spend money or pay a bill you actually end up getting more money back than the amount you expressed. As a result, once you bust loose, you actually enjoy and look forward to spending money and paying bills and fully enjoy the experience, instead of dreading it or having the negative sort of experience you have now.

If your Phase 2 journey is like mine, and it may not be, it will be tough to really feel Appreciation when interacting with many illusions you've been judging harshly. I'll talk more about this in later chapters, but for now I'll just say you do your best. You use words that reinforce The Truth and do your best to feel The Truth within them. As an example, you can use words like these:

- "Wow, it's amazing that I can fool myself into thinking/feeling _____."
- "Wow, look at that. I can actually convince myself that _____."
- "Man, _____ seems so real, but it's just an illusion."

I can absolutely promise you that even if expressing Appreciation feels empty, fake, or like bullshit at the start, it does open up and then expand over time. More on this later.

Here's another example of expressing Appreciation. Let's say tomorrow morning you stop at a coffee shop on the way to work and *buy* yourself a vanilla latte for four dollars. As you give the clerk the four dollars, you could say something like this to yourself—and do your best to really *feel* it—"Wow, this is so cool. I created this coffee shop. I created the espresso machine, the beans, the milk, the steamer, the syrup, and the cup. I created the clerk and all the people who appeared to be in the coffee shop with me." Then, as you sip the sweet, hot liquid, you could say—and feel—"Wow!" again. Why? Because there's no coffee shop, no espresso machine, no beans, no milk, no steamer, no syrup, no cup, and no hot, sweet liquid. It's all smoke and mirrors—all an illusion. You just convinced yourself it was there, it was real, and it tasted good.

That's an amazing, magnificent, magical, mind-blowing, supernatural accomplishment!

Appreciate it!

Key Point

Everything that happens in your business (not just financial illusions) can (and will) be Appreciated in off-the-charts ways, no matter what judgmental story you make up about it to convince yourself it is real.

In Phase 2 of The Human Game, besides shifting your focus from spending money and paying bills to expressing Appreciation, there are two additional opportunities you can give yourself that support you in busting loose from The Business Game.

First, you can give yourself the gift of Appreciating all the money you appear to receive from others. Right now, when you *receive* a paycheck, a bonus check, a dividend check, a commission check, or any other expression of Appreciation in the form of money, how do you respond? Do you feel tremendous Appreciation for it—for yourself as the Creator, for the creation, and for The True Creative Process? Or do you take it for granted, swear under your breath because the check isn't larger, or instantly compare the amount to your *bills* or your wants and find it lacking? No matter what your current response is, you now have the opportunity to convert it to an expression of Appreciation and start getting the three dollars back for every one dollar you put in the slot machine, to continue that metaphor.

Key Point

Express Appreciation for money that appears to flow out of—and into—your business and personal accounts.

For example, I own and run several businesses and have partnerships in several others. In Phase 1 of The Human Game, I looked at those businesses and the *payments* I received from them as the source of my financial abundance. In Phase 2, I know they're *not* the source of my abundance (my Consciousness is), but I still express Appreciation to myself in the form of money from them. Here's how I do it. When I write myself a check from one of the company accounts or receive a check from one of my partnerships, I follow the same steps I just outlined. Why? Because the checks aren't real, the companies aren't real, and the customers who bought products and services that supposedly gave the companies the ability to pay me aren't real; it's all just a magnificent creation and illusion, and I Appreciate the whole story hugely!

Beyond my businesses and partnerships, I also receive royalties on books I've written and audio albums I've recorded that are published and sold by others, plus other commissions and other financial rewards of various kinds. When I receive those checks, I express Appreciation for them, too.

Similarly, if you own your own business, are the CEO of a business, or are responsible for sales for a division or project, and you look at money that appears to flow into your business, division, or project, you have the opportunity to express Appreciation for that illusion of inward flow in the same way—instead of ignoring it, taking it for granted, or judging it as not enough or below plan.

The second additional opportunity you can give yourself is to fully Appreciate what you've already created and have been enjoying in your hologram versus judging it, taking it for granted, or focusing on what you don't have. If you judge what you currently have by saying it's bad, it's not enough, it sucks, it's not what you want, you want more, you want something different, and so on, what are you doing? Reinforcing the illusion that it's real and that you really are limited. If you focus on what you don't have, what are you doing? The same thing.

Everything you're currently experiencing in your hologram is there because your Expanded Self created a complex pattern in The Field, energized it, and popped it into your hologram, making it appear absolutely real. There was no accident or mistake. Whatever you've experienced and are experiencing now was brilliantly designed and popped into your hologram to perfectly support you in playing The Human Game and The Business Game exactly the way you wanted to play it—*no matter how you'd judge or label it from your old perspective.*

Again, all illusions Truthfully deserve to be Appreciated for all their magnificence! I'll discuss this in greater detail in later chapters, but for now let me say that you can create anything you choose once you move deeply enough into Phase 2 and knock out enough of the cloud cover, but first you must thoroughly Appreciate what you've already created. If you don't Appreciate what you've already created, it's like putting a dollar into the slot machine and getting nothing back. Why do that when you can get three dollars back instead (metaphorically)?

Key Point

It's possible and very easy to fully Appreciate what you already have, even if you may choose to create something else at another time.

By the way, just as a sidebar before we conclude this chapter, do you think it's any accident that the term *appreciation* is used in the traditional financial community to describe an increase in value of an investment or portfolio? As part of Phase 1 in The Human Game, we hide clues to The Truth all over the place, but make sure we don't really see them. If you make the leap into Phase 2, you'll see clues like that everywhere and find it quite amusing and fascinating.

When you're ready to discover The Process—the crown jewel that you'll combine with Appreciation to transform the patterns you've installed in The Field to limit the flow of financial abundance to yourself, turn the page to begin Chapter 12.

Assembling the Drill – Part 2

This recognition is freedom, freedom from that "I," from that egoic pattern of striving, anxiety and suffering. It's the release into peace and joy and wellbeing.[1]

—*Dasarath Deb*

In the preceding chapter, by moving into the practical side of The Busting Loose Model and discovering the magic of the Appreciation tool, (using another metaphor) you jumped into the driver's seat and buckled your seat belt in preparation for a fast and wild ride through Phase 2 of The Human Game. To expand on that metaphor, it's time to put the key in the ignition, start the car, put your foot on the gas, accelerate toward busting loose from The

---

[1] Dasarath, as quoted by Katie Davis, *Awake Joy* (Kihei, HI: Awake Spirit Publishing, 1993), p. 105.

Business Game, and open into a consistent direct experience of The Truth of who you really are.

In this chapter, to expand on your awareness of the Appreciation tool, you'll discover the other three tools composing the final parts of the drill bit you'll use to knock out the Phase 1 cloud cover. The other tools are:

2. The Process
3. The Mini-Process
4. Transformational Vocabulary

I want to give you some general background, and then we'll go into a detailed discussion of each of these additional tools. In Phase 1, there are five steps to pull off The Phase 1 Miracle:

1. Your Expanded Self created patterns in The Field and applied tremendous amounts of power to pop them into the hologram as Phase 1 Miracle illusions.

2. Your Expanded Self totally immersed you within those illusions.

3. You looked at the illusions, interacted with them, lied to yourself about them (i.e., told yourself stories that reinforced Phase 1 dynamics), and judged them, which means you added glue to hold the lies/illusions in place.

4. You repeated the dynamic described in step 3 over and over with every resource at your disposal from within your own personal perspective and experience, as well as from what appeared to be outside of you (parents, siblings, coaches, teachers, friends, associates, bosses, employees, partners, police, the media, the forces of nature, the economy, the stock market, the tax authority, etc.).

5. You repeated the dynamic described in steps 1 to 4 relentlessly until you were absolutely convinced the illusion *was* real and you *were* the opposite of who you really are within it.

Therefore, in Phase 2, the whole game is to reverse those dynamics. To reverse those dynamics and knock out the cloud cover, your Expanded Self will follow five steps:

1. Create patterns in The Field designed to support you in *reexperiencing*—in various ways, shapes, and forms through amazing stories—the key limiting and restrictive patterns you created to lock yourself into Phase 1.

2. Energize those patterns and pop you into the middle of the stories inside the hologram.

3. Work with you to interact with the story line details and characters and tell The Truth about them (which dissolves judgment over time); reclaim the power that has been propping them up and keeping them repeating in your hologram; Appreciate yourself as their Creator; and Appreciate the creations/illusions themselves.

4. Repeat the dynamic in step 3 over and over with every resource at your disposal from within your own personal perspective and experience, as well as with what appears to be outside of you (parents, siblings, coaches, teachers, friends, associates, bosses, employees, partners, police, the media, the forces of nature, the economy, the stock market, the tax authority, etc.).

5. Repeat the dynamic in steps 1 to 4 over and over until however much of the cloud cover you want to knock out in Phase 2 gets knocked out.

As I mentioned, the Phase 2 game was designed to be played so you'd knock out the cloud cover one tunnel at a time, one chunk at a time, *over a long period of time*, so you can ultimately enjoy and appreciate what I call "the journey of expansion" in off-the-charts ways. The following examples help explain what I mean:

Chocolate: If you love the taste of chocolate and you buy a big bar of it, do you want to shove the whole bar into your mouth at once and gobble it up? No. You want to break it into small pieces, chew them slowly, and savor each flash of taste, right?

Champagne: If you love the taste of fine champagne, do you want to open the bottle and guzzle the whole thing in one gulp? No. You pour some into the glass, being careful not to let the foam overflow and waste the precious liquid, and you then take small sips to fully savor each flash of taste, right?

Movies, Plays, Novels: Do you want a really great movie or play to be two minutes long, or a really great novel to be one page long? No. You want the movies and plays to unfold over a couple of hours so you can enjoy the fullness of the stories. And you want a novel to be substantial in length for the same reason.

Mountain Climbing: If you love mountain climbing and you've decided to experience the thrill—and challenge—of reaching the summit of Mount Everest, do you want to take a helicopter to the top or to snap your fingers at the bottom and instantly be at the top? No. You want to climb the mountain, however long it takes, however difficult it might be, to savor each second of the climb.

Baseball, Tennis, Golf: If you love watching or playing baseball, do you want the game to end after one inning? If you love watching or playing tennis, do you want it to end after one serve? If you love watching or playing golf, do you want it to end after one hole? No! Why? Because extending it out over time allows you to have more fun and have more experiences to Appreciate.

It's the same thing with playing in Phase 2 of The Human Game!

To share one last example to hammer this point home: If you entered Phase 2 and instantly reclaimed all your power, wisdom, abundance, and True Joy, it would be the equivalent of scheduling the Super Bowl between the New England Patriots and the New York Giants; getting all the players, coaches, referees, support staff, and fans to the stadium; having millions watching on television worldwide; and then having the referee snap his fingers and say, "Okay, the Patriots just won 37 to 10. You can all go home now."

The players don't want to go home. The coaches, referees, and support staff don't want to go home. The players and fans don't want to go home. Everyone wants all four quarters of the game to be played, no matter what ups and downs might be experienced, how difficult the playing might get, or what the final outcome is. The players want to play because they love the game. Well, as a Player of The Human Game, you don't want to "go home" the minute you enter Phase 2, either (even though part of you might say you do). You want to play because you love playing The Human Game, even if you don't feel that way now with the sun of who you really are blocked from view by the Phase 1 cloud cover.

Key Point

There is a popular spiritual maxim that goes like this: "Life is a journey, not a destination." That's very True of the Phase 2 journey!

Because of your limiting experiences in Phase 1 and your cumulative frustration with them, it's understandable that you'd want all your power, wisdom, abundance, and True Joy back instantaneously, especially when you get a taste of what's possible in Phase 2. I felt that way too when I first entered Phase 2. However, you must understand that the Phase 2 game doesn't work that way— nor do you *really* want it to work that way, even if the idea seems attractive.

Okay. Let's begin our discussion of The Process.

The Process, Tool 2

The four tools combine to create your Phase 2 drill bit. Each one plays an important part, but The Process could be called the heaviest lifter of the group, especially in the early stages of Phase 2. Think of it as the sharp point of the drill bit that actually comes into contact with the solid, dense cloud cover.

The Process is the most extraordinary tool I've ever developed or used. Being able to apply The Process is what all the preceding chapters and puzzle pieces have been building to, and one of the major gifts you came to this book to receive. However, as you'll see, an explanation of The Process would not have made any sense, and you wouldn't have been fully empowered to use it to maximum advantage without the foundation of the other puzzle pieces that were delivered in the preceding chapters.

Applying The Process is easy. It's also a lot of fun once you get your feet wet and become comfortable with it. Like learning any other new skill, however, it may feel strange and awkward at first.

Power is hidden inside *all* the illusions you experience while playing The Human Game. However, the greatest amount of power, the biggest lies, and the biggest illusions are located where you feel discomfort. As you now know, who you really are is an Infinite Being who is in a constant state of True Joy. As such, it's *impossible* for you to experience discomfort of any kind. It's impossible for you to feel fear, anxiety, frustration, impatience, embarrassment, shame, anger, depression, or anything else you'd label as a negative emotion.

The only way you can appear to feel discomfort (negative emotion) is if you create such a pattern in The Field, add an enormous amount of power to it, pop the illusion of it into your hologram, and convince yourself it's real. And the more discomfort you feel, the more *negative* you feel, the more intense the *negative* emotions seem— this all shows you how much further away you pushed yourself from who you really are, how much harder you had to work to convince yourself the illusion was real, and how much more power you had to apply to pull it off.

Think of it this way. If you're 10 feet tall and I want to convince you that you're 9 feet, 11 inches tall, it wouldn't be that hard, would it? But if you're 10 feet tall and I want to convince you you're 3 feet tall, that's a big job. Why? Because the gap between The Truth and the lie is so large. Similarly, if you want to convince my wife she can't play golf well, it's no big deal, because she knows she doesn't play golf well. But if you want to convince Tiger Woods he can't play golf well, that's a gigantic challenge because, again, the gap between The Truth and the lie is so big!

Key Point

The bigger the illusion, the bigger the lie, the more effort and power are required to make it appear real.

Therefore, to support you in drilling through the cloud cover, your Expanded Self will create and activate patterns that pop extremely uncomfortable stories into your hologram for you to experience and apply The Process to.

However, please hear me when I say the themes and content of those uncomfortable stories *won't be new*. You will reexperience stories with themes and content you've experienced all your life. In Phase 1, those patterns/stories repeated endlessly in your personal life and business—with different people, places, and things at the forefront—without you getting anywhere through the repetition. You were like a dog at the track endlessly racing but never catching the rabbit, or a hamster running endlessly on its wheel but never getting anywhere. However, in Phase 2, when the stories are recreated by your Expanded Self in similar or different disguises, you'll have the opportunity to apply The Process with them, and when you do that, you drill through the cloud cover and you get somewhere amazing!

As we discussed in Chapter 2, from the moment you were born, you began hiding your tremendous power, wisdom, abundance, and True Joy from yourself and convincing yourself you were the opposite of who you really are. You also convinced yourself most of the hiding places for The Truth were so painful, dangerous, scary, and deadly that they had be avoided at all costs. You convinced yourself if you went into some of those places, something horrible would happen—you'd die, lose yourself, lose your marriage or kids, be shamed or embarrassed beyond your ability to cope, whatever it was. You know what your "don't go there" places and emotions feel like, because you've experienced them throughout your life.

Once again, in Phase 2, your Expanded Self will take you back to the places like that and support you in transforming them by telling The Truth about them, reclaiming the power that has been propping them up as illusions and causing them to repeat, and increasing your feelings of Appreciation for yourself (as Creator) and your creations.

Once you've applied The Process enough, dug enough tunnels, poked enough holes in the solid, dense cloud cover, and allowed more and more of the sun of who you really are to shine through, your hologram starts to change; then it changes some more, and the pace of change starts to accelerate, which is when it gets really cool. As you expand more and more, and collapse more and more limiting patterns in The Field, the power, wisdom, abundance, and True Joy that are your natural state start shining through more and more, and your life and business become more and more miraculous.

I'm now going to explain how to apply The Process. Please keep in mind a very important point: There's a core structure to The Process, and there are guidelines for how to work within that structure. The core structure should be respected each time you apply The Process. If you don't respect the core structure, it won't support you in drilling through the cloud cover.

However, the guidelines for working within the structure are just that—guidelines—and you have a lot of freedom and wiggle room to modify them to your liking. In short, there's no one way, best way, rule, or magic formula for how to apply The Process. Like everything in The Human Game, it must be customized for your unique needs as a unique Infinite Being on a unique mission—and must be allowed to change over time as you change, if that's what you choose to create.

I'll highlight the core structural components for you and share the guidelines I've developed for myself, my clients, and students from the Business School of Consciousness.[2] Then I encourage you to follow the lead of your Expanded Self as you evolve The Process for yourself. Play with it, experiment with it, and make it your own. What I did when I first started applying The Process and what I did in later stages of playing the Phase 2 game were very different.

I'm now going to give you an overview of the steps for applying The Process, and then we'll discuss each step in detail. Remember, it will all start with experiences being popped into your hologram that cause you discomfort—perhaps great, perhaps minor.

An Overview of the Process

When you experience discomfort of any kind, follow five steps:

1. Dive right into the middle of it.
2. Feel the discomfort as fully as you can.
3. When it naturally reaches a peak of intensity, tell The Truth about it.
4. Reclaim your power from it.
5. Express Appreciation for yourself and the creation.

In Phase 2, you can apply The Process each time you feel discomfort of any kind—emotional or physical—especially as it relates to business and finances. This means if you feel discomfort because, for example, you had quarterly results that didn't meet expectations, you lost your biggest client, a key employee quit, a team member made a big mistake that really cost you, or the stock market crashed.

You can also apply The Process as you experience discomfort and find yourself asking questions like these (from a business or personal perspective):

- "Can I afford that?"
- "Should I sign that contract?"

---

[2] www.business-school-of-consciousness.com.

- "Should I hire that person?"
- "Should I fire that person?"
- "Should I buy that?"
- "Would it be prudent to buy that right now?"
- "Do I really need that right now?"
- "What would my spouse think if I bought or did that?"
- "What would my partner/boss/board think if I did that?"

Key Point

If you feel any discomfort at all, you have the opportunity, *but not the mandate*, to apply The Process.

Notice that I said "the opportunity, *but not the mandate*, to apply The Process." This is so important! In Phase 1, so many of us memorize rules and formulas for what we *should* do and how we *should* act and then we put tremendous pressure on ourselves (and cause ourselves a lot of stress) to force ourselves to do everything perfectly. The Phase 2 game and applying The Process aren't like that. The Phase 2 game and applying The Process are *not* about forcing yourself, out of willpower or self-discipline, to do things. The Phase 2 game and applying The Process are not about pressure, stress, being overly anal-retentive, being an overachiever, or being perfect. I'll share more about this later.

Okay, let's now begin a detailed discussion of the guidelines for each step of The Process.

Step 1: Dive Right into the Middle of It

The tremendous power that's disguised as discomfort is very real and very tangible. You can feel it. You might experience it as a gigantic vibrating ball of energy. You might experience it as a hurricane or tornado of energy. It might feel like a whirlpool or undercurrent of rushing water. It doesn't matter how you experience it. We're all different, and we all have different ways of experiencing emotions, energy, and power. Just notice what's there for you. Whatever your experience of the discomfort is, *in Consciousness* (i.e., in your imagination), you dive right into the middle of it (or run or walk or jump or whatever form of movement works for you). I use the words "dive into it" simply because that's how I experienced it on my journey.

However you choose to do it, fully immerse yourself within the feelings of discomfort. In the beginning, it might be easier if you apply The Process with your eyes closed. Later, it won't matter and you'll be able to do it on the fly, even while engaged in conversation with others.

Step 2: Feel the Discomfort as Fully as You Can

Once you're fully immersed in the feelings of discomfort, sense them as fully as you possibly can. Just feel them, the intensity, the waves, the raw power in them, whatever the experience is like for you. If you can escalate the intensity and allow yourself to feel even more of what's there, do it—because the more you feel, the deeper the drill bit can go into the tunnel you're digging through the cloud cover.

I say this because in Phase 1, many of us create a dynamic where we automatically decrease the intensity of all our emotions before we allow ourselves to feel them. For example, the true intensity of an emotion might be at level 100, but we knock it down to level 60 before we allow ourselves to feel it because level 60 feels safer. Therefore, using that example, if you were feeling only the 60 units, there would actually be 40 additional units of power available to you to apply The Process with. If you feel comfortable allowing the intensity to amp up, do it. If you don't feel comfortable doing that, it's no big deal. You'll go back and get the rest of the power later. You can't do it in a wrong way. Why? Because as you'll discover in more detail later, your Expanded Self is right there with you making sure it's always done just right!

Key Point

When you apply The Process, do your best to just feel the discomfort as much as you'll allow yourself to—without thought, logic, intellect, judgment, labeling, or analysis of what's happening. Just *feel it* to the best of your ability in the moment. Your best will naturally expand over time.

The intensity you feel, no matter how you might judge or label it, *is* your power. It *is* who you really are. It *is* what you had to apply to the pattern to pop that experience into your hologram and convince yourself it was real. If you get to the point where you feel like you're going to be overwhelmed by the sensations of discomfort, you can stop, but I invite you to stretch yourself. The feelings of danger are just an old trick you used in Phase 1 to keep yourself away from your power and The Truth. You can ignore the trick—completely safely—if you choose to. Your Expanded Self would never give you more than you can handle, no matter how it appears.

The core structural component of step 2 is experiencing the feelings as fully as you possibly can. *How* you do it and *what* you see, feel, hear, and create for yourself in the experience are all up to you, and can evolve and change over time. As I've explained, there are no rules or formulas for anything in Phase 2 of The Human Game.

Step 3: When It Naturally Reaches a Peak of Intensity, Tell The Truth about It

As you immerse yourself in the feelings of discomfort and feel them as fully as you possibly can, you'll notice the discomfort reaching its own natural peak of intensity—or you'll notice yourself reaching the limit of how much you're willing to feel in that moment. Trust yourself on knowing when the peak or your limit has been reached. Resist the Phase 1 temptation to get overly analytical and beat yourself up by saying something like this to yourself: "I have to find the perfect peak point, and if I miss it I've screwed it up and I'm an idiot." You just do your best and trust your Expanded Self, especially at the start. It'll get easier as you apply The Process more and more.

When the intensity naturally reaches its peak, you tell The Truth about it. What does that mean? You affirm who you really are, how powerful you really are, that you created it, it's not real, it's just a creation of your Consciousness. To do that, you must come up with a phrase to describe who you really are that resonates with you and supports you in feeling as powerful and infinite as you possibly can. Following are some examples you can use or adapt, or you can make up your own phrase. The words don't matter. How they make you *feel* is the only thing that matters. The first phrase is what I have used throughout my Phase 2 journey. The other phrases are examples my coaching clients and students in the Business School of Consciousness use:

- "I am the Power and Presence of God."
- "I am the Power of Infinite Intelligence."
- "I am the Power of Pure Consciousness."
- "I am the Ultimate Power in the Universe."
- "I am a Being of Pure Light."

Once you choose a phrase (and it may change and evolve over time), you then add your affirmation of The Truth after it and expand the phrase. Here is an example of how you could tell The Truth about an illusion that's making you feel uncomfortable, using the label I chose for who I really am: "I am the Power and Presence of God creating this. It's not real. It's completely made up. It's just a story, a creation of *my* Consciousness appearing real. It's just True Joy in disguise."

Step 4: Reclaim Your Power from It

After you tell The Truth about your creation, you then reclaim your power from it by using words, seeing images, feeling feelings, or a combination of all three. For example, you could simply use words like this (which I did): "I reclaim my power from this creation *now!*"

Or you could *see* power flowing into you, or you could *feel* power flowing into and through you, or you could experience some combination of words, images, and feelings. Just trust whatever you *feel* moved to do. There's no magic or actual power in the words, images, or feelings you choose as you do this step. It's simply a way of acknowledging that this is the moment when the power will be reclaimed.

Step 5: Express Appreciation for Yourself and the Creation

In the fifth and final step, you take a look at the illusion, at the total-immersion "movie scene" you created to stimulate the feelings of discomfort, and you Appreciate how magnificent that creation was, how amazing you had to be to create it, and how amazing it is that you could actually believe it was real when it was really just special effects, smoke and mirrors. We discussed how to do this in the previous chapter, but I want to return to The Movie Theater Crutch I shared in Chapter 2 and invite you to use it for support in the Appreciation step of The Process.

Imagine, once again, that you're sitting in a movie theater watching a movie on the screen that's making you feel extremely uncomfortable. Imagine there's a man, woman, and child in the movie scene you're watching. Now, imagine that in the back of the same theater, leaning against the back wall, are the three actors who played the man, the woman, and the child in the scene, the director of the movie, the makeup artist, and the special effects engineer. Let's call this group the creative team.

While you're sitting in your seat squirming with discomfort, what is the creative team doing? Celebrating! Appreciating! They know it's not real. They know it's all made up. They know it's all just a story. They know no one *really* gets sick, hurt, or abused, lives, dies, or makes a million bucks. Since they don't take the action seriously or judge what's going on in the story line, they're free to simply celebrate and Appreciate their creative contribution to such an effective illusion.

Now, let's apply this metaphor to the Appreciation step of The Process. Whenever you're immersed within an illusion that's making you uncomfortable, it's the equivalent of you sitting in the theater feeling very uncomfortable about the action on the screen. When you begin to move into feelings of Appreciation when applying The Process, it's the equivalent of you getting up out of your seat in that theater, walking to the back of the theater, joining the creative team, and sharing their Truthful perspective on and their Appreciation of the illusion on the screen.

Did you see the movie *Jurassic Park*? If not, I'll tell you that it was a story about dinosaurs, and the Hollywood animators did an extraordinary job of creating dinosaur images on the screen that looked unbelievably real. How do you think those animators felt the first time they saw their creations, the illusions they worked so hard to create, up there on the big screen? They felt *huge* amounts of Appreciation for themselves and their creations. That's how you'll feel more and more as you apply The Process, expand, knock out cloud cover, and begin feeling the sun of who you really are shining into your hologram.

In essence, in the final step of The Process, you simply want to do your best to affirm and feel "Wow!" about the illusion you've been working with, and bask in the why of that Wow, and in all your magnificence as Creator. I call this "The Wow Effect." As with everything else in Phase 2, your best will naturally expand over time.

In the beginning, with one or more of the steps (especially the Appreciation step), everything may sound or feel empty or fake. That's okay. Do it anyway and keep doing it. Over time, everything becomes more and more and more real and True, and it all feels more real and True to you—naturally.

Key Point

You must always do your best to really *feel* The Truth behind all the words you say, the images you see, and the feelings you feel to support each of the steps as you apply The Process. As with everything else in Phase 2, your best will naturally expand over time.

Does this seem too simple to be really capable of drilling through the cloud cover? If so, be aware that it's not just about what you're doing as you apply The Process. You're applying The Process side by side with your Expanded Self, who is leading you to patterns in The Field and helping you work on them.

In Phase 1, your Expanded Self did everything in His or Her power to keep you thinking the illusion was real, that you were opposite of who you really are within it, and to keep you away from a direct experience of who you really are. In Phase 2, your Expanded Self does everything in His or Her power to reverse that and support you in knocking out the cloud cover and expanding back into a direct experience of who you really are. By applying The Process over time, you drain the power from the patterns that have been limiting and restricting you, including while playing The Business Game. You also dissolve the beliefs, judgments, and consequences stored in those patterns (i.e., the glue you applied in Phase 1 to hold the illusions in place).

Do the steps of The Process seem confusing? If so, they won't after you have been using it for a while with the help of your Expanded Self. I've taught The Process to tens of thousands of people all over the world. It always takes some practice, but everyone gets it quickly and then evolves it over time to make it their own. You will, too! The toughest parts, from my experience (and they may be easy for you since we're all different), are finding the courage to dive into the discomfort the first few times if it feels scary or dangerous, and fully appreciating a creation you're still judging as being bad or negative. However, all of it will come in time with practice.

Here is the five-step procedure for applying The Process again for easy reference and review. When you hit the peak of intensity with any discomfort you feel, you dive into the heart of the discomfort and say something like this, using your own words (and/or utilizing images and feelings):

1. I am _____ creating this." (Fill in the blank with the description you chose for who you really are.)

2. "It's not real. It's completely made up." (Feel the meaning of the words as much as you can.)
3. "It's just a story, a creation of *my* Consciousness, True Joy in disguise." (Feel the meaning of the words as much as you can.)
4. "I reclaim my power from this creation *now*."
5. Now Appreciate how amazing you had to be to create the illusion being Processed and to convince yourself it was real, how amazing the creation was, and how beautifully it served you in Phase 1 and in Phase 2 up to that point.

Let's now go through The Process with a specific example. Feel free to create your own example as we go along if the one I share doesn't work for you in terms of bringing up discomfort.

Suppose you are the CEO of a company. You spent the previous year building a relationship with a large and important client named Sally James. She'd been sending you a lot of business and had the potential to send you even more in the years to come. Everything had been going great with her. As your CEO responsibilities grew, you turned Sally's account over to a trusted associate named Bill to handle for you.

Imagine you arrive at the office one morning, check your voice mail, and hear Sally's voice asking you to call her about an urgent matter. Your heart begins to pound and fear begins to roll through you. You call her and she proceeds to rant and rave for 37 minutes about what a lousy job Bill has done with the account, how her confidence in your company has been shaken, and how she's thinking of sending her business to a competitor. The fear begins to expand, and anger at the associate (and at yourself for turning the account over to Bill or not keeping a close watch on him afterward) gets added into the mix. In short, you're *very* uncomfortable!

In this example, at the moment your heart starts to pound when hearing the voice mail message, during the chat with Sally as she rants and raves, and after your conversation with her ends and you are filled with feelings of fear and anger, you have the opportunity to apply The Process. To do that, you'd start out by simply feeling the discomfort. In *Consciousness*, you'd simply dive right into the middle of it and feel it as fully as you can. There would be no need to think about it, analyze it, label it, describe it, or say, "I'm angry at myself, I'm angry at my associate, and I'm afraid of losing the account." Just feel the feelings! Allow them to reach their natural peak or your personal intensity limit in the moment.

When you feel the peak, apply the rest of whatever version of The Process guidelines you're using at the time—doing your best to *really feel The Truth in each step*, however you do it. In the example that follows, I'll share what I'd do and say, but again, there's no magic in my approach. It's just what I'd do. While keeping awareness of the scene with Sally and the associate in mind, I'd say to myself, slowly, with lots of pauses in between the lines, and feeling The Truth of the words as I say them: "I am the Power and Presence of God creating this. . . . It's not real. . . . It's completely made up. . . . It's just a story, a creation of *my* Consciousness appearing real. . . . It's just True Joy in disguise. . . . I reclaim my power from this creation *now*."

Then I'd move into the Appreciation step and say and feel something like this, being as specific or general as I felt moved to be in the moment: "Wow! Isn't it amazing that I can create the illusion of Bill dropping the ball like that, make it seem so real, and feel so vulnerable, stupid, and afraid about it!"

There are no rules or formulas in Phase 2, but in general, you don't apply The Process to an illusion once and that's it. For reasons I'll discuss in greater detail later, you go back into the same illusion, in the same or different disguises, over and over and over, as you slowly but surely peel back all the layers that were required to make that illusion persist in the hologram and make you so uncomfortable—until it ultimately collapses.

So, after applying The Process in a situation like our example once, in Consciousness, I would then replay the scene in my imagination (the voice mail message, the call with Sally, the feelings during and after). If I still felt any discomfort as I replayed it, I would apply The Process again—and keep doing it as many times as I felt moved to in the moment, if I continued to feel uncomfortable when replaying the scene in my imagination.

That's it. That's The Process. After you get comfortable with it, depending on the details in the scene that trigger discomfort and the personal choices you make in applying The Process, the whole thing can take as little as a minute or as long as you choose to extend it. It ultimately becomes quick and easy. It doesn't take hours or your entire day. Plus, as I mentioned, applying The Process is actually quite a fun and joyful experience you'll actually look forward to. I do, and so do all my clients and students who apply it.

If I'm at home by myself and I feel discomfort, I generally apply The Process with my eyes closed while reclining in a zero-gravity chair I have in my home office. If I'm engaged in conversation with other people, say at dinner or a party, and I feel discomfort, I look away and apply The Process, or I look down and touch my fingers to my forehead like I'm deep in thought, or I excuse myself and go to the restroom to apply The Process there. You'll figure out how to do it in various situations. It's not hard and just takes some common sense and practice.

Key Point

You don't always have to apply The Process in the heat of the moment.

Even though it ultimately becomes quick and easy to apply The Process, there will still be times when you'll decide it's not convenient or possible to do it in the heat of the moment when the discomfort gets naturally triggered. That's fine. If that happens, you have two choices:

1. Defer it and apply The Process later, when it's convenient, by simply replaying the trigger scene in your imagination, recreating the feelings of discomfort, and applying The Process to them then.

2. Ignore the opportunity and know that another one will come another day.

There's an additional application of The Process I want to share with you that you're going to love. Sometimes, when you feel discomfort, you just feel a vague, unfocused sense of discomfort in the moment. At other times, something gets popped into your hologram that causes you discomfort in the moment, but then you take it into the future and that sets off a chain reaction in your mind: "Oh no, if this happens, that will happen, then this, then that, then that, then . . . Arghhhhhhh!" And you find yourself *imagining* a potential disaster happening in the future.

Consciousness is Consciousness. Illusions are illusions. It doesn't matter if they're in your hologram or in your imagination, so if you feel discomfort about an imaginary event in an imagined future, you can apply The Process to the experience. I call it "Stretching." In this scenario, you just go into the imagined disastrous future in your mind, see and feel as much of the potential disaster as possible, and then apply The Process to it. By doing that, you'll support your Phase 2 journey in three ways:

1. You keep drilling through the cloud cover, although in a different way.
2. Once the patterns have been drained of power and the judgment has been dissolved, the fear and feelings about the future disaster will be gone *permanently*.
3. By experiencing the *disaster* in your imagination (i.e., in Consciousness), there's no need for you to pop it into your hologram and experience it in more tangible form.

Key Point

Until a pattern is collapsed, it will continue to *appear* real, act real, and appear to have power over you.

Understanding something is an illusion intellectually and collapsing the illusion while having a direct experience of The Truth of it are very different experiences. Knowledge has no power in Phase 2. Direct experience has all the power.

The Process is the closest thing to a miracle I've ever experienced while playing The Human Game. If you commit yourself and work it through to the end, patterns that have plagued you, caused you pain, or limited your finances, business success, joy in playing The Business Game, and the flow of abundance to you will simply disappear from your hologram. Things that used to scare you to death will make you laugh. Things that used to automatically trigger in you anger, fear, embarrassment, frustration, or feeling weak or small will simply be gone—*poof*—and you'll feel joyfulness, peace, and power instead. It's truly remarkable.

In Phase 2, discomfort is just a flashing red light, like a police siren, that says, "There's power here! There's power here! There's judgment here! There's a big lie here! There's opportunity to knock out cloud cover here! Come get me! Come get me!" So you go get it and magic happens over time.

In Phase 1, you wanted to make bad feelings go away. In Phase 2, you say, "Bring them on," so you can use them to drill through the cloud cover.

Even though there are four more chapters in this book (plus the three additional bonus chapters you can download, mentioned in Chapter 16) and our journey together isn't over, I'd like to suggest that you take some time as soon as possible to get your feet wet by applying The Process. You may be feeling discomfort about something this very minute—a bill, a personal problem, or an employee issue. Or maybe something new will get popped into your hologram later today or tomorrow.

We'll be discussing The Process again in the chapters that follow, but now it's time to discuss the other two tools that complete your Phase 2 drill bit.

The Mini-Process, Tool 3

As you move into Phase 2 of The Human Game, you'll notice two scenarios unfolding related to business and finances (and other creations unrelated to money):

1. Illusions that cause you to feel discomfort.
2. Illusions that don't cause you to feel discomfort but that are still limiting and restricting you.

When you feel discomfort, you apply The Process. When you don't feel discomfort but you see limiting illusions at work, you apply the Mini-Process. Here's an example to help you distinguish between the two scenarios. If you look at a business or personal checking account statement and feel uncomfortable because the balance seems low, you apply The Process to it.

However, if you look at the balance on your checking account statement and you *don't* feel uncomfortable (because it seems large enough to make you feel "prosperous" or "okay financially" in that moment, or however you'd label it), you apply the Mini-Process. Why? Because your checking account isn't real, the deposit and withdrawal numbers on the statement aren't real, and the balance isn't real, so you know you're looking at a limited creation, an illusion. Even though the illusion is okay with you, you still have the opportunity to drill through the cloud cover, and you use the Mini-Process to do that.

The Mini-Process is the same as The Process except you don't dive into the discomfort as in step 1 because there isn't any discomfort there. So, you simply follow the remaining steps:

1. "I am _____ creating this." (Fill in the blank with the description you chose for who you really are.)
2. "It's not real. It's completely made up." (Feel the meaning of the words as much as you can.)
3. "It's just a story, a creation of *my* Consciousness appearing real, just True Joy in disguise." (Feel the meaning of the words as much as you can.)
4. "I reclaim my power from this creation *now*."
5. Now fully Appreciate how amazing you had to be to create the illusion being Processed and to convince yourself it was real, how amazing the creation was, and how beautifully it served you in Phase 1.

Transformational Vocabulary, Tool 4

As part of The Business Game, we have numerous ideas, concepts, and words that are used to reinforce the illusion of financial limitation. To complement the use of the Appreciation, The Process, and the Mini-Process tools in Phase 2, you want to modify your vocabulary and self-talk to support your ever-growing expansion and opening into your natural state of infinite abundance.

Therefore, you want to watch your conversation and especially your self-talk carefully and transform ideas, concepts, and words like the following by replacing them with a Phase 2 alternative while feeling The Truth and meaning of the new wording as much as you possibly can as you do it:

Phase 1 Term	Phase 2 Replacement
Cost	Request for appreciation in the form of money
The bill	Request for appreciation in the form of money
Expense	Expression of appreciation in the form of money
Overhead	Fixed monthly expressions of appreciation in the form of money
Price	Requested expression of appreciation in the form of money
How much?	What is the requested appreciation for this illusion/creation?
Payment	Expression of appreciation in the form of money

You get the idea. Just like with applying The Process, the Phase 2 alternative wording may feel empty or fake at first, but it will become more and more real the more you use it and the deeper you move into Phase 2.

In addition, as you describe other illusions (with self-talk and when talking to other aspects of yourself), you want to also use language, as much as possible, that accurately reflects or describes The Truth (instead of reinforcing the illusion). Here are some examples to get your creative juices flowing:

- "I created the illusion of _____."
- "I created him/her to say/do _____."
- "I experienced the illusion of feeling _____."
- "_____, so to speak."
- "In the story line, _____." (This is one of my favorites!)

Let's get real for a minute. If you go into a store, bank, or restaurant and speak in this way, or do so to an employee, associate, vendor, client, board member, friend, or spouse who knows nothing about Phase 2 or busting loose from The Business Game, you might worry they'll think you're nuts. I have three things to share about that:

1. "They" aren't there. They're made up. They're just aspects of *your* Consciousness saying and doing what you create them to. They will not judge, criticize, or even notice your use of Phase 2 supportive language unless you create them to. If you do create others to judge you for using Phase 2 language, you're most likely reflecting back your own judgments, but that will pass. If you don't, you can just have fun with it!

2. If you feel uncomfortable about using the Transformational Vocabulary tool, you have the opportunity to apply The Process. Why? Because all discomfort has its roots in lies and illusions!

3. If, despite what I just shared, you're unwilling to use Transformational Vocabulary under certain circumstances with others, you still have the opportunity to use whatever language you choose outwardly, while inwardly, silently, through your self-talk, reminding yourself of The Truth.

Many Phase 2 Players tend to discount the value of the Transformational Vocabulary tool, thinking it pales in importance compared to the other three tools, but I must tell you it's a very important part of your drill bit and is also critical to drilling through the cloud cover. Language, as it was repetitively used in Phase 1 by others and ourselves (inwardly and outwardly), was a big part of how we pulled off The Phase 1 Miracle. Reversing that dynamic, then, is an important key to expansion in Phase 2.

Key Point

In Phase 2, The Human Game is The Human Game. There is no split between your personal and business lives. You use the tools to drill through business illusions. You use the tools to drill through personal illusions. As you knock out cloud cover, your entire Human Experience is transformed.

When you combine the four tools—Appreciation, The Process, The Mini-Process, and Transformational Vocabulary—into one unified drill bit, and drill away through the cloud cover day in and day out, amazing things start to happen. To discover more about what using the drill looks like, exactly how to use the drill on a daily basis, and what to expect as you start tunneling through the cloud cover on your journey toward busting loose from The Business Game, turn the page to continue with Chapter 13.

Stranger in a Strange Land

Toto, I have a feeling we're not in Kansas anymore.[1]

—Dorothy in The Wizard of Oz

*S*tranger in a Strange Land, a science fiction novel by Robert Heinlein, is the story of Valentine Michael Smith, born during, and the only survivor of, the first manned mission to Mars. Michael was raised by Martians, and arrives on Earth as a true innocent, knowing nothing of human ways, and feeling quite disoriented by all of it.

Players who move into Phase 2 of The Human Game (including me when I first leaped) often have a similar experience—except the feeling in Phase 1 is like being a stranger in a world you thought you

[1] Judy Garland, speaking as Dorothy in the movie *The Wizard of Oz* (1939, Warner Home Video); based on L. Frank Baum, *The Wonderful Wizard of Oz* (Chicago: George M. Hill Company, 1900).

knew. In Phase 1, the goal was to convince yourself the illusion was real and you're the opposite of who you really are within it. You grew accustomed to the look and feel of playing in Phase 1.

In Phase 2, however, the goal is to reverse all of that, and support you in knocking out the cloud cover and expanding back into a direct experience of who you really are. Therefore, everything in Phase 2 works exactly opposite to how it works in Phase 1, and everything that happens to you in Phase 2 is being driven by an opposite force that looks and feels very different. As a result, Phase 2, especially at the start, can feel surreal, strange, and disorienting— especially as it applies to what you experience with employees, customers, clients, products, services, sales, marketing, decision making, cash flow, problem solving, and so on.

Therefore, starting in this chapter and continuing in the chapters that follow, I'll be offering what I call "navigation support" for living in and moving through the new world you'll discover as a Phase 2 Player.

First, Phase 2 has two segments:

1. *The Expansion Segment*, in which you spend most of your time, effort, and energy using the tools and drilling through the cloud cover.

2. *The Play Segment*, in which you spend most of your time and energy playing The New Business Game for the sheer pleasure of playing, with no limits and no restrictions of any kind.

We'll be discussing The Expansion Segment in this chapter and the next, then we'll move into a discussion of The Play Segment.

In Phase 1 of The Human Game, your focus was on what appeared to be outside of you. In Phase 2, in The Expansion Segment, the focus shifts to what's going on *inside* you. Phase 1 was all about hiding your power, wisdom, abundance, and True Joy, and convincing yourself the illusion is real and you're the opposite of who you really are within it. In The Expansion Segment of Phase 2, it's all about:

1. Reclaiming power.

2. Reaffirming The Truth.

3. Dramatically increasing your levels of Appreciation for yourself as Creator and for all your creations.

4. Expanding and unlimiting yourself.

5. Remembering and having a direct experience of the fact that the illusion is *not* real.

6. Giving yourself a guided tour of how you pulled off The Phase 1 Miracle in your own unique hologram.

These six points are what I call the "Phase 2 work."

In Phase 1, what's happening in your hologram (the story line details) is very important to you. In Phase 2, the story line details are irrelevant. Why? Because they're all being created by your Expanded Self for the sole purpose of supporting you in doing the Phase 2 work and the Phase 2 work alone. Nothing else matters.

In Phase 2, it doesn't matter if you create the illusion of quitting a job or keeping it, hiring someone or not, experiencing sales highs or lows, making or losing money, expanding or contracting your product line, growing or shrinking your team, or deciding to do X instead of Y. It doesn't matter if your business appears to thrive or struggle. It doesn't matter what your checking account balances, net worth, or financial statements look like (or how they change). This is a very difficult concept for many Phase 2 Players to get initially, but it's The Truth, which is why I mention it here, and you *will* have a direct experience of it once you expand to a certain point.

In Phase 2, the only thing that matters is how what's going on in the story line supports you in doing the Phase 2 work. The goal in Phase 2 is to get you to the point where you can bust loose from The Business Game and play The Human Game and The New Business Game without any limits or restrictions. Because that treasure is so precious and goes beyond anything you can imagine to be possible for yourself right now, everything else pales in comparison—and whatever problems appear to get created on the road to getting that treasure will take care of themselves once enough cloud cover gets knocked out.

Key Point

In Phase 2, nothing has any significance, importance, meaning, stability, or solidity except to the extent that it supports you in using the tools and drilling through the cloud cover.

This concept is tricky. On the surface, it's easily understandable from a logical perspective. However, there are subtleties to it that don't become clear until you've had numerous Phase 2 experiences that *show you* The Truth of it and give you a direct experience of that Truth. For now, just allow the seeds to be planted. They'll be watered, be nurtured, and grow tall at a later date.

In Phase 1 of The Human Game, you were taught to be proactive, go out there and make things happen, take massive action, set goals and achieve them, get the job done, and be as productive and efficient as possible. In Phase 2, it's the exact opposite. In Phase 2 you make a transition into living in what I call *reactive mode*. You wake up in the morning and wait to see what gets popped into your hologram and what you feel motivated or inspired to do in response to it. There are two scenarios to reactive mode living and working:

1. When an illusion that appears to be *outside of you* seems to require a response, a decision, or an action.
2. When you feel an *internal* motivation or inspiration to act.

In either scenario, when you feel motivated or inspired to do something, you do it. If you don't feel motivated or inspired to do anything, you wait until you do. You live that way all day long. Then you go to bed at night, wake up the next morning, and do it again. As difficult, impossible, or counterintuitive as this may seem at first glance, especially if you're used to being in take-action mode, in Phase 2 you slowly but surely move into a space where you have no goals, agendas, or desired outcomes. You have no one-year plans, five-year plans, or ten-year plans. You squeeze your focus way back and take your business activities one *moment* at a time.

It's like you're a handyman. When you're a handyman, you wait for someone to call with projects for you to complete. When you're called, you go to the home or office and consider what needs to be done. You then choose a tool from your tool belt or truck and do what needs to be done. When you're done with one tool and one project, you choose another tool to complete another project, always using the right tool for the job. Sometimes you use a screwdriver, sometimes a paintbrush, sometimes a hammer, wrench, drill, or saw.

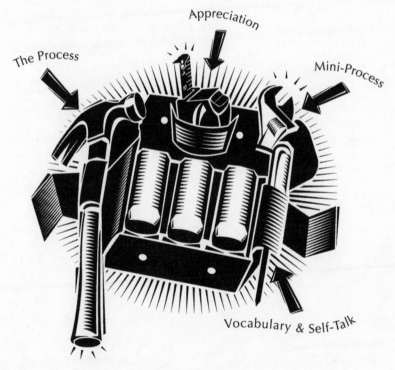

Your Phase 2 tool belt.

As you're taking life and business one moment at a time and living in reactive mode, if an experience from either of the two scenarios gets popped into your hologram that causes you discomfort, you have the opportunity (but not the mandate) to pull The Process tool from your belt and use it. If something gets popped into your hologram that doesn't cause you discomfort but points to a limiting pattern in The Field (like a bank statement, financial statement, monthly report on the value of your stock portfolio, bill, etc.), you have the opportunity to pull the Mini-Process tool from your belt and use it.

If you find yourself thinking or speaking (including to yourself) with limited Phase 1 language, you have the opportunity to pull your Transformational Vocabulary tool from your belt and use it. Every time you feel moved to do it (you get to do it 24/7), you can pull the Appreciation tool from your belt and Appreciate the magnificence of your creations, yourself as the Creator of everything you experience, and The Human Game itself.

If you have a decision to make, you do what you *feel* motivated or inspired to do, trusting it's the perfect choice since you're being guided every step of the way by your Expanded Self. If you have discomfort about the decision, you have the opportunity to apply The Process to the discomfort and continue applying it until you have little or no discomfort about the decision when you focus on it. Then, from that expanded state, you do what you *feel* motivated or inspired to do, trusting it's the perfect choice.

In short, here's how you live in reactive mode in Phase 2:

- Wait until something inside or outside you appears to require an action, decision, or response from you.
- Ask yourself, "Is there discomfort?"
- If yes, before responding or acting, you have the opportunity to apply The Process one or more times until you . . .
- Do what you *feel* motivated to do in that moment (including nothing).

- If there's no discomfort, you have the opportunity to simply do what you *feel* motivated to do in that moment (including nothing). Phase 2 is all about feelings!

Key Point

You could say that if you *feel* motivated or inspired to say or do something and you actually say or do it, it's what your Expanded Self wanted you to do. Your Expanded Self is driving the bus in Phase 2. You can't make a mistake, mess anything up, or blow it. You just do your best to trust your Expanded Self and flow with what you *feel* inspired or motivated to do, moment to moment. Your best will naturally expand over time.

In Phase 1, you convinced yourself there was power in the hologram, that you, the Player, were driving the bus, and that the burden and responsibility for getting things done was on your shoulders. It wasn't True in Phase 1, for the reasons we've discussed, and it won't be True in Phase 2, either. The illusion that you had power and were driving the bus was cleverly created by brilliant patterns in The Field that were designed to support you in pulling off The Phase 1 Miracle.

Key Point

In Phase 2, you no longer need to worry about what to do, how to do it, when to do it, what the best strategy or person is for the job, and so on. As you knock out clouds and expand, you'll relax more and more into knowing that your Expanded Self, who is much more qualified to make those decisions, will make them more wisely and better than you ever possibly could!

As you expand in Phase 2 after knocking out more and more of the cloud cover, slowly but surely over time you let go of everything related to driving the bus or being proactive in your business (and personal life). You slowly but surely relax into the Phase 2 game and The Truth of who is *really* in charge and what's *really* going on. This isn't something you can rush or shortcut. It's not something you can do by intending it, using willpower, or applying self-discipline. It's something you open into, naturally, over time, as you drill through the cloud cover. I can assure you from deep personal experience (on my own journey and from the journeys of other Players), that this is an *extremely enjoyable* way to live and play The New Business Game.

To discover specific details about the journeys of other Phase 2 Players as they've played The New Business Game, including the details of my own journey, please visit the following page on my web site to access the special Bonus Chapters: www.bustingloose.com/chapters.html.

If resistance, anxiousness, anxiety, or worry come up as you consider letting go of the illusion of power or control over events and experiences in your hologram, or as you actually begin to let go, you have the opportunity to apply The Process to it. You were never in control in Phase 1, anyway. There never was any power in the hologram, regarding your thoughts, actions, or decisions. It was all an illusion. Your Expanded Self was always in control and always had the power, so by letting go and trusting your Expanded Self in Phase 2, you're just affirming The Truth, living from it, and expanding beyond all the stress, pain, and limitation you experienced while pretending the opposite was true.

You don't have to go looking for patterns to work on or sections of the cloud cover to drill through. You just follow the lead of your Expanded Self, who will take you where He or She wants you to go. As we discussed, your Expanded Self knows where the patterns with the most power are hidden. Your Expanded Self knows where to put the dynamite charges in the limited "building" you constructed in Phase 1 so you can collapse it when you're ready. As we also discussed, to continue the metaphor of demolishing a building, you don't have to put a dynamite charge on every brick of the building, just on the key foundational bricks supporting the most limiting and restricting patterns you created in Phase 1.

Applying The Process to drill through the cloud cover requires an enormous amount of courage, patience, discipline, commitment, and diligence. Why? Because as I explained in Chapter 10, your Expanded Self will lead you to reexperience Phase 1 Miracle patterns that stimulate incredibly intense feelings of discomfort within you. In Phase 1 of The Human Game, you ran away from discomfort like that, or tried to repress it, muffle it, or make it go away. In Phase 2, you dive into the heart of it, and it takes tremendous courage, discipline, and commitment to do that, maintain the "bring it on" attitude, and continue applying The Process to the discomfort day after day, even if you feel like giving up.

Key Point

As you do the Phase 2 work, you must always remember the treasure that awaits you at the end of the journey. It's worth it!

Applying The Process also requires you to be absolutely realistic in terms of how much you can do and how fast you can do it. Once you get a taste of the transformative power of the drilling tools, you may want to use the tools on everything in your business and personal life—all at once—and you may also want everything to change in your hologram—all at once—and neither choice is Truthfully best for you, nor is it supportive.

Remember, the goal in Phase 2 is *not* to instantaneously knock out the cloud cover and transform your hologram in one fell swoop. Your Expanded Self is going to lead you to patterns with the most power in them and support you in transforming them through many applications of The Process over time until the power, judgment, and lies within them have been fully drained. In some cases, I've drained patterns in days or weeks. With other patterns, it took months, a year, or even longer. Your Expanded Self will also support you in fully Appreciating those creations and yourself as the Creator of them. As you move more deeply into Phase 2, the Appreciation tool becomes more and more important, as you'll see.

Key Point

In Phase 1, you're taught "fast is better." In Phase 2, speed is irrelevant. Your ultimate goal is to bust loose from The Business Game and play The Human Game and The New Business Game without limits or restrictions. The timetable has no importance with a treasure like that at the end of the rainbow, and it will be absolutely perfect for you, no matter how long it takes.

There will also be times when you'll feel discomfort, but then after you apply The Process you'll feel joyous and expanded when you come out the other end. Then, a few seconds, minutes, or hours later, you'll find what appears to be the exact same uncomfortable thought or feeling returning. It may feel the same but it never actually is. It's never a boomerang. It's always something new. Whenever you apply The Process, something is always happening within the tunnels you're digging through the cloud cover. You're not kidding yourself or pretending. It's real, even if you don't feel like anything is happening and you don't feel any different immediately afterward.

Key Point

Once you drain power from a pattern, it stays drained. Once you dissolve lies and judgment, they stay dissolved. Once you dig a tunnel through the cloud cover, it stays dug and never collapses or fills itself in again. Once you poke a hole in the cloud cover and the sun starts to shine through the tunnel, it continues to shine. Once you expand, you stay expanded. You don't ever shrink or slide backward.

In Phase 2, you apply The Process to apply The Process, you drill to drill, and where it goes it goes. In the purest form of expression, you don't apply The Process to change, fix, or improve your hologram, although if your journey resembles mine, you'll still find yourself applying The Process with an agenda—for a while, before that pattern ultimately weakens and drops away. This is such a critical point to get and it may be challenging for you at the start. You don't apply The Process to make something *bad* go away or something *good* show up or increase in quantity. You don't apply The Process to triple the sales of your business, double your income, get out of debt, increase the productivity of your employees, get a promotion, outfox a competitor, feel better, or produce *any* specific result. As you knock out the cloud cover, all such story line details will take care of themselves as the sun begins to shine more brightly in your hologram.

It can be extremely tempting, when you want something good to happen in your business, or something *bad* appears to happen in your business—with cash flow, finances, employees, the economy, stock market, or a competitor—to apply The Process, then start looking at your hologram to see if something changed *as a result*. But that doesn't support you in busting loose from The Business Game. This gets tricky, it's subtle, and there's quicksand here you want to avoid, so please listen closely. If you want to change, fix, or improve something in your hologram, what are you doing? Judging it! You're saying, "This is not okay as it is. I want it to be different." As we discussed, judgment is the glue that keeps the Phase 1 illusions locked in place, so if you judge an illusion, what happens? You keep strengthening the glue that's keeping that creation in your hologram. In effect, you keep saying, "This is real! This is real!" And the illusion *must* therefore stay locked in place.

Key Point

If you find yourself thinking, "I want _____," or "I wish _____," or having a preference or desire to put your own stamp on something that already is, *you are judging*, which means you're uncomfortable, which means you have the opportunity to apply The Process.

Key Point

You can't judge an illusion, knock out the cloud cover that defines it, and collapse its pattern simultaneously. It's simply not possible.

Now, having said that, I must add something important. If you're judging something, wanting to change, fix, or improve something in your business in Phase 2, you can't stop judging from intent, intellect, willpower, or self-discipline. That doesn't work. But whenever you're judging something or wanting to change, fix, or improve it, you're uncomfortable, so you can apply The Process to it, and over time through the cumulative use of The Process, judgment will start to weaken, then drop away on its own as a natural consequence of expansion.

Let's go more deeply into this key concept. In Phase 1, there's the illusion of a cause-and-effect relationship between actions and results. We convince ourselves "If I do X and Y I'll get Z." In Truth, as you now understand, there's no such relationship *from within the hologram*. That is, there's no cause *in the hologram* that creates an effect *in the hologram*. The True cause is always outside the hologram. The True cause is always your Consciousness, a pattern in The Field, and your power.

If you apply The Process and then look for a change in your hologram *as a result*, what are you doing? You're looking for proof of The Truth and you're therefore energizing the belief, "I have doubts about this. I'm not sure this is True." You're looking at a creation and saying, "Hey you, *bad* creation, go away and then I'll believe," or

"Hey you, *good* creation, come to me or increase and then I'll believe." And when you do that, nothing can change in your hologram and you can't knock out cloud cover or expand. Why? Because your "prove it to me first" dynamic will continue to feed the doubt and the limiting patterns—and, even if you did give yourself some proof, it wouldn't do any good anyway because there's still so much power in beliefs about the opposite being true. Do you see that? If not, you will after you leap into Phase 2 and play the game for a while. In Phase 2, your goal is to see and really *get*, at a very deep and profound level that goes way beyond understanding, that nothing in the hologram is real and that *you* have all the power. The goal is *not* to strengthen the illusion.

When I've shared this with live event attendees, coaching clients, and Business School of Consciousness students throughout the world, they generally understand the concept, but some say, "I don't like my present situation. That's why I want to bust loose from The Business Game. Of course I want to change my hologram. Of course I want to fix it. Of course I want to improve it. How am I supposed to reconcile the conflict here?" Did that thought cross your mind, too? If so, let me share three additional insights with you to complement what I just said about judgment:

1. You can't fix, change, or improve an illusion. It's not real. There's nothing to fix, change, or improve. It's all smoke and mirrors!

2. As you use the tools, drill through the cloud cover, and expand in Phase 2, you'll get to a point where you're feeling massive Appreciation for everything exactly the way it is, without any desire to change, fix, or improve anything.

3. When you reach the point just described, that's when the door will open for a new pattern to be inserted into The Field, but not before. In Phase 2, in general (as an Infinite Being, you could create something different) as long as you want something to change, it won't!

Look at this from another angle. Suppose you try to apply The Process with an agenda: "I want to knock out some cloud cover so I can double my personal income," or "I want to knock out some cloud cover so I can wipe out my debt," or "I want to knock out some cloud cover so I can double sales for my business." Suppose you succeeded in creating your desired result. All you're doing is trading one illusion for another. All you're doing is trading one *limited* creation for another *limited* creation. That's not your goal in Phase 2. Your goal in Phase 2 is to bust loose from limits, restrictions, and The Business Game *entirely*. You want to reach the point where you can play The Human Game and The New Business Game without any restrictions or limits at all. As long as you want to change, fix, or improve your hologram, as long as you have an agenda, a goal, or a desired outcome, you're reinforcing the strength of the illusion and adding power to the very patterns you have the opportunity to drain and bust loose from.

Plus, consider this as it relates to why you ultimately expand through the desire to change, fix, or improve your hologram. Every single creation you pop into your hologram is an absolute miracle. There's nothing there. It's all smoke and mirrors. Yet it appears absolutely real because of how talented and powerful a Creator you are. Having $50,000 in the bank isn't better than having $500 in the bank. Being a millionaire isn't better than being broke or being $25,000 in debt. Busting loose from The Business Game and opening up to the infinite abundance that is your natural state isn't better than playing the Phase 1 game and being locked into financial limitation.

All the examples I just gave you, and the many others we could discuss, are *different*, but they're all *equal creations* and equally magnificent when viewed from the expanded perspective of The Truth. Is a major character in a movie who has a $5 net worth worse off than another major character in that same movie who is worth $10 million? No. Neither character is real. They're all made up, as are the net worth numbers that supposedly apply to them. It's the same with the illusions in your hologram. And you *will* have a direct experience of this Truth once you expand to a certain point.

All your creations, all illusions, are perfect exactly as they are. They wouldn't be in your hologram if there weren't a pattern in The Field that got energized to create them exactly the way they are. There wouldn't be a pattern in The Field if your Expanded Self didn't put one there—intentionally, based on a brilliant plan—to support you perfectly on your journey, no matter what definition, label, or judgment you might apply to the creation.

The only reason certain creations appear *better* to you is because you're locked into a Phase 1 perspective where you're judging them, making up stories about them, and convincing yourself the stories are real. I realize this may be tough to accept right now, but it's The Truth and that's what you created me to share with you. As I mentioned, all the concepts I've been sharing with you here will become more and more real as you knock out more and more cloud cover and expand more and more while doing the Phase 2 work.

Your hologram *will change* as you do the Phase 2 work. You could look at those changes and judge them as *better*. However, The Truth is, your business and personal life don't get *better*. They just become *different*, and the differences allow you to play different games for the pure pleasure of playing them. When you knock out enough cloud cover and regain enough of your infinite wisdom to be able to see this—really see it—and get it at a very deep and profound level (which you will if you commit to playing the Phase 2 game), that's the signal you're getting very close to busting loose from The Business Game!

This is subtle but very important and a major hurdle you'll have to jump if you commit to playing the Phase 2 game. As I mentioned, if you're like I was and like many of my students and clients have been, despite what I just shared, you may be tempted on many occasions to apply The Process with an agenda of wanting to change, fix, or improve your hologram—and you may give in to that temptation. If that happens, so be it. It's not a big deal. As I explained, you can't mess up your hologram or make a mistake in Phase 2. However, if you try to apply The Process with an agenda, or you try to change, fix, or improve your hologram, you'll see it simply doesn't work. Then, as you continue to do the Phase 2 work and expand, the desire to fix, change, or improve your hologram will ultimately fall away—naturally.

Key Point

If you find yourself judging or wanting to change, fix, or improve anything in your hologram, go with it, embrace it, let it be, feel it fully, but take advantage of the drilling opportunities it offers you as you feel moved to do.

Other clients and students say to me, "That *sounds* great, but it's just not practical for me. I own my own business, and I *must* focus on numbers, goals, and outcomes," or "I have a job where my boss expects me to set and achieve goals on a regular basis," or "I have overhead and a family to feed. I can't afford to be so la-di-da and frivolous." If thoughts like that crossed your mind, take a deep breath and allow me to remind you of several Truths that will get more and more real for you as you expand and move more deeply into Phase 2. In the examples I just gave:

- There is no business.
- There are no numbers.
- There are no goals or outcomes.
- There is no job.
- There is no boss.
- There is no overhead or family to feed.
- There's no such thing as being frivolous or la-di-da.

It's *all* made up. It's *all* just a creation of your Consciousness. There's no power outside of you—not in anyone, not in anything. *You* have all the power and your Expanded Self will use it brilliantly in Phase 2—with your job, business, boss, family, and everything else—to support you in doing the Phase 2 work and busting loose from The Business Game.

In Phase 2, as you knock out cloud cover and expand, all of the items on your to-do list that seem so important will take care of themselves, easily, effortlessly, and joyfully. Why? Because your Expanded Self will see to it once the limiting patterns and illusions have done their job of helping you drill.

Whether you own your own business, work for someone else, or are unemployed; whether you're single or married with children—whatever your situation is, you can still take life one moment at a time, still live in reactive mode, and still use the drilling tools to bust loose from The Business Game without an agenda, goals, or an investment in specific outcomes or results. I do it every day and have been for over five years even though I own multiple businesses, am married, and have two young children. I'll show you exactly how I do it in the chapters that follow, and offer additional guidelines you can follow. There's absolutely nothing unique about me in this respect.

I'd now like to chat with you about what to expect as you begin using the drilling tools on your journey deep into the heart of Phase 2. We'll begin by discussing what will appear to be the challenging or difficult aspects of the Phase 2 game (in this chapter and the next), then we'll move into the expansive and transformative aspects of what to expect.

Challenging Experiences to Expect in Phase 2

Expect the following seven challenges in Phase 2:

1. Expect to be uncomfortable—a lot!
2. Expect weird things to happen.

3. Expect others to act out of character.

4. Expect to have all your core beliefs challenged.

5. Expect to frequently feel confused, frustrated, overwhelmed, and disoriented.

6. Expect to be profoundly impatient.

7. Expect instability and unusually rapid change in your hologram.

Expect to Be Uncomfortable—A Lot!

As we discussed, the strongest Phase 1 patterns are hidden where you feel the most discomfort. Therefore, to create opportunities to drain power from those patterns and transform them, you must feel uncomfortable a lot of the time, especially at the start of your Phase 2 journey. That's just the way it is. In fact, you'll know the moment you actually enter Phase 2, because one or more things will be created and popped into your hologram that are unusual and intense and cause you a great deal of discomfort. Discomfort is the name of the game in Phase 2 during the early stages, and I can't define how long the early stages will last.

In Phase 1, the knee-jerk reaction to tremendous discomfort can be something like this:

- "I hate this."
- "Get me out of here."
- "Why is this happening to me?"
- "I can't handle this right now."
- "Go away!"

If you have thoughts or feelings like that, it's just what I call "Phase 1 residue." It was originally designed to support the Phase 1 goal of limitation and convincing yourself you're the opposite of who you really are. In Phase 2, the opportunity you give yourself is to apply The Process to such feelings, drill through the clouds, and march ever closer to The Busting Loose Point.

Expect Weird Things to Happen

The six primary goals for Phase 2 are:

1. Rediscovering The Truth about who you really are and what's really going on.
2. Reclaiming your power.
3. Constantly staring illusions in the face and telling The Truth about them.
4. Giving yourself a guided tour of how you pulled off The Phase 1 Miracle in your unique hologram.
5. Constantly increasing your Appreciation for yourself as the Creator of everything you experience.
6. Constantly increasing your Appreciation for your creations.

To achieve those goals, experiences must be created that seem weird to you. What does *weird* really mean, anyway? A definition I recently saw in a dictionary is: "Of a strikingly odd or unusual character; strange." If you're an Infinite Being who convinced yourself you're the exact opposite of who you really are, and you suddenly start showing yourself who you really are and how powerful you really are, don't you think what you'll see must appear strange, strikingly odd, or of an unusual character from a Phase 1 perspective? You bet! As far as I'm concerned from my personal experience of my own life and with thousands of clients and students worldwide, the weirder it appears, the greater the opportunity for expansion you create for yourself. In Chapter 15 (and one of the bonus chapters available for download mentioned in Chapter 16), I'll be sharing numerous stories of just how weird things can appear.

The other thing you may notice is that things may get so weird you'll wonder if they really happened or you just imagined them. My experience in my own life and with clients has been that in the early stages of Phase 2, whenever you have a major experience of The Truth, seeing how powerful you really are, and the degree to which you really are creating everything that's happening to you, it has a strong surreal aspect to it. Ultimately, the weirdness, if it appears to be uncomfortable, will transform into an experience of True Joy and massive Appreciation.

Expect Others to Act Out of Character

In Chapter 7, I explained that other people, playing the roles of actors in your total-immersion movie, serve three purposes in your hologram:

1. Reflect something back you're thinking or feeling about yourself or a belief about the illusion you've energized.
2. Share supportive knowledge, wisdom, or insight with you.
3. Set something in motion to support you on your journey.

Therefore, your Expanded Self will be handing scripts to the actors in your total-immersion movie experience and creating them to say and do all kinds of things to support you in doing the Phase 2 work. Therefore, expect to see people saying and doing all kinds of weird things, inconsistent things, out-of-character things—all to support you on your Phase 2 journey.

You may feel tempted to try to figure out why such things are happening or which of the three purposes the words and actions of the other aspects of yourself are supporting. Do your best to let go of the desire to figure those things out. If your Expanded Self wants you to benefit from a reflection, knowledge, wisdom, insight, or something being set in motion by an actor in your hologram acting in an unusual or out-of-character way, he or she will make it obvious and crystal clear to you. You won't need to go digging for it or racking your brain for answers. You just keep drilling, and the rest takes care of itself.

Expect to Have All Your Core Beliefs Challenged

As you know, each limiting pattern in The Field has one or more beliefs inside it, along with judgment and consequences. None of them are True. They're all lies. They're all just made-up stories. Therefore, if you're going to bust loose from The Business Game, the key beliefs you have about how The Business Game works, how you must play it, and what it takes to win it (i.e., the beliefs that have been keeping you locked into limitation in the illusion) will be pushed, poked, prodded, and ultimately collapsed through the unfolding Phase 2 stories you find yourself immersed in. That *must* happen.

Key Point

You can't simultaneously continue believing the lies you convinced yourself were true in Phase 1 and bust loose from The Business Game. It's not possible. They're mutually exclusive activities. In Phase 2, you trade lies and illusions for experiences of The Truth.

Expect to Frequently Feel Confused, Frustrated, Overwhelmed, and Disoriented

If you're going to be experiencing a lot of discomfort in Phase 2, if you'll be seeing a lot of weird things, and if everything you thought was True but isn't gets challenged to its very core, do you think you might feel confused, frustrated, overwhelmed, and disoriented at times?

Of course!

I laugh about it now, but there were many times in my first year of doing the Phase 2 work when I looked up to the sky and said to my Expanded Self, "You've overestimated my ability to deal with this. This is too much. I can't handle it. I need a break. Please make it stop or let me plateau for a while."

The good news is those feelings qualify as discomfort, right? So if you feel confused, you can apply The Process to it. If you feel frustrated, you can apply The Process to it. If you feel overwhelmed, you can apply The Process to it. If you feel disoriented, you can apply The Process to it. It all just provides additional opportunities to drill and knock out cloud cover!

Key Point

Your Expanded Self knows you better than you could ever possibly know yourself. He or She never gives you more than you can handle. Even if you think you're overwhelmed or past your limit, you're not and you *can* handle it. You'll be just fine and will ultimately have massive Appreciation for such experiences.

Expect to Be Profoundly Impatient

If your journey is like mine and like many other Players whose journeys I'm aware of, you'll want to have all your infinite power, wisdom, abundance, and True Joy back immediately after leaping into Phase 2. You won't want to have to use the tools, drill through the cloud cover, and experience expansion and transformation *over time*. I call that profound impatience.

If you feel that way, the reason is simple. You're so fed up with all the limitation and restriction you experienced in Phase 1 that when you're reminded of who you really are and what's really possible for you, you want all the goodies *yesterday*. That's a reasonable response. It's to be expected. As I said, I felt that same way myself!

From my experience, if that dynamic runs within you and you're feeling profound impatience, there's not much anyone can say or do that will suddenly make you feel patient or more patient—nor do you want to make the impatience go away, because impatience is discomfort, and what can you do with discomfort? Apply The Process!

However, I would like to offer you several metaphors and examples you can tap into when using the tools and drilling or by themselves to support you in reminding yourself of The Truth and expanding through any impatience that surfaces.

First, have you ever seen a movie or television show about a prison break? The odds are you have. Let me speak generally about what often happens in movies and television shows like that. One or more prisoners who have really long prison sentences, maybe even life sentences, decide they want to break out. They have limited time and tools they can use to do it, so they use what's available to them.

In one such movie I saw, a prisoner made a makeshift shovel out of a large spoon, and began to dig a tunnel out of his cell through a hole behind his toilet. Now, in a scenario like that, the prisoner knows it's going to take a really long time to dig his way out. He knows he can dig only when the guards aren't looking and that his makeshift shovel isn't very powerful, so he's *very patient*. He wants out of jail yesterday, yes, but he knows that isn't going to happen, so he has a lot of patience as he digs and makes what appears to be slow progress. You have the opportunity to remind yourself of the similarities between this prison break example and your own escape from Phase 1 limitations and restrictions.

If your journey is like mine, and it may not be, you may also feel quite impatient about the need to use the tools so repetitively to drill through the cloud cover. "Okay, I've been applying The Process for a while now," you might think to yourself. "How much longer do I need to keep doing the same thing over and over and over and over and over again?"

Let me share a few things about the profound impatience dynamic to support you in expanding through it. Then, I'll continue the discussion in the next chapter. First, the really ironic thing is that in Phase 1, many Players will work very hard trying to create successful businesses, careers, financial independence, wealth, or a strong flow of passive income. They'll work their butts off for decades, *not achieve the goal*, and not really complain that much along the way. But if those same Players play the Phase 2 game for three months and haven't busted loose, man, are they angry!

Next, I want to give you a couple of things to pop some of the impatience that contributes to an attitude like I just described. If you're a mountain climber and you choose to climb a mountain face that's icy, you're going to have to repetitively kick your boot with a sharp point on it into the icy snow to support your climb. You're going to have to repetitively raise your arms, swing an ice ax overhead and plant it in the ice, then pull yourself up with it. If you love mountain climbing, are you going to complain, "Why the hell do I have to keep kicking my boot into this snow? Why do I have to keep putting my ice ax into it, over and over, in order to climb? Why is this ice even here in the first place?" No.

If you like to play golf, do you say, "Why do I have to keep using this damned putter over and over and over and over again to sink the ball in the hole?" No.

If you like taking walks with your dog, do you say to yourself, "Why the hell do I have to keep putting one foot in front of the other over and over and over and over again to walk?" Or if you like jogging, do you complain about having to keep doing the same thing at a faster pace? No.

If you're a tennis player, do you say, "Why do I have to keep hitting this blasted ball over the net? Damn it!" No.

Does the gymnast ever say, "Why do I have to keep holding myself up on these damned rings or swinging my body around this blasted horse?" No.

In each of these examples, the repetition is expected; it's part of the game, part of what the players love most about it. It's the same thing with using the tools to drill in Phase 2. You're playing a game you love (even if it doesn't seem like you're loving it), and the repetitive use of the tools is part of that game.

When you feel impatient, it's just the judgment and Phase 1 residue that gets overlaid onto your experience. The impatience isn't real; it's just another Phase 1 Miracle illusion, and it will weaken and drop away. But the odds are, from my experience in my own life and with other Players, you will take yourself there—many times!

I tell Players to expect that the journey of expansion in Phase 2, the process of knocking out cloud cover, busting loose, and radically transforming holograms, will take many *years*. If it takes less time, celebrate it if you want (although you probably won't at that point), but expect it to be a long journey. In my case, the first enormous breakthroughs in Phase 2 didn't come until I'd been playing for two years. Amazing expansion and transformation came in the three years that followed, and I'm continuing to have extraordinary experiences at the time of this writing, more than five years into the Phase 2 game. These time frames are not rules or formulas, just what I created, but it's very supportive to keep them in mind.

Expect Instability and Unusually Rapid Change in Your Hologram

As we discussed, in Phase 2 your Expanded Self will create patterns in The Field, energize them, and pop out illusions designed to support you in drilling through the cloud cover, poking holes, and allowing the sun of who you really are to shine through into your hologram. As a result, you'll likely notice a greater degree of instability and rapid change in the stories that unfold.

To give you a general example to illustrate a point, if your Expanded Self creates a pattern in The Field for a scene in your total-immersion movie experience that's meant to last 20 minutes and give you the opportunity to apply The Process three times and expand in certain ways from doing it, once the 20 minutes are up and you've applied The Process three times, whatever was going on in that scene isn't needed anymore and it can change or morph on a dime into something radically different—including in ways that don't appear to make any sense.

Similarly, if your Expanded Self writes a scene in which another aspect of yourself called an employee, partner, vendor, client, banker, or accountant is supposed to say A and do B to support you in doing the Phase 2 work and ultimately have an experience of C, once you experience C, that other aspect of yourself can morph on a dime into someone new, including in ways that don't make any sense or that appear inconsistent with the character's personality, history, and so on, as I explained earlier.

In fact, sometimes, other aspects of yourself may be created to not even remember saying or doing what they said and did. And after they morph once, they can be created to morph again, in weird and wild ways, to support the goals of another scene. It can actually get quite wild when you experience this level of morphing of other characters in your total-immersion movie experience in Phase 2!

I can't tell you exactly what Phase 2 will look or feel like for you. It's different for everybody. But your Expanded Self knows how to bust you loose as a unique Infinite Being playing a unique Human Game. What I can absolutely guarantee is if you have the courage, persistence, commitment, and discipline to do the Phase 2 work and stick with it—even when it feels scary, uncomfortable, and awkward—you'll come to love it. And the transformations that ultimately take place in your hologram, in your business, and in your internal experience are extraordinary.

Two critical points I want to make before we close this chapter. First, do your best to be gentle and patient with yourself as you do the Phase 2 work, and when you can't be, apply The Process because you're uncomfortable. You don't have to become a master at using the tools overnight. You may find yourself saying things like this to yourself:

- "I'm just not doing it right."
- "I just had the opportunity to apply The Process and I didn't do it. Shit!"

- "I'm never going to able to do this."
- "I just don't have what it takes to stick it out."
- "No matter how hard I try, it never works for me."
- "I can't do it!"

Recognize such voices as old limiting creations that served you well in Phase 1 but don't serve you any longer. Apply The Process to them. You just do what you can do and trust that everything is working out perfectly, no matter what's happening. You're *always* doing it perfectly, no matter what it looks like or what story you could tell yourself about it!

Key Point

Never underestimate what it took to convince yourself that the illusion was real and you were the opposite of who you really are.

For however many years you've been alive, you've used every ounce of power, creativity, inventiveness, cleverness, and trickiness you had as an Infinite Being to convince yourself the illusion was real and you were the opposite of who you really are within it.

You beat yourself over the head unmercifully, so to speak, saying, "The physical world is real, the physical world is real, money is real, money is real, my checking account is real, my checking account is real, the power is outside of me, the power is outside of me, I really am limited, I really am limited," until you were absolutely convinced. You were relentless to take yourself from infinite to finite. Now you must reverse all of that and take yourself from finite back into infinite. It's going to take time, energy, effort, and discipline. Be prepared for that and give yourself a break, or apply The Process if you judge yourself for being too slow, or if it feels like there's too much to do, or whatever else comes up for you.

Key Point

You as the Player don't need to proactively make things happen or produce results in Phase 2. You simply do the Phase 2 work, and as you do it, more and more cloud cover gets drilled through, and more and more of the sun of who you really are shines in. When that happens, your hologram changes on its own and extraordinary results get produced—naturally—through the unfolding of amazing stories.

To me, Phase 1 was exhausting. It was so complicated. There were so many choices and options, so much work to do, so many things to make happen, so many details to analyze, process, and manage to prosper in my businesses. But then my levels of joyfulness, peace, and satisfaction soared off the charts as I moved more deeply into Phase 2 and expanded beyond all of those old patterns (and they continue to rise). You'll create the same dynamic for yourself.

One of the other things I love and Appreciate so much about the Phase 2 game is that it's so simple! You have only four tools on your tool belt, and it's obvious when to use each one. You live in reactive mode, waiting to see what you feel motivated or inspired to do in response to what pops into your hologram. Then you simply trust your Expanded Self and do what you *feel* motivated to do, including pulling out the right tool for the job and using it.

After you do that day in and day out, you'll wake up one morning and notice something has changed in your hologram. Maybe something that used to drive you crazy now makes you laugh. Maybe someone who always appeared to be a jerk to you suddenly starts appearing to be kind and supportive. Maybe money starts showing up from unexpected places. One thing will change, then something else, then something else. Then the pace and quantity of change will start to accelerate into what I call "miraculous territory." But it all comes from the patient, persistent, and detached application of the drilling tools on a daily basis.

For more details on what The Busting Loose Point actually looks like, including the details of my own story about how I crossed it, you can access the special Bonus Chapters from this book here: www .bustingloose.com/chapters.html.

Key Point

Everything you've discovered so far will get more and more real and your experience of its Truth will deepen as you continue to knock out cloud cover and expand.

When you're ready to discover a new twist on the old saying, "When the going gets tough, the tough get going," as it relates to busting loose from The Business Game, turn the page and continue on to Chapter 14.

When the Going Gets Tough

It's not that I'm so smart, it's just that I stay with problems longer.[1]
—*Albert Einstein*

There's an old Phase 1 saying, "When the going gets tough, the tough get going." I always interpreted that saying to mean that when things get really difficult in life, if you're strong and tough, you dig in, find some form of inner strength you didn't know you had, really find out what you're made of, and keep yourself going until you ultimately overcome the difficulty.

In Phase 1, that saying was often used to reinforce Phase 1 dynamics by motivating people to persist along a difficult path that *never* improved and just caused endless pain. Despite that, however, there is a similar sort of experience you can have while playing the

---

[1] Albert Einstein, in "About.com: Quotations," http://quotations.about.com/cs/inspirationquotes/a/ProblemSolvi1.htm.

Phase 2 game. I experienced it on my Phase 2 journey more than once. Beyond the challenges I discussed in the previous chapter, there can be times along the road when the journey *appears* to get so challenging, intense, and overwhelming that you feel like throwing in the towel and giving up—despite knowing the extraordinary opportunities that are possible once the cloud cover is knocked out. I call those experiences "dark nights of the soul."

Ironically, it's at such dark moments that you're often the nearest to poking a hole through the cloud cover and experiencing the greatest expansion and transformation. When I experienced dark nights like that, I frequently had angry one-way conversations with my Expanded Self where I said things like this: "My Phase 1 was too difficult. This Phase 2 journey has been too difficult on top of that. If this is the way it's going to be, get me out of here. I've had enough. I can't do this anymore."

On my Phase 2 journey, I must have felt deep feelings of futility and hopelessness like that 100 or more times. After I kept applying The Process and expanding through them, however, I began to see and feel something fascinating. I began to see and feel that those feelings of futility and hopelessness were *not* real-time. I began to see and feel that they were replays of the way I felt from birth to age three (and then later in life as the patterns replicated themselves), when the biggest pattern I created to pull off the Phase 1 Miracle was being created and locked in. I discovered that while there was a real-time Phase 2 drama unfolding that was triggering me to feel those old feelings, the real-time drama was a replay of the original drama and the feelings were a replay of the original feelings, so cleverly disguised that I had no idea of The Truth for a long time.

When I dug a tunnel deep enough to poke a hole in the cloud cover on that pattern (that I now call my "Octopus Pattern"), and I could experience The Truth of it, my Appreciation for myself as Creator of such amazing and superbly disguised experiences (the original *and* the replays), and the experiences themselves expanded to such a huge degree that it blew me away. If you'd like to learn more about that experience, what I now call my "Octopus Pattern," visit the following page on my web site to download a special audio I created for you: www.bustingloose.com/octopus.html.

Dark nights of the soul are *not* required to bust loose or knock out the cloud cover, but many Players experience them, which is why I wanted to devote this time to discussing what they are and what they mean, and to offer support in case you take yourself to a place like that.

If you have a dark night of the soul experience, what's *really* going on? A *huge* lie is in motion. And when huge lies are in motion, there's an enormous storehouse of power propping them up, an extraordinary opportunity to drill and poke a huge hole through the cloud cover, and an opportunity to experience extraordinary expansion and transformation in your hologram as a result.

Another version of the dark night of the soul is where you feel like giving up not because it's so tough, but because you're having serious doubts about me personally, The Busting Loose Model, or both. Do you remember when I discussed the Sean Connery movie *Entrapment* to illustrate the elaborate security system we had to install in Phase 1 to keep us away from The Truth and our power, wisdom, abundance, and True Joy? If not, you can review it near the end of Chapter 4.

Well, to continue that metaphor, imagine that you've built an elaborate security system like the one in that movie to protect a valuable jewel in your museum. Further imagine that an unusually skilled thief was able to get through all your security measures, has the jewel in his hand, and is about to leave the museum with it. If you had one last chance to protect the jewel from being stolen, what might you say to the thief if you were there? "It's a fake! That's not the real jewel!" Right? That's your last shot, your last-ditch effort since all else failed.

If you find yourself playing the Phase 2 game for a while in a dedicated, committed way, and you experience doubts about me personally or The Busting Loose Model itself, it's just your Expanded Self showing you how effective your security system was (and can be), what a great illusionist you are, by throwing a last-ditch effort in your face—a last-ditch effort that can be extremely effective! Just apply The Process and keep applying it, and the feelings will weaken and go away. They might return again, or they might not. If they do, just apply The Process again, as much as it takes, and it'll ultimately take care of itself—permanently.

To make our Phase 1 Miracle illusions appear real and fool ourselves into thinking we're the opposite of who we really are, the illusions have to be made extremely complex, rich with detail, and multilayered. If you could take a peek at the software and all the layers that were created within it to make the *Jurassic Park* dinosaurs (or any amazing special effect) appear real, you'd be astounded.

I like to use the metaphor of an onion to illustrate the concept of something having many, many layers that combine to create a solid-looking object. To deconstruct or dissect the key illusions your

In Phase 2, we keep going back and back and back into illusions until we've peeled back all the layers our Expanded Selves want us to examine.

Expanded Self takes you to in Phase 2, you keep going back and back and back into the heart of the illusion and peeling back more and more of those layers.

Why would your Expanded Self want you to peel back many or all of the layers of an illusion like that? Because each time you peel back a layer and see its composition clearly (the beliefs, judgments, consequences, repetition throughout your business life and personal life, etc.), your Appreciation for how you created the illusion rises until your overall Appreciation for the entire illusion and your role as Creator of it skyrockets.

Here's an example of how to think about this. I love the television show called *24* with Kiefer Sutherland. I discovered the series after it had been on the air for two years, so there were two seasons of DVDs available. I bought the DVDs for the two seasons I missed, watched them, and loved the shows. Then I discovered the bonus material that came on additional DVDs in the boxes. In the bonus material, there were interviews with the creators of the show, the actors, and the production staff. They showed you what the set for the show looked like, and they also showed you how several extremely convincing illusions and special effects were created. My Appreciation for the show was already high after watching the episodes, but it soared even higher after watching the bonus material. Why? Because I got to "peel back the layers" and see more and more of how the illusions that I Appreciated so much were created. If you've had a similar experience, you know what I mean. If not, I hope you get the idea.

A similar dynamic takes place as you peel back the layers on how you created your Miracle illusions in Phase 1 to Appreciate how they were constructed, how it all worked, and so on. Each time I experienced a dark night of the soul on my Phase 2 journey, I came out on the other side, after poking a hole through the clouds with it, in an off-the-charts Appreciative state about myself as Creator and about the illusion itself, including the story line details, layers, actors, and special effects that combined to create it.

Let me now share another metaphor to hammer this important point home. Think for a moment about steel. Steel is a very hard and solid substance. If you want to mold steel into a specific shape—a car door, desk leg, or tabletop —you first have to heat it up to a very high temperature until it gets soft. Then you mold it, cool it off again, and lock it into that shape permanently. However, if you later wanted to remold that steel into a new shape, you must repeat the entire sequence—heat it up again, get it soft, then remold it and cool it off.

To expand on that metaphor, when you pulled off the Phase 1 Miracle, it was like heating up the steel, molding it into a limited and restricted shape opposite of what it really is, then cooling it off and locking that shape in. In Phase 2, when you want to remold that shape into an infinitely powerful, wise, abundant, and Truly Joyful shape, you have to heat it back up again to make it soft and moldable. What you experience as discomfort, intensity, or even dark night of the soul experiences in Phase 2 is the "heat" you had to generate to do that!

Let me share one more metaphor with you before we close this chapter. Let's go back to the metaphor of the sun and clouds, including drilling, tunnels, and poking holes. Imagine that your Expanded Self takes you to a section of the cloud cover in Phase 2 and says, "Let's begin digging here." So He or She inserts patterns into The Field with story lines designed to support you in drilling, pops you into those stories, and lets you begin using the tools to drill.

Imagine you've been doing that for a while and you've drilled out three-quarters of the length of a specific tunnel and are near to poking a hole through. However, you don't know you've drilled out three-quarters of the tunnel, so it's possible you'd feel frustrated and like you've been drilling and drilling and drilling without getting anywhere, even though you've come a long way, right? You might even feel like giving up and throwing in the towel, even though you've come so far and a breakthrough is near, right? Remember this image when the going gets tough, if it does. No matter how you feel at any moment, as long as you're using the tools, you're inside a tunnel somewhere in the cloud cover, you're drilling, and you're making progress toward poking a hole through.

Finally, there are times on the Phase 2 journey when you drill and drill and drill and poke a hole through, and something is transformed in a big way in your hologram when the sun starts to shine. You bask in that sunshine, so to speak, feeling expanded and Truly Joyful. But then you get taken to another section of the cloud cover, another pattern, and it can feel like the rug just got pulled out from under you, like maybe you didn't really poke a hole through or get anywhere at all.

What's happening in situations like that is you *did* drill out a tunnel, you *did* poke a hole, and you *did* experience expansion and transformation. It was all real and True, but then your Expanded Self said, "Okay, let's go to another section of the cloud cover and start drilling there so we can expand and transform things even more." It feels like the rug has been pulled out from under you, like you lost something or never really had it, but that's not True. You're just drilling in a new tunnel that feels dark and cold in comparison to how warm it felt when you were basking in the sun. Despite feelings like that, you are on your way to even greater expansion, even greater transformation, and even more sunshine streaming into your hologram, even though it doesn't feel that way.

By the way, if you want to watch a movie that will really hammer home the points I've made in this chapter (in a multisensory way) about why the Phase 2 journey needs to be so intense, relentless, and difficult, why the "heat" needs to get so high when we're working on collapsing really big illusions and lies, check out *The Game* with Michael Douglas. It'll blow you away!

When you're ready to shift gears from the theoretical sort of discussion we've been having and discover specific, nuts-and-bolts, day-to-day, practical details of what happened to me as I drilled through my cloud cover, and what happened to other Phase 2 Players as they drilled through theirs, turn the page to begin Chapter 15.

Recreating Yourself, Your Team, Your Customers, Your Business, and Everything In Between

Instead of instilling fear, if a company offered a way for everyone in the business to dive within—to start expanding energy and intelligence—people would work overtime for free. They would be far more creative. And the company would just leap forward. This is the way it can be. It's not the way it is, but it could be that way so easily.[1]

—*David Lynch, Film Director*

---

[1] David Lynch, *Catching the Big Fish: Meditation, Consciousness, and Creativity* (New York: Tarcher, 2006), p. 74.

Did you jump forward to this chapter without reading all of the preceding chapters? If so, for your sake, please go back and finish the others before reading this. You won't be able to bust loose unless you receive all the puzzle pieces I have for you and the whole busting loose map pops into view. Then you can use that map to actually bust loose. Trust me on this!

When you knock out enough cloud cover and expand to the point where you start playing The New Business Game, I call it crossing The Busting Loose Point.

The Busting Loose Point

🔑 **Key Point**

Every Infinite Being creates his or her own unique Busting Loose Point and what comes before and after crossing it.

In the past few chapters, I explained that living in Phase 2 means using the four drilling tools day after day without an agenda, an investment in results or specific outcomes, or a desire to fix, change, or improve your hologram (to the best of your ability until it becomes natural and applying The Process when it's not). I explained that in Phase 2 you live in reactive mode, taking your experiences a moment at a time, waiting to see what gets popped into your hologram, then responding as you *feel* motivated or inspired to—before or after applying The Process when discomfort arises.

When you do that enough—and I can't tell you what "enough" means for you, because we're all different—you reach The Busting Loose Point where you can cross into a new world and a new way of living. You're now ready to discover specific details of what The Busting Loose Point is all about and see what the world looks like once you cross it. Keep in mind, however, that while your Busting Loose Point may have several things in common with mine and with those of the other Players whose stories I share, you'll ultimately customize your Busting Loose Point and what follows to support yourself as a unique Infinite Being playing a unique Human Game and New Business Game.

Also keep in mind that what I'm sharing in this chapter isn't theory or a narrative of something I simply *believe* is possible. I reached The Busting Loose Point, crossed it, and I'm actually living in the ways I discuss in this book. My journey is far from over, however. I'm still stepping into more and more of a direct experience of who I really am as I play The Human Game and The New Business Game. I don't know what's around the corner in my hologram, nor do I want to know. I prefer to allow the magnificence of Phase 2 to unfold on its own and surprise and delight me. I must say that even though I have no idea what it will look like as I move more deeply into Phase 2, going as deeply into it as I have at the time of this writing has been more incredible than anything I'd ever experienced before or ever thought I would experience in my business or personal life.

When you cross The Busting Loose Point, you've collapsed most or all of the foundational patterns that kept you locked into financial limitation, and you've expanded and opened to the infinite abundance that is your natural state. At that moment, you *know*—at a very deep and profound level—you're creating absolutely everything you experience. You *know*—from deep within your Being (in a way I can't transmit to you in words)—that you have the power to create absolutely anything and pop it into your hologram to play with. You *know*—from deep within your Being—that numbers aren't real, money isn't real, your accounts aren't real, and the apparent flow of money through your hologram isn't real, but your natural state of infinite abundance *is* real. You *know*, from deep within your being, that "others" are just you in disguise and there's no separation between you. In short, you have total trust and confidence in The Truth of who you really are. This is a very real and very attainable state of Consciousness, even if it seems like science fiction right now.

If you take a close and objective look, most of what you'd say has frustrated or been challenging for you as you've played The Business Game boils down to one thing: Phase 1 "Power Outside Beliefs."

What do I mean by that? I mean that in Phase 1, there are so many variables involved in building and sustaining a successful business that you believe you can influence (in the story line) but cannot control because there is power outside of you driving them:

- Employees, partners, vendors, boards of directors, stockholders, prospects, clients, and customers, who are outside of you, are separate from you, have their own power and decision-making ability, and are not controllable by you . . . and that's a problem.

- Competitors, who are outside of you and separate from you, and you never know what they'll do . . . and that's a problem.

- The economy, which is outside of you and separate from you, and you have no say in what happens with it or how those happenings impact you.

- Lawsuits, which are beyond your control—and you can even do everything right and still get sued unfairly.

On and on it goes, with Phase 1 "you're the opposite of who you really are" dynamics creating instability and struggle.

Now that you know The Truth, that *you* are creating everything you experience—everything, down to the smallest detail; that there's no power outside of you, not in anyone or anything; and that you can reclaim that power by knocking out the cloud cover, the world suddenly looks quite different, doesn't it?

In the Introduction, I shared that busting loose from The Business Game tends to take on certain predictable shapes and forms, even though it's unique for every Player. Let's take a look at these common shapes and forms now, point by point.

- Living in an inner space that's joyful, exciting, peaceful, and serene—no matter what's going on around you, what happens in your business or elsewhere in the world, or what anyone else says or does.

In Phase 1, being happy as you play The Business Game, and enjoying the playing itself, is rarely on the menu. It may be given lip service or be secretly desired, but in general it's long gone when the pressure to produce specific results, build a sales and profit machine in the first place, keep the sales and profit machine running (and preferably growing), and put out fires rears its ugly head.

You may recognize these popular battle cries: "I'll take a vacation when _____." "I'll just work these ridiculous hours until _____, then I'll slow down." "What do you want me to do? The buck stops with me and this must get done or else _____."

In Phase 2, all of that changes—in *huge* ways. In Phase 2, after you've knocked out enough cloud cover (and before that in spurts), the roles reverse and your fun, joy, ease, and what I call "lifestyle friendliness" become your top priorities (and your Expanded Self's, too). This is where True Goals really start to come into play, as opposed to the Hypnotic Goals ("rabbits") that drove so much of your Phase 1 experience. When you're in that space, results take a backseat.

In addition, once you expand into more and more of a direct experience of who you really are, it doesn't matter what's going on outside of you in the story line. Even when you create experiences you could have once labeled as challenging or difficult (assuming you still do . . . and you may not), you'll remain in a joyous place, a serene place, an excited and exciting place—just like a mountain climber, football player, actor, or gymnast when they pursue what they love to do, even when it's really tough to do.

All of this will radically transform your experience of playing The Business Game, and it will also overflow into your personal life in cool and unexpected ways.

• Playing The Business Game for the sheer pleasure of playing, without any specific, conscious agenda, goals, or attachment to producing specific results—yet creating extraordinary results anyway, financial and otherwise.

In Phase 1, you can't run a business without a business plan, marketing plan, goals, agendas, and targets. "How can you expect to hit a target if you don't know what it is?" is the popular battle cry on this one. "How can you get somewhere if you don't know where you want to go?"

The mechanics of manifestation.

Study the manifestation illustration for a minute, looking from left to right to remind yourself of the True Creative Process that drives everything you experience as you play The Business Game. If you take all the statements and teachings about goals, intentions, plans, targets, and so on, you can see they hold True if you elevate them to your Expanded Self. Your Expanded Self *must* have plans, targets, goals, intentions, and desired outcomes. If He or She didn't, no patterns would get created in The Field, get energized, or be popped out as illusions appearing to be real. Of course there must be intention to create outcomes *somewhere*, but you now know that the power of intention rests with your Expanded Self—not with you, the Player.

The True Creative Power shaping what happens to you as you play The Business Game and The Human Game has *always* rested behind the scenes with your Expanded Self. Any time a plan appeared to work or appeared to fail, any time you appeared to achieve a goal or fall short, any time your intention manifested or didn't, it was always details in patterns in The Field that determined the outcome. You had your role to play, and you played that role brilliantly, but it wasn't you, your actions, your thoughts, your intentions, your plans, your goals, or your targets that did it. It's for this reason that two things will happen as you knock out cloud cover and expand in Phase 2:

1. You'll ultimately let go of trying to tame, manipulate, or control the hologram and trying to set goals, targets, and agendas, and you'll relax into your role as a Player who plays for the sheer pleasure of playing.

2. Despite letting go of the illusion of control, you'll still produce extraordinary results in your business. Why? Because your Expanded Self will be writing extraordinary patterns in The Field and popping you into the middle of those stories to play.

   Having a strong, positive impact on your customers and the world at large through the distribution of your products and services—but again, without any effort, specific intent, goal, or agenda to do so.

Many Players who play The Business Game play it because they want to help people or change the world through the distribution of their products and services. They have an incredible passion for what their business and mission are all about. If that describes you as a business owner or employee and you want to continue playing that game, you will in Phase 2, but with a big difference. What difference? It will just happen, without you exerting what feels like effort, intending to do it, devising plans for how to do it the best or most efficient way, and so on.

Your Expanded Self will simply create patterns in The Field with "change the world and impact lives" stories in them; your Expanded Self will energize them, and boom, out will pop those stories with you as the star, enjoying every second of them! You'll play your role in those stories, as I explained, but without concern for the story line, driving the bus, or making anything specific happen. You'll just go along for the ride.

Look at it like this. You may or may not actually enjoy roller coasters, but for the moment, imagine you do. If you choose to ride a roller coaster at Disney World or another amusement park, it's all about the fun, the ride, the feelings you have as the car moves up, down, and around curves. When the ride starts, you get into your seat, buckle yourself in, and wait for the ride to start with great excitement and an expectation that you're going to have lots of fun. You know you're not in charge. You know you don't get to choose or control how the car moves. But you don't care, because you know that in advance and you just want to ride the ride and have the experience.

The same thing happens when you start playing The New Business Game. You'll just buckle yourself in, live with tremendous excitement and anticipation of having a blast, and allow the ride to run its "planned by someone else" course without you being in charge or trying to move it anywhere. You relax into it, go where you're taken—and have the ride of your life day after day! That's how I live, and how you'll live, too, once you knock out enough cloud cover.

- Doing *only* what you love to do, what *really* floats your boat, as part of playing The New Business Game—all day, every day.

I'll discuss this in greater detail later in this chapter and also in the next chapter, but for now let me say that as you knock out the cloud cover and your vision and experience of The Truth expands, your focus will shift from numbers, Hypnotic Goals, outcomes, and the details of The Business Game story line to True Goals, simply doing what you really love to do, and having a blast doing it. You'll also give yourself permission to allow what you love to do to change as you change.

There's a popular expression, "Been there, done that." This is not a rule or formula; it's just the way I'm creating my journey—but as I've knocked out more and more cloud cover, my "been there, done that, want to do something new" cycle has accelerated. As I've expanded, so has my desire to do things in ways I've never done them before, things I've never done at all before, and things no one has ever done before. I have no attachment to finishing what I start or being consistent or predictable.

As an example, I still enjoy playing The Teaching Game, but at the time of this writing, I'm feeling tremendous excitement about continuing to do that in new ways, such as through novels, film, and innovative uses of technology and multimedia (text+audio+video)—instead of just through the more traditional channels of public speaking and nonfiction books like this.

At some point, I may lose interest in playing The Teaching Game and The New Business Game, and I may find myself doing things I can't even conceive of now, would never be able to predict, or have never thought of before. I'm excited to see what I will create!

- Working only when you want to, and having more free time and freedom than you can possibly imagine right now, while still effectively playing your chosen role in your business—no matter how large or small the business may be.

In Phase 1, while playing The Business Game, even if you're the boss, you generally do *not* have total control over your schedule and time. That was certainly true for me. In Phase 1, you don't have the luxury of working only when you want to, producing only when the creative juices are flowing, and having the free time and freedom to pursue other nonbusiness interests or passions.

To hammer this point home with an extreme example, consider J. Paul Getty, who, at the time he was the world's richest man, wrote this about his friend Hal Seymour:

> Hal considered himself to be very wealthy in personal freedom. He was always able to do things he wanted to, and always had time in which to do them. He seldom missed a chance to remind me that, in these regards, I was much poorer than he. Before his death a few years ago, he frequently wrote me letters which opened with the wryly humorous but meaningful salutation: "To the Richest Man in the world from the Wealthiest . . . ." I'll have to admit that I envied Hal his abundance of time—which is one of the forms of wealth that people tend to disregard these days. Rich as I may be from a material standpoint, I've long felt that I'm very poor, indeed, in time. For decades, my business affairs have made extremely heavy inroads on my time, leaving me little I could use as I pleased. There are books that I have wanted to read—and books I have wanted to write. I've always yearned to travel to remote parts of the globe which I've never seen.[2]

Why would the world's richest man (and so many others who play The Business Game in Phase 1) create "poverty" like that? Because in Phase 1, with the "convince yourself you're the opposite of who you really are" dynamics in place, it has to be that way. Who you really are has total control over His or Her time and can do as He or She pleases in every moment. So, in Phase 1, you must experience the opposite of that most or all of the time. In Phase 1, there are so many things outside your control that create endless items on your

[2] J. Paul Getty, *How to Be Rich* (New York: Jove Books, 1965), p. vii.

to-do list, including so many urgent ones, that living in your natural state simply isn't possible.

In Phase 2, however, after you knock out enough cloud cover, the game is about having more and more of a direct experience of who you really are, including total control over your time and absolute freedom to say, be, and do anything. As a result, your Expanded Self creates patterns in The Field, writes new stories for you that reduce the number of items on your to-do list, reduce or eliminate the need for you to be involved if those items stay on the to-do list for your business, or whatever else you choose to free up your time and energy to focus only on what you really love.

Along these lines, it might interest you to know that while the home office for the international operations of Manpower, Inc. was in Milwaukee, Wisconsin, my grandfather, as part of living his own "ultimate lifestyle," lived in Chicago, Illinois, and worked from there. In the story line, it had to do with Gramps having exceptional delegation abilities, but in Truth, his Expanded Self simply created patterns in The Field to support that level of freedom and personal preference.

I created something similar on my own Phase 2 journey. As I continued to knock out cloud cover and expand, I recreated and simplified my business model to include fewer moving pieces, fewer people, and other aspects of myself to do the few remaining things I chose to include in my model that I didn't want to do myself. I awaken most mornings with many cool and fun things I *could* do, but few, if any, things I *must* do. When I create an illusion that appears to be a must or to have a deadline (which could easily be redesigned if I wanted to do so), I don't look at them as musts or deadlines, and I don't force myself to do them. Why? Because I love doing them. They're fun for me. They're not work.

I describe the place I live these days while I play The New Business Game as being in "creative ecstasy." I pursue only creative projects that I absolutely love, in general with no deadlines or pressure. When the creative juices are flowing, I play with those projects. When they're not flowing, I don't and I do whatever else

I feel moved to do in those moments, including many non-productive things like playing video games, reading novels, or watching movies or episodes of television shows I enjoy. I have as much time as I choose to spend with my family and friends.

- Playing The New Business Game while being completely un-affected by and unconcerned about the economy, the stock market, the tax authority, gas prices, competitors, employee turnover, industry trends, technological innovations, lawsuits, or other factors that now make you feel vulnerable.

Boy, is this a biggie! And it may be one of the most challenging aspects of The Busting Loose Model for you to accept right now, although you *will* have a direct experience of it if you choose to play the Phase 2 game.

To pull off the Phase 1 Miracle, you had to create illusions like the economy, competitors, the stock market, the tax authority, lawsuits, and so on, then use them to limit yourself, restrict yourself, and convince yourself you were the opposite of who you really are. But that's no longer necessary in Phase 2, so *once you knock out enough cloud cover*, you're free to recreate (or eliminate) all those illusions to support you in playing The New Business Game for maximum fun, challenge, and pleasure.

There are an infinite number of possibilities for how you can recreate those illusions. Take the stock market for example. If the stock market crashes and you have no money invested in it, does it affect you in a limiting, restricting, or bad way? No. If the stock market crashes on November 11th and you had sold everything on the 10th when the market was at a peak, does the crash affect you in a limiting, restricting, or bad way? No. If the stock market crashes on November 11th and you had *sold short* a bunch of stocks on the 9th, does the crash affect you in a limiting, restricting, or bad way? No. All of these options and many more could be chosen for you to experience with anything that appears to be happening in the hologram outside of you.

As it relates to the tax authority, if you have access to an unlimited source of money through your direct experience of The Truth of who you really are, what does it matter how much Appreciation in the form of money you express for the illusion of taxes? You don't have less after you make that expression, so it becomes irrelevant. You can still choose to play The Minimize Taxes Game if it would be fun for you (and that game *can* be lots of fun), but if you do that, it won't be about saving money or having more money. It'll be about the fun you get from playing that specific game.

As it relates to industry trends, technological innovations, lawsuits, and other factors that may now make you feel vulnerable, once you knock out enough cloud cover, your Expanded Self will simply start writing new stories about those creations, inserting new patterns in The Field, and popping out new illusions to support you in playing however you want to play, without the need for those creations to appear at all, or if they do, without limiting or restricting you or reinforcing Phase 1 dynamics. And let me tell you, when this starts, it'll absolutely blow your mind!

- Having support teams (employees, partners, board members, vendors, stockholders, investors, etc.) effortlessly and joyously unite, work together, motivate themselves, and hold themselves accountable for high levels of performance.

As you now know, in Phase 1 other people were created to appear separate from you, independent of you, and to have their own power and decision-making authority in your hologram. That created lots of challenges, frustrations, and failures for you, and it brilliantly reinforced Phase 1 dynamics as you played The Business Game.

In Phase 2, however, to hammer the point home yet again, other people (i.e., other aspects of *your* Consciousness), don't need to reinforce Phase 1 dynamics any longer, so they'll be given new scripts and be recreated to say and do new things that brilliantly support your ability to knock out cloud cover, expand, and ultimately play The New Business Game for the sheer pleasure of playing, with no limits and no restrictions.

The Human Game and The Business Game, by definition, are team sports. Everyone you see who appears to be outside of you is on your team. Therefore, in the examples that follow, when I use the word *team*, it includes *all* the other aspects of yourself that have impact on your business—employees, partners, board members, stockholders, customers, prospects, vendors, and so on.

Speaking of employees, while you can play any game in Phase 2 if it's fun or supportive for you, you won't *need* to intellectually devise or tweak systems to motivate employees, hold them accountable, keep them loyal to you and playing on your team, keep secrets from them (out of fear of the wrong people finding out), prevent them from stealing from you, modify their habits or behavior, or increase their productivity. Why? Because your Expanded Self will be writing new stories with new characters who will say and do new things, all designed to help you play as you choose to play, with no need for any Phase 1 limiting dynamics to be a factor.

Speaking of customers (and prospects), you can create and play with whatever you want; you and/or your salespeople won't *need* to use techniques to sell, convince, or persuade them to buy your products or services. You and your team can simply say and do whatever you/they feel moved to say and do, and you'll recreate your customers and prospects to play whatever roles you want them to, including buying whatever amounts of products or services you want them to buy, at whatever price (i.e., expression of Appreciation) you want them to "pay." Do you find that mind-blowing? Maybe. But it's True nevertheless.

Unless it's fun for you or other aspects of you, there will be no *need* to do market testing, focus groups, polls, or research to uncover what products or services your customers and prospects want, what features they most want, or how to price them for maximum profitability. You will simply live in reactive mode and create your team to do the same—to whatever degree your script specifies. You'll offer the products and services you feel moved to offer, with the features you feel moved to include, at whatever price (i.e., request for an expression of Appreciation) you feel moved to set—and you'll create other aspects of yourself to pop into your hologram, buy them, and interact with your business in the ways you want them to—no matter what you end up choosing to do. Pretty mind-blowing, isn't it? Wait until you actually experience it!

Think of it this way. As an actor, Christian Bale has the ability to play an infinite number of roles that include an infinite number of lines and actions. In the role of Bruce Wayne and Batman in the movie *The Dark Knight*, he's limited in certain ways and says and does things that come from the Batman script and support the goals of *that* story. Now imagine that Christian is a member of your team in Phase 1 of The Business Game, and think of this as an analogy to him playing the role of Batman. However, when the filming of Batman is over, Christian is no longer limited by that character, script, or role and is free to play any other role, follow any other script, say and do an infinite number of other things to support the unfolding of new stories. Now think of Christian's new freedom as an analogy to playing a new role on your Phase 2 team in The New Business Game.

In Phase 2, you have an infinite number of ways to experience the illusion of your team. You may keep the same team members in place but rewrite the scripts they act from. You may create new aspects of yourself and move them into key roles on your team. It doesn't matter. Your Expanded Self will write whatever stories He or She chooses to support you in having a blast playing The New Business Game.

For example, if you've had customers that have been extremely difficult to deal with historically, you may completely rewrite their scripts and they'll suddenly change, often without any logical or cause-and-effect reason for that change. Or you may choose to simply "fire them" as clients while enjoying one of the many freedoms that come from having absolute certainty about your infinite abundance, instead of being constrained by your Phase 1 certainty about limitation and scarcity. As you continue to play the Phase 2 game and continue to expand and change, your team will continue to expand

and change, too—as reflections of you and your Consciousness. It's actually quite an extraordinary experience!

There's another aspect of recreating your team I'd like to share now. In Phase 1, if another aspect of your Consciousness was saying or doing something you didn't prefer, you'd interact with them, engage with them, and attempt, through various means, to change their behavior. In short, you'd try to manipulate them, the story line, and the hologram from within the hologram. Sometimes it appeared to work. Sometimes it didn't.

In Phase 2, while that option is still available and may be taken from time to time as the perfect support on your journey, it's no longer *necessary* and will be used less and less as you expand. In Phase 2, if other aspects of your Consciousness are saying or doing something you don't prefer, they're being created to say and do it to support you in doing the Phase 2 work. If you don't prefer it, you're judging it and you're uncomfortable, so you have the opportunity to apply The Process. Once you've done that and drilled however your Expanded Self wanted you to drill in those moments, your Expanded Self will change the script and their behavior will change—without you needing to engage or interact with them directly about the issue. I've created an audio to give you additional detail on this phenomenon. You can download it here: www.bustingloose.com/engage.html.

This is so important, so powerful, and so difficult to grasp intellectually until you expand enough by knocking out enough cloud cover to actually experience it yourself. But it's one of the absolute keys to busting loose. Once the illusion of separation drops away, man, what's possible and the opportunities for playing The New Business Game are just off-the-charts cool!

- Having amazing things come to you in joyful, fun, surprising, and effortless ways, instead of you having to go get them, work hard, or push, push, push to make things happen.

As I noted earlier, there are no rules or formulas in Phase 2. Everything is customized by you, for you, to support you in playing

The Human Game and ultimately The New Business Game the way you want to.

The way I've chosen to play The New Business Game, I live purely in reactive mode, waiting for things to come to me and responding as I feel moved to when they do. That's really fun for me, especially since I was so highly proactive in Phase 1 and was so exhausted and frustrated by it. If I feel a motivation to go somewhere, do something, or set a new possibility into motion by taking an action, I do it (no rules or formulas), but in general, I go about my business, do what I love to do, and wait for New Business Game opportunities to come to me, giving myself permission to change my mind and shift gears at any time, as I mentioned earlier.

Living that way, even when I do choose to respond to an opportunity and play my role in the unfolding story, it comes from a playful, joyous, easygoing place, just to use that language. There's no pushing, no investment in outcomes, no agendas, and no trying to produce specific results—just flowing from moment to moment, living in reactive mode, and playing!

All of this, and much more, is possible for you and *will happen for you* once you knock out enough cloud cover. As I noted in the Introduction, there's nothing unique or special about me. I've just been playing The Human Game and The New Business Game longer in Phase 2!

Let's continue our discussion of redesigning your business, your team, and yourself by doing an in-depth Phase 2 analysis of money. Once you cross The Busting Loose Point, there's no longer a *need* to check or pay much attention to your bank balances or financial statements, although you can if it would be fun for you. If you do continue to look at numbers (I do), you'll look at them with amusement and Appreciation while knowing The Truth about them. There's no longer any *need* to track or measure the apparent flow of money. *Cost* is irrelevant. *Bills* have no significance. Why? Because you have absolute certainty about what's really going on and that the supply of money available to you and the number of possible stories through which it can manifest to support you in playing The New Business Game are infinite.

Key Point

After crossing The Busting Loose Point, you just express Appreciation for all the creations you choose to experience (in the illusory form of cash, checks, credit cards, or other transfers) with absolute certainty that your infinite abundance is real and that the money will take care of itself—however it takes care of itself.

When you expand to the point where you have a direct experience of your infinite abundance—*and not before*—money *does* take care of itself—however it takes care of itself. You have no limits or restrictions of any kind related to money. However, you cannot rush your journey to that experience or make it happen out of intellect, willpower, self-discipline, desire, or intention. You can only use the drilling tools and expand to the point where it becomes True for you as a direct experience and direct knowing.

In Phase 1, you convinced yourself if you want to buy or do something, you must have the money before you can buy or do it. In Phase 1, if you have the money, great. If you don't, you have to save up or wait until you have enough to buy or do what you want, or borrow the money and pay it back with interest. After you cross The Busting Loose Point, that dynamic reverses itself. You feel motivated or inspired to express Appreciation for specific creations *first*, you decide to express the Appreciation (it's really your Expanded Self scripting it), and the money takes care of itself—however it takes care of itself. I keep saying "however it takes care of itself" because, as you'll see, there's no fixed or set way for that to happen after you cross The Busting Loose Point. Why? Because infinite is infinite, and no limits really means no limits. I'll give you several examples of how it *can* look later in the chapter, but they will just be examples, not rules, formulas, or limits.

> ### Key Point
>
> After you cross The Busting Loose Point, money will still appear to come from the hologram (although it doesn't need to) but you'll *know* it doesn't. You'll *know* it comes from you, your Consciousness, a pattern in The Field, and your power. The story line of how it appears to show up is just how you chose to express your infinite abundance for maximum enjoyment and fun.

Expressing Appreciation in the form of money then becomes like breathing. You don't worry about where your next breath will come from, do you? You don't measure or track how much air is available to you right now—or how much will be available to you in the future. You don't try to get more air or protect the air you already have. You just breathe without thinking about it, and you have total faith that air will always be there for you. Living from your natural state of infinite abundance works the same way. You just breathe your abundance as the supply appears to move in and out.

Here's another way to look at what opening into your infinite abundance looks and feels like after you cross The Busting Loose Point. I call it *Cosmic Overdraft Protection*. In banking, there's a Phase 1 creation called overdraft protection. Your checking account is linked to a credit card or other account. If you write a check and there isn't enough money in your checking account to cover it, the funds automatically get transferred from your credit card or the other account and the check is made good.

Imagine what life would be like for you and how it would change if you had overdraft protection where the other account was your natural state of infinite abundance that had an unlimited supply of money in it. Imagine what your life would be like and how it would change if you had absolute confidence in your Cosmic Overdraft Protection and you could just follow what brings you joy, fully immerse yourself in creative ecstasy, do what you want to do, Appreciate your creations, write checks as expressions of that

Appreciation, and know that all those checks would be made good, too. This is a metaphor, but there are also True aspects to it.

Key Point

Metaphorically, you qualify for Cosmic Overdraft Protection the minute you cross The Busting Loose Point.

When I share this concept with live audiences, I often get blank stares, disbelief, even anger or accusations of me motivating people to be "financially irresponsible" and just go around "writing rubber checks that bounce." Such comments, thoughts, and feelings come out of what I call Phase 1 residue. From that perspective, they seem perfectly reasonable and accurate. However, when you cross The Busting Loose Point, you're in a radically different place where the old rules no longer apply. At that point, there's no such thing as rubber checks, bounced checks, insufficient funds, and so on. I know this is tough to accept right now, but it's True nevertheless.

When I first got near The Busting Loose Point, saw what was beyond it, and knew—intellectually—that everything I just shared was the absolute Truth, I still could *not* live and breathe it. The thought of blindly expressing Appreciation and writing checks without tracking the numbers, just trusting that the money would take care of itself, scared me every time I considered actually doing it.

Despite how much cloud cover I'd knocked out at that point, how much power I'd reclaimed, and how much I'd expanded, I still kept power in patterns in The Field that caused me to fear getting bounced check notices from my bank, getting angry phone calls from vendors, my credit rating going to hell, and so on—and those fears kept me from crossing The Busting Loose Point. In other words, I was in a sort of no-man's-land.

Then, one day, after applying The Process extensively to those fears, I had a revelation when my Expanded Self said this to me:

"As long as you understand about breathing your abundance but don't actually start breathing, you're saying, 'My infinite abundance isn't really there,' or 'It may not really be there'—and you continue to feed power into your financial-limitation patterns. At some point, you have to make a decision about what's real and what's not, draw a line in the sand, cross it, and never go back. You can't stay in no-man's-land and also fully open into your infinite abundance."

I *knew* those words were True and I so badly wanted to bust loose, but it still felt unsafe, like jumping off a cliff without a net. I continued applying The Process to my fears until one day I woke up and said, "I'm jumping off the cliff today. I have no choice but to trust that my Expanded Self is going to support me perfectly as I 'fall.' " On that day, I started acting as if my infinite abundance was real, as if I really had Cosmic Overdraft Protection, as if every time I put a dollar into the slot machine, I'd get three dollars back. I stopped watching the numbers. I stopped logging onto my online banking resources. I stopped studying my financial statements. All of this was just part of my Expanded Self's script, details in patterns in The Field, of course.

Once I made that decision in the storyline, I created numerous opportunities to express Appreciation in the form of money. Sometimes I expressed it in a joyful and expanded state. At other times (a lot at first but then less and less), when I first saw the *bill* or signed a check, fear still came up in varying intensities, so I applied The Process. Through it all, I kept breathing. I kept acting as if The Truth was The Truth—and my infinite abundance was real. That's what I did for another six months until I finally crossed The Busting Loose Point, and was never short of financial "air" again!

Note that what I just described is not the same thing as the popular phrase "fake it till you make it." That concept is a Phase 1 creation that does not and cannot work in Phase 2. In fact, it never really works in Phase 1, either, although many people swear by it. The reason I was able to make the transition I just described was because I'd knocked out so much cloud cover, reclaimed so much power, and expanded so much; most important, I was being fully supported in making the leap by my Expanded Self.

Once you cross The Busting Loose Point, your natural state of infinite abundance expresses itself however you choose to express it. As I mentioned in the past few chapters, infinite means infinite. It means no limits whatsoever. Money can *appear* to move through your hologram in any amount, at any time, and with any story line for how and why it moves as it appears to move.

If you look at my life as an example, since I've created the illusion of owning businesses that offer products and services, I could choose to express my infinite abundance by creating other aspects of myself to play the role of customers expressing Appreciation for those products and services in whatever quantity I choose. I could also choose to express Appreciation for myself in the form of money by selling one of the businesses and creating the illusion of receiving a large check.

Everything you experience is a creation of your Consciousness from a pattern you inserted into The Field, and your Expanded Self can insert *any* pattern into The Field. It doesn't have to make sense or be logical (these are just limited Phase 1 creations). Once you pass The Busting Loose Point, you can create *anything* you want to play with just for the sheer pleasure of playing with it.

⚷ Key Point

Infinite is infinite. There are no limits of any kind once you cross The Busting Loose Point. It's just a question of how you want to play The Human Game and The New Business Game and what would be fun for you.

So, once you cross The Busting Loose Point, does it mean you go around expressing Appreciation in the form of money for inventory, advertising, marketing, salaries, and so on without giving it a second thought? Your Expanded Self certainly could create that, or He or She might create another illusion/story that would be more supportive for you. There's no judgment in Phase 2—no right, wrong, should, should not, good, bad, better, or worse. You can literally create whatever you want.

Key Point

Each time you apply The Process, you expand, change, and actually become a different person who desires different things. That's another reason for taking life one moment at a time in Phase 2. Why plan for the future, even just a few days forward, when you don't know who you'll be or what you'll want when you get there (when you create it)?

Most of the examples I just gave you involve the illusion of money still appearing to move through the hologram in visible and countable fashion. It may seem like if you created such illusions, you'd still be playing The Business Game and still be focusing on piling up money. However, once you cross The Busting Loose Point, that's not what it's about. For example, at the time of this writing, I still have multiple businesses, and money still appears to move through them. However, I don't care about the numbers or how big they appear to be. It's no longer about products, services, customers, sales, profits, income, salary, and so on. It's about me and my fun and enjoyment. I'm just playing in creative ecstasy, expressing massive Appreciation for myself, the creations I genuinely want to experience—*and the rest takes care of itself* out of Phase 2 dynamics. The rest of it just happens!

Key Point

What you do in Phase 2 doesn't matter. *How* and *why* you do it and the overall level of fun you experience are all that matter.

The ultimate goal of Phase 2 is to play The Human Game and The New Business Game without any limits or restrictions. That really does mean *no limits or restrictions.* You can create and play with anything, no matter how much like Phase 1 it may appear from a certain perspective.

I just watched a documentary about how coral reefs around the world are in danger and may disappear in the next 20 or 30 years if we don't do something to reverse their decline. You can play save-the-reef games or prevent-global-warming games or get-the-world-to-recycle games or create-electric-cars games.

You can create the illusion of being an actor, musician, professional athlete, CEO of a multimillion-dollar or multibillion-dollar corporation, or talk show host—just for the sheer pleasure of doing it—even if you don't currently have the skill, track record, connections, or whatever else you imagine would be needed to do it.

In Phase 2, you can play *any* game in the amusement park if it floats your boat—or create entirely new games to play that no one has ever thought of before (which is what I believe many Players will do as they move more deeply into Phase 2). However, keep in mind that when you chose to come here and play The Human Game and The Business Game, you had certain rides and attractions in mind and will therefore *choose to limit yourself* to what really interests you.

Key Point

In Phase 2, you can play any game you want, even if it still appears to be a Phase 1 game. You just play differently. You can also create entirely new games no one has ever thought of before.

As you knock out more and more of the cloud cover, and afterward as you play The New Business Game, you may change companies or careers, sell your business, buy another business, start your own business—and things can change a lot!

When I first created the illusion of releasing these concepts to the public, I created two women buying one of my Home Transformational Systems. Both women were practitioners of holistic healing or what you might call alternative medicine techniques. After completing the system, they both sent me e-mails expressing ideas like this in a total panic: "My whole career is based around the body being real, illness being real, and my techniques being able to really heal people. If nothing is real, what am I supposed to do, quit?"

I wrote them back and said this: "You can do anything you want in Phase 2. If you really enjoy playing The Healing Game, you can certainly continue playing. You'll then continue creating people coming to you with all sorts of illnesses and you'll continue creating all kinds of healing techniques to help them—all in support of you playing The Healing Game with maximum fun and enjoyment. However, if you're doing that work out of obligation, because someone pushed you into it, to make money, or for some other reason, and it really *isn't fun for you* or perhaps even bores you, either now or at some point in the future after you continue expanding, you also have the opportunity to make another choice."

One of the women discovered she really did have a genuine love for The Healing Game and continued playing it. The other woman ultimately quit and went in a different creative direction as she moved more deeply into Phase 2.

I have several friends who love trading stocks and commodities. I know others who love buying and selling real estate. I know others who love teaching how to buy and sell stocks, commodities, and real estate. Looking at those activities from one perspective, they're pure Phase 1 Business Game activities. However, when played after crossing The Busting Loose Point, they become completely different games and are played in completely different ways. If you decided to play the stocks and commodities game after crossing The Busting Loose Point, for example, you'd create the illusion of up-and-down movements in the markets, buying, selling, profits, and losses in a way that would be fun for you. It would all be about *your fun*. There would be no limits or restrictions on what's possible for you to create and experience.

If you chose to play The Real Estate Game after busting loose, you'd create the illusion of land, homes, buildings, buyers, sellers, and transfers of property appearing to move in ways that would be fun for you for the sheer pleasure of playing that game—and you might do it in a way no one has ever done or even thought of before. There would be no limits or restrictions on what you did or how you did it.

If you chose to teach others how to play the "make money through trading stocks, commodities, and real estate" games, you'd create as many people as you wanted to come into your sphere of influence and attend your seminars, hire you to speak, or buy your books, tapes, courses, consulting, and coaching services—and you might do it in a way no one has ever done or even thought of before. There would be no limits or restrictions on what's possible.

The numbers associated with playing all those games—sales, expenses, income, profits, asset value, net worth, and so on—would be irrelevant unless it would be fun for you to look at them and track them *from a Phase 2 perspective.*

As long as you continue playing The Human Game, you'll choose rides or attractions from the amusement park to play with or create entirely new ones. Therefore, as long as you continue playing The Human Game and The New Business Game, you'll still be creating and playing with illusions that come from patterns in The Field. You'll still allow things to appear to unfold over the illusion of time, versus snapping your fingers and making them appear instantly. Why? Because the illusions you create and pop into your hologram will be thrilling for you to experience in exactly that way.

Key Point

In Phase 2, nothing is about *other people* anymore. It's all about you, your fun, your joy, your expansion—and everyone else comes along for the ride to support you in playing your games.

When you start playing The New Business Game and creating new illusions and stories to play with, if your journey is like mine (and it may not be), you might surprise yourself by what you create. Let me give you an example. In the Introduction, I discussed my experience with Blue Ocean Software, helping build it and sell it for $177 million. When I first started working with Blue Ocean, I was the fifth employee, and the company had generated sales of $1.2 million the year before I joined. When we sold the company, we had 77 employees and sales of $44+ million.

In Phase 1, I had a lot more fun at Blue Ocean when we had fewer employees and lower sales. As we grew and added more people, then a board of directors, then allied with a venture capital firm as we started marching toward going public, everything got so much more complicated, conflicting agendas surfaced, personality conflicts soared, and it wasn't as much fun for me.

In general, as we play The Business Game in Phase 1 (although there are exceptions), bigger is better, more money is better, higher sales and profits are better, and so on. However, when limitation and scarcity fall out and you start playing The New Business Game, so many things change. You might surprise yourself, using this same example, by choosing to keep your business at a certain level and *not* grow it. You could also grow it and write a story that makes the growth totally enjoyable for you. There are no limits or restrictions. It's all up to you.

Key Point

Opening to your infinite abundance means letting go of thoughts and concerns about how you will receive it or how you must act to receive it.

When I was playing The Business Game in Phase 1, I immersed myself deeply within creations called the mail-order business and direct-response marketing. I spent 18 years playing those games and became a masterful player. Based on what I'm seeing unfold in my own Phase 2 experience, I don't see myself doing any one thing for a long period of time again. The way my Phase 2 experience is unfolding, it's more like surfing. I create a particular wave coming in that looks interesting, so I get up on my board and start riding it until it I feel like getting off. Then I wait until another starts to roll in, jump on when I feel so moved, then ride that wave for as long as I choose to, then get off again—continuously creating new kinds of waves to ride as I continue expanding.

Everything I just described may sound exciting to you, but does it still seem hard to believe, like a pie-in-the-sky fantasy? If thoughts like that crossed your mind, it's perfectly understandable for you to feel that way, given the Phase 1 limiting beliefs in which you still have huge amounts of power. I assure you, however, it's absolutely real, and if you leap into Phase 2 and use your drilling tools in the ways I've suggested, you *will get there*. As I've said, if you still have doubts but make the commitment, your Expanded Self will give you proof that all of this is True through the experiences you create and pop into your hologram. I absolutely guarantee it.

Let's take a moment to ground what I just shared by returning to science. I explained earlier that once you pass The Busting Loose Point, you no longer need to pay attention to numbers or to count, measure, or track the flow of money in your life (unless you choose to do it from a Phase 2 perspective for the fun of it). Let's take another look at that concept from the perspective of quantum physics. You know that science looks at The Field as a source of unlimited power and infinite potential. When Consciousness focuses on The Field, a specific creation—a single possibility—collapses out of it, as determined by the intention of Consciousness.

Who you really are is pure Consciousness. Who you really are is infinite power and infinite abundance, just as science defines The Field to be. You can't see or experience anything in your hologram that doesn't originate from a pattern you inserted into The Field. Therefore, in your hologram, if you decide you want to look at the balance in your checking account, the balance in another account, or other numbers that appear important, what must happen? Your Expanded Self must create a pattern in The Field with specific details relating to the account and the numbers He or She wants you to see. Power must then be applied to the pattern, and the details must be popped into your hologram so there's something for you to see. Otherwise, nothing would be there! The minute your Expanded Self does that, going back to quantum physics, infinite potential *must* collapse into a finite, limited creation, right? And whatever you see must be less than who you really are and what your natural state of infinite abundance really is.

Stick with me here, because when you get the significance of this it'll blow your mind. What would happen, after you pass The Busting Loose Point, if you simply didn't look at or focus on accounts, statements, or numbers at all? If you don't look, there's no need for a collapse from infinite to finite, right? There's no need to create a pattern in The Field with details about limited numbers or imaginary accounts and pop it into your hologram for you to see, is there? You're just pure Consciousness then, just an Infinite Being playing in creative ecstasy with infinite potential, right?

You're just expressing Appreciation in the form of money for the creations you choose to experience while living in a highly expanded state. That's why you don't need to pay attention to the numbers in Phase 2 if you don't want to, and why you can simply express Appreciation for your creations with absolute trust and confidence that the money will take care if itself—*once you knock out enough cloud cover!*

You may want to reread the last few paragraphs again before you continue. This is where you can truly go after you cross The Busting Loose Point!

Now, you could say to yourself, "Well, why not keep *looking* at the numbers but create patterns in The Field for a 'limited' $10 million or $1 billion in my imaginary account? That would be fine with me." You could certainly create that if you wanted to after crossing The Busting Loose Point, but why would you want to if you had full confidence in your Cosmic Overdraft Protection? Let me share an example to illustrate the importance of what I just said.

Suppose, to fund the operation of your business in a way that would be really fun for you (because that's what it's all *really* about), it would only require your business having illusory sales and profits of $X. Why would those numbers need to be larger? If you're an employee and choose to continue that experience in Phase 2, and to have a blast on the job and have the lifestyle you prefer, suppose it would only require compensation, in whatever form, of $Y a year. Why would you need any more?

The "more, more, more, bigger, bigger, bigger" dynamic is a cornerstone of Phase 1 and is a brilliant creation to lock in the Phase 1 dynamics. But in Phase 2, when the focus shifts to play and fun, and your vision clarifies to seeing The Truth instead of illusions and lies, all of that changes.

When you open into a direct experience of The Truth, you're no longer concerned about so-called sales, profits, expenses, cash flow, stock prices or options, lines of credit, the interest rate you get on parked cash, or the value of an investment portfolio. If you have access to an infinite supply of money that can appear to flow to you in any amount, at any time, within any story line, why would any of that matter to you? This is not something you can understand intellectually. It goes way beyond that. You can't think your way into this state of Consciousness, so to speak. You can only expand to the point where you have a direct experience of it, which you will if you play the Phase 2 game.

In my case, in my personal life and with my businesses, I do as I please. I express Appreciation in the form of money for *everything* I feel moved to express Appreciation for. I do that *not* because I've piled up so much illusory money in my illusory accounts that I feel rich enough to do it. I do it because I've expanded to the point where I have absolute certainty about who I really am, where money really comes from, and my ability to create whatever I need on a dime by simply entering details into patterns in The Field and energizing them.

Yet, if you totaled up how much money it appears to take to fund my businesses and lifestyle, the number isn't as large as you might expect. If that changes, and I choose to play other games that require higher expressions of Appreciation in the form of money, I'll create the illusion of that amount of money appearing to flow through my hologram according to the details of a story that would be fun for me. The same will be True for you!

Key Point

Limited is limited no matter how big the numbers appear to get, whereas infinite is infinite. Who you really are is infinite, and infinite is where you will be after crossing The Busting Loose Point.

I'd now like to share one last critical puzzle piece before we close this chapter. In Phase 1, we look at financial abundance as something outside of us, as observable story line details in the hologram. The observable details might be a big bank account, a big net worth, a big and beautiful house, a fancy car, lots of stuff and toys, freedom, and so on. But that's *not* what infinite abundance really is.

Infinite abundance is a *feeling*!

When you knock out enough cloud cover and open into a direct experience of your infinite abundance, that experience will be at the feeling level. In a way I can't transmit through words, you will feel The Truth as it relates to abundance. Once you expand to the point where you experience that feeling consistently—as your natural state—patterns in The Field will start being rewritten by your Expanded Self and you *will* notice story line details changing. But the story line details are not evidence or proof of The Truth or your abundance. The *feeling* is!

Key Point

Infinite abundance is a *feeling*, not story line details that can be observed in the hologram.

Once you pass The Busting Loose Point, it'll look how it looks for you. As you open up more and more into a direct experience of who you really are, you'll experience whatever you experience. As I explained, there are no rules or formulas for how Phase 2 looks or unfolds. That's the really exciting part. I don't know what it's going to look like for you, and it doesn't matter. As I explained, after you cross The Busting Loose Point, it's all about playing with what you want to play with, exactly how you want to play with it.

Remember, too, that no matter how excited you may feel about what life and business can be like after crossing The Busting Loose Point, it pales in comparison to what the actual experience is like. I can't adequately express in words (though I did my best) the fun, joyfulness, exhilaration, peace, relaxation, and freedom I experience as I breathe my abundance and play The New Business Game. As I explained in the Introduction, busting loose from The Business Game can't be described. It must be experienced.

Do you see now why I had to give you all the puzzle pieces I did before we got to this chapter? If I didn't, you'd never have believed or understood the magic of The Busting Loose Point. Despite the foundation I laid for you in previous chapters, you may still have some doubts you'll need to expand through. If you felt impatient with me at various points during earlier chapters and wished I'd hurry up and get to the point, perhaps you'll feel some Appreciation now for why the book was created to unfold as it did.

Well, my friend, our journey, for now, is almost at its end. You've received nearly all the pieces of the puzzle this book was designed to offer you, the big picture has popped out into full view for you, and you can see it clearly. Now there's a decision to be made. When you're ready to take a look at that decision, turn the page and continue on to the final chapter, Chapter 16.

Red Pill or Blue Pill?

The world is round and the place which may seem like the end may also only be the beginning.[1]
—*Ivy Baker Priest (1905–1975), Public Official*

Nothing splendid has ever been achieved except by those who dared believe that something inside them was superior to circumstance.[2]
—*Bruce Barton, Advertising Executive, Religious Writer,*
Copywriter, and U.S. Congressman

The popular movie *The Matrix* includes some extremely supportive and Truthful material in it that directly applies to the Phase 2 journey and game. If you haven't seen it, I strongly encourage you to go out and rent a copy of the first movie in

[1] Ivy Baker Priest, in *Bits & Pieces* (Chicago: Ragan Communications, October 2004).

[2] Bruce Barton, in *Bits & Pieces* (Chicago: Ragan Communications, April 2005).

the trilogy as soon as you finish this book. You have to filter out some of the Phase 1 dynamics highlighted in the story line (especially the "good versus evil" battle) but once you do that, what's left is pure Phase 2 gold.

The journey of Neo, the main character in *The Matrix*, tracks very closely with the journey Phase 2 Players experience. At the beginning of the movie, Neo is going about his business playing within limits and restrictions in a world he thinks is real. Then along comes another character named Morpheus who tells him the world he thinks is real is really an illusion. At first, Neo doesn't believe Morpheus; he can't believe Morpheus because The Truth Morpheus shares is too alien for the belief systems Neo has in place at the time.

Morpheus then tells Neo he is "The One," which means Neo has more power than he can possibly imagine and a glorious destiny. Neo isn't able to accept that, either. But Morpheus then guides Neo on a journey of discovery through which Neo ultimately opens into a direct experience of The Truth of who he is, the power he has, and what he's really capable of while still playing within his illusion.

In one of the early scenes of the movie, when Neo has been drawn to Morpheus in search of The Truth, Morpheus offers Neo the choice of a red pill or a blue pill. "You take the blue pill," Morpheus says, "the story ends, you wake up in your bed and believe whatever you want to believe. You take the red pill, you stay in Wonderland, and I show you how deep the rabbit hole goes." Neo hesitates, then leans forward to take the red pill. Morpheus pauses, then says, "Remember, all I'm offering is The Truth, nothing more." Neo then swallows the red pill and begins his journey of expansion.

Just like Neo found his way to Morpheus, you found your way to me and this book because of your desire to know The Truth. Like Morpheus, I've offered you what is as close as I can get to The Truth, through The Busting Loose Model. Like Morpheus, I've taken you on a journey of discovery and shown you how deep the rabbit hole goes—how you too can open into a direct experience of The Truth of who you are, the power you have, and what you're really capable of while still playing within your illusion. Perhaps like Neo at the start of his journey, you're not *yet* ready to fully accept what I've shared with you. Or perhaps you're right there with me, anxious to begin your Phase 2 journey. Or perhaps you're somewhere in between.

As it appears to you right now, you may think you, the Player, have a choice to make about taking either the blue pill, which means staying in Phase 1, or taking the red pill, which means leaping into Phase 2. However, The Truth is that your Expanded Self has already chosen which pill you'll take (perhaps He or She has already given it to you), and your Expanded Self has a plan for you, regardless of which pill you end up swallowing or when you swallow it. As that plan gets executed, you will be taken into a direct experience of who you really are.

Will you end up taking the red pill? The blue pill? The blue pill now with a plan to take the red pill later? Only time will tell. But I can tell you that The Busting Loose Model isn't casual reading, dip-your-toe-in-the-water stuff, something you wander into accidentally. You wouldn't have created me and *this particular book* and popped it into your hologram unless one of the following is true for you:

- You're ready to enter Phase 2—now—and this book is your Launch Point.
- You plan to enter Phase 2 soon and want to get your feet wet before reaching the Launch Point and leaping off it.
- You want to play the Phase 1 game awhile longer but with enhanced awareness of The Truth about what's *really* going on.

As you wait to see how your story line unfolds after completing the book, the obvious questions are: What now? What's your Expanded Self going to do? How will you know what the decision is?

If this is your Launch Point into Phase 2, you'll know. You'll get what I call a "knock me over the head so I can't miss it" sign. Perhaps you already have gotten such a sign. You'll actually feel as if someone flipped a switch in your life and everything changed in that instant. You'll start seeing the "weird things" I discussed actually showing up in your hologram. You'll start experiencing unusual and intense discomfort, and you'll feel a natural motivation to apply the tools to drill through the cloud cover. Perhaps it will look and feel different for you, but *you will know* if and when you make the leap into Phase 2.

If you're getting ready to make the leap into Phase 2 and want to get your feet wet first by exposing yourself to The Busting Loose Model, things will appear to move the way they always did before you created this book, but you'll feel a subtle shift, a heightened level of anticipation, excitement, and awareness of what's going on around you as you wait to arrive at the Launch Point—like an astronaut waiting to enter the rocket ship and take off on an amazing journey into space.

If you're going to continue playing the Phase 1 game a while longer but with enhanced awareness of The Truth about what's really going on, things will appear to stay pretty much the same for you, but you'll notice yourself seeing the Phase 1 game with at least some of the X-ray vision this book helped you turn on—to one degree or another. Even if you still have doubts or feel skeptical about what you discovered here (or about me personally), or you feel like you've completely rejected The Busting Loose Model, your life—and business—will never be the same. You can't go on a ride like this, take it to the end, and not get off profoundly changed. It's just not possible. You may or may not be consciously aware of the impact these pages have had on you, but they've had deep impact—in one way or another.

I'm now going to share something with you that might surprise you. Through the preceding pages, I've discussed numerous intellectual concepts and metaphors with you. We've talked about Phase 1, Phase 2, illusions, Infinite Beings, judgment, games, cloud cover, the sun, holograms, illusions, and so on. As interesting, powerful, and transformative as they may already seem to you, all the concepts and metaphors only offer the following five forms of value:

1. Opening a gateway into Phase 2, which makes busting loose and playing The New Business Game possible.

2. Motivating you to leap through that gateway into Phase 2—if it's your time.

3. Providing a context in which it makes sense to use the drilling tools.

4. Motivating you to use the tools.

5. Creating a common language to use when discussing The Busting Loose Model and the Phase 2 game.

Think of it this way. Suppose I was invited onto a television show to be interviewed about The Busting Loose Model. Suppose the host said to me, "Hey, Robert, I understand you have this incredible tool called The Process that can help our audience. Tell me about it." Suppose I gave him the first step: Dive into the middle of discomfort and feel it fully. He'd get that instantly, as would his audience. Suppose I then gave him the second step: When the discomfort naturally hits a peak of intensity, tell The Truth about it. He'd likely ask, "Well, Robert, what *is* The Truth about it?" I'd tell him, "It's all an illusion, a creation of *your* Consciousness, a story masquerading as real, True Joy in disguise." I'd start to lose him and most if not all of his audience, right? As I move into the other steps—reclaiming power, appreciating yourself as Creator, and the creations themselves—I've lost the entire audience and the host completely, right? They have no idea what I'm talking about, and they would have zero motivation to leap into Phase 2 or use the tools.

When you have *all* the components of The Busting Loose Model in place, however, the tools and their components make sense, and you'll naturally feel motivated to leap into Phase 2 and use them, if it's your time. If that happens, nothing else matters!

If you leap into Phase 2 and use the tools on a regular basis to knock out cloud cover and expand, you can discard *all* the concepts and metaphors I've shared—if you choose—like someone with an injured leg ultimately discards the crutches once the injury is healed. For this reason, you also don't need to *believe*, fully understand, or fully agree with everything I've shared here. If you make the leap into Phase 2 and combine the tools to create and use your drill bit, the rest will take care of itself!

If you reach the Launch Point immediately or soon, you have your tool belt. You'll know when and how to use the drilling tools on the belt. If you become a Phase 2 Player, there are five key points I've already discussed that I will repeat now. You may not be able to fully accept or get all five points until you've knocked out a bunch of cloud cover, but I'm repeating them anyway so they will be freshly installed in what I call your "incubator." Here is a summary of the five key points, and then I'll discuss them individually:

1. Patience
2. Remembering
3. Trust
4. Appreciation
5. Expansion

Patience

As we've discussed, the Phase 2 journey is divided into two segments: The Expansion Segment and The Play Segment. In The Expansion Segment, you use the drilling tools to knock out cloud cover so you can:

- Remember who you really are.
- Reclaim power.
- Reaffirm The Truth—even when the illusion looks, sounds, tastes, smells, and feels exactly the opposite.
- Dramatically increase your Appreciation for yourself as the Creator of everything you experience, your creations, and the magnificence of The Human Game.
- Give yourself a guided tour of how you fooled yourself so brilliantly in Phase 1.

- Reexperience The Truth of who you really are so you can stay and play The New Business Game in The Human Game amusement park without limits and restrictions.

As I explained, drilling through the cloud cover is *not* to be accomplished overnight. The tools were designed to be applied over time, taking as long as your Expanded Self chooses to perfectly support you in playing The Human Game exactly the way you want to play it—and savoring each step in your expansion as you'd savor a fine wine, meal, novel, or play.

Your experience may be entirely different, but if you're like me, despite your new knowledge and awareness, there may still be many, many times when you become impatient, you want to make something you judge as bad go away or lessen in intensity, or you desperately want to get off the ride because it seems like it's getting too wild for you. If that happens—and again, it may *not* for you—be gentle with yourself. Give yourself a break. Realize that judgments and feelings like that are perfectly understandable in the light of the transition that is taking place from Phase 1 to Phase 2. Simply apply The Process to your feelings of discomfort and allow it to take you where it takes you. Ultimately, the feelings of impatience and discomfort will weaken and drop away.

Remembering

As much as possible, especially when the going appears to get tough, always remember three things. If you're like me—and again, you may create something different for yourself—remembering these three key points will help you persist and continue doing the Phase 2 work even if part of you feels like throwing in the towel.

1. *What's really going on.* You're reclaiming power, expanding, and changing in huge ways, even if it doesn't always look or feel like it.

2. *The Truth about the hologram in Phase 2*. Once you enter Phase 2, nothing in your hologram *or that happens in your business* will have any significance, meaning, importance, stability, or solidity except to the degree to which it supports you in using the drilling tools and doing the Phase 2 work.

3. *Your ultimate destination*. Playing The Human Game without limits or restrictions and The New Business Game is a treasure that is more valuable than any treasure you've ever heard about, read about, or seen in the movies, or that you could possibly imagine from your current perspective. The little I sketched for you about what it's like pales in comparison to what's really possible for you in Phase 2.

I also invite you to remember that you can't judge a creation— hate it, dislike it, or want to change it, fix it, improve it, or make it go away—*and* collapse and transform it simultaneously. Those are mutually exclusive events. At the start of your Phase 2 journey, you'll have tons of judgments as you're led to patterns in The Field and work to transform them. However, as you do the Phase 2 work, you'll see judgment naturally fall away as you continue to expand.

Key Point

In Phase 2, you must expand to the point where you can fully Appreciate an illusion *exactly as it is* before the door will open to transform it.

Remember that Phase 2 is not about logic, intellect, thinking, or trying to figure things out. It's about *feelings* and *direct experiences* of The Truth.

I also invite you to remember that as you move more deeply into Phase 2, everything I've shared with you in this book, even the things you're certain you fully understand and get (or absolutely disagree with), will become more and more real to you—and your understanding and grasp of them will deepen in ways you can't imagine right now. Look forward to these "aha" moments of expansion and remember to savor each one fully.

I also invite you to remember that the Hypnotic Goals that take up so much of your attention now may or may not still be there after you knock out cloud cover and expand. It's the True Goals that become the focus in Phase 2—what you really want. If your journey is like mine, this will be something that's fascinating to watch unfolding.

Finally, I invite you to remember that if you still have doubts about anything I've shared in this book (or about me personally), but make the commitment to play the Phase 2 game, your Expanded Self will give you proof that all of this is True (and that I'm legitimate) through the experiences you create and pop into your hologram. I absolutely guarantee it.

Trust

As quickly as you're able to do it, and you *will* be able to do it as you knock out cloud cover and expand, I invite you to let go of the illusion of wanting to control or manipulate the hologram. Let go of the Phase 1 trick of needing to be proactive and taking massive action to make things happen or get things done. Let go of goals, agendas, and investments in results and outcomes.

Trust your Expanded Self and simply follow its lead. Relax into the Phase 2 game and allow your Expanded Self to lead you to the treasure. When you're unable to fully trust or let go, give yourself a break and recognize it's just another opportunity to apply The Process, because distrust and holding on are just different forms of discomfort.

Appreciation

As Phase 2 unfolds for you, you're led to patterns in The Field, you collapse and transform them, and your story lines change. Do your best (and your best will expand) to Appreciate the magnificence of it all—you as the Creator of everything you experience, your creations, the entire Human Game, The Business Game, and the beauty and majesty of the expansion you experience in Phase 2.

As your wisdom, power, and abundance expand, Appreciate each moment of the opening and expansion. As more and more becomes possible for you in the hologram, Appreciate those ever-expanding possibilities.

As you experience discomfort, do your best (and your best will expand) to Appreciate the tremendous gift it brings (as opposed to the pain it appeared to bring in Phase 1) and the beautiful opportunity it gives you to knock out cloud cover and expand. If the going appears to get tough and you feel fried, burned out, or overwhelmed, Appreciate what a magnificent job you did of fooling yourself, since it's not possible for you to feel that way—only to create the illusion of feeling that way and convince yourself the illusion is real.

As you see—and experience—more and more of The Truth of who you really are and what your natural state really is, do your best (and your best will expand) to Appreciate yourself as the Player and your Expanded Self (The Real You) for how well you supported yourself in playing The Human Game through Phase 1 and Phase 2.

As you shift into living in reactive mode, taking your business (and personal life) one moment at a time, doing what you *feel* motivated or inspired to do (before or after applying The Process when you're uncomfortable), Appreciate the simplicity of the Phase 2 game and how much more joyous and relaxing your experience ultimately becomes as it simplifies down. In Phase 2, you have only four tools to manage, and the "what to do" and "how to do it" are very simple and easy—unlike your experience in Phase 1.

As you cross The Busting Loose Point, open to the infinite abundance that's your natural state, and ultimately begin playing The Human Game and The New Business Game without limits or restrictions, Appreciate the magnificence of that achievement, and revel in the joyfulness and creative ecstasy you open into.

As you experience all of this and much more beyond what I've sketched out for you, if you feel like thanking me or Appreciating me for writing this book and supporting you in playing the Phase 2 game, it's fine to include me, but *I'm always second in line.*

Remember, if you're aware of it, *you* created it, down to the smallest detail—including me and this book. If you do find yourself Appreciating me or this book, please put yourself first in line, thank and Appreciate yourself (and your Expanded Self), then include me if you still feel moved to. You created the illusion of me and this book because you decided that would be the most fun way to remind yourself of The Truth. The journey and wild ride we've taken together isn't about me. It's about *you.* I didn't do anything for you. You did it for yourself!

Expansion

If you swallow the red pill, leap into Phase 2, and use the drilling tools to knock out cloud cover and expand, you'll absolutely bust loose from the old Business Game, begin breathing your infinite abundance, and start playing The New Business Game.

However, the transformations in your Human Game experience won't stop with expansion in business and money, as cool as those are on their own. As I explained in the preceding chapter, expansion in Phase 2 extends into every nook and cranny in your hologram. As I've suggested, by doing the Phase 2 work, you'll also see expansion and the potential for creating extraordinary experiences in all areas of your life. You'll also give yourself opportunities to apply the drilling tools to patterns and sections of the cloud cover that have nothing to do with business.

You're now poised to begin the ultimate adventure available to anyone playing The Human Game and The Business Game. You're about to go on a hunt for a treasure more valuable than gold, more valuable than jewels, more valuable than all the oil deep underground, more valuable than the trillions of dollars on deposit in the banks of your hologram.

You're on the brink of opening into sources of power beyond anything you can imagine, True Joy beyond anything you can imagine, peace beyond anything you can imagine, fulfillment be-yond anything you can imagine, abundance beyond anything you can imagine, and creative ecstasy beyond anything you can imagine.

Here's another interesting tidbit for your incubator. Once you knock out enough cloud cover, you'll have a direct experience of The Truth that:

- Throughout Phase 1, no matter what it looked or felt like to you as the Player and how uncomfortable you were, and regardless of the various struggles you had as you perceived it, your Expanded Self (which means you) has *always* been having a blast playing The Human Game and The Business Game.

- Throughout Phase 2, no matter what it looks or feels like to you as the Player and how uncomfortable using the drilling tools appears to get for you, and regardless of the various struggles you may feel you have along the road to expansion, your Expanded Self (which means you) will *always* be having a blast playing The Human Game and The Business Game.

To hammer this point home, recall the experience of the Hollywood moviemaking creative team. If you're sitting in a movie theater watching a so-called horror movie, tragedy, or intense drama, where *bad* things appear to be happening to the characters, you may judge those experiences and think to yourself, "Oh, that's terrible!" But what was the experience of the creative team as they made the movie and when they watched the final cut? Joy, celebra-tion, Appreciation, and satisfaction, right? In general, they had the time of their lives playing their parts when making the film!

For example, when you see a character being stabbed and bleeding on the screen and think, "Oh, that's awful," the Hollywood special effects wizard who created the illusion is thinking, "Yes! Look how real the injury and blood look. I really nailed that one!" When you see a character who appears to be suffering emotionally or physically, the actor playing the role is thinking as he watches the film, "What a convincing performance! Way to go!" The same thing is true for you and your Human Game total-immersion movie experience. No matter what you see or experience in your hologram, your Expanded Self is having a blast and is saying, "Wow! I really pulled that illusion off. So cool. What fun!" As I explained in earlier chapters, as you use the drilling tools and expand in Phase 2, you'll feel more and more like the Hollywood creative team yourself—no matter what illusions you create and immerse yourself within.

You now have at your disposal everything you *need* to swallow the red pill, open a gateway into Phase 2, leap into Phase 2, start drilling through the cloud cover, and expand into a direct experience of The Truth of who you really are and what you're really capable of. If there's something else you *want* to support you through your Phase 2 journey (be it person, place, or thing), your Expanded Self will hand it to you on a silver platter. You won't need to go looking for it or work hard to find it.

The real journey for you is just beginning, as incredible as the journey offered by this book may have seemed to you. As you prepare to close the book and move on to see what's next in your story line, know that I wish you an ever-expanding experience of The Truth—the power, wisdom, abundance, and True Joy that is your natural state, and that is now absolutely within your grasp.

I have one final comment for you before we part ways—for now. The original draft of this book included three additional chapters, which were removed from the final book at the request of the publisher. One chapter included an advanced-level discussion of how your perspective changes as you move through Phase 2; another consisted of frequently asked questions by Phase 2 Players and my answers; and the third contained detailed stories and examples from my own Phase 2 journey and the journeys of other Phase 2 Players. Since I felt you might find the chapters supportive, I've made them available from my web site. Just visit this page to download your copies: www.bustingloose.com/chapters.html.

APPENDIX

Additional Support Resources

In this Appendix, I'd like to share with you additional resources that can support you in playing the Phase 2 game. I have divided the resources into ten groups:

1. Key Points
2. Movies and Television Shows
3. Phase 2 Player Communities
4. Books
5. Home Transformational Systems
6. Live Events
7. Mailing Lists
8. Twitter
9. Facebook
10. People, Resources, and Tools

Key Points

Throughout the book, I highlighted what I called Key Points. As a unit, they represent the core foundation that The Busting Loose Model rests on. If you'd like to have a list of all the Key Points so you can refer to them as a group, print them out and create wallet-sized reminder cards, post them in your environment to remind yourself of The Truth, or whatever use might support you on your journey, please visit the following page on my web site: www.bustingloose.com/keypoints2.html.

Movies and Television Shows

I find it helpful when integrating new ideas, especially radical ones, to have visual and emotional examples of what the new way of thinking and living can look and feel like—or to hammer key points home in powerful ways. That's why I recommend many different movies and television shows to Phase 2 Players. The list is constantly expanding. To download the most current list, visit here: www .bustingloose.com/movies.html.

Phase 2 Player Communities

There are four Phase 2 Player Communities that may interest you if you become a Phase 2 Player:

1. *Dynamite the Box Blog.* This is a blog I created to share multimedia streams of Consciousness, thoughts, feelings, experiences, and resources regarding playing The Human Game and The New Business Game in Phase 2—and to invite Players to comment on those thoughts: www.dynamitethebox.com.

2. *The True Joy Experience Blog.* This is a blog I created to share multimedia streams of Consciousness, thoughts, feelings,

experiences, and resources about opening into and living within the True Joy state, the ultimate in Phase 2 expansion: www.truejoyexperience.com.

3. *The Official Phase 2 Player Community*. This is a central location where Phase 2 Players can meet, interact with each other, share Phase 2 stories, help each other in many ways, receive support directly from me on playing the Phase 2 game (live and via audio, video, and text), and so much more. Based on feedback and requests from Phase 2 Players, this community is constantly expanding and evolving: www .phase2players.com.

4. *Business School of Consciousness*. This educational resource was created to give players of The New Business Game, and those seeking to expand into playing that game, a place to gather, interact with each other, share stories, help each other in many ways, receive support directly from me (live and via audio, video, and text), and more: www.business-school-of-consciousness.com.

Books

The following books are highly recommended for Phase 2 Players. I've included Amazon.com links for them, which I hope will still work as time passes. If not, simply look for them yourself at Amazon .com or your favorite bookstore.

The Field, by Lynne McTaggart

This book summarizes the latest research on The Field: what it is, how it works, and related additional scientific research. It's a very technical book, a difficult read for some, but you'll find it to be an invaluable resource if you want to go beyond what I've offered in this book as it relates to the science: www.bustingloose.com/field.

The Holographic Universe, by Michael Talbot

This book is a very easy and entertaining read that goes into much more detail on the hologram metaphor than I've given here. One of the most valuable aspects of the book is all the stories and illustrations of the holographic and "unreal" aspects of what we call reality. I strongly urge you to pick up a copy immediately and dive right in: www.bustingloose.com/Talbot.

Star Trek: The Next Generation

One of my favorite television shows was *Star Trek: The Next Generation.* Those shows included a character named Q, from an advanced race of beings who are omnipotent. While he's much more mischievous or devious than Infinite Beings really are, seeing that much power in motion can be supportive to Phase 2 Players. There's also a line of *Star Trek* books available with Q as the starring character. Look for them at your favorite bookstore, or check here for a listing of the books on Amazon.com (I hope the link will still work): www.bustingloose.com/qb.

Cradle to Cradle, by William McDonough

I talked about being able to play The Human Game and The New Business Game without limits or restrictions, and making up games no one has ever even thought of before. Bill McDonough is an amazing man and a friend of mine. He's not consciously playing the Phase 2 game (at the moment), but he's a great example of making up games to play that no one has even thought of before. This book summarizes many of the projects he's involved with related to recycling and the green building movement, and can be quite supportive and inspiring to you. The early part of the book brilliantly illustrates the limitations of Phase 1, and the rest describes the new games Bill created to play. Even the paper the book is printed on represents playing a game that's never been thought of before! www .bustingloose.com/cradle.

Home Transformational Systems

Books are great, and there's so much more that can be done live and with multimedia. You may be interested in exploring one or more of the following multimedia systems that were culled from my live events and enhanced for experiencing in the privacy of your own home. You may also want to refer someone you know or care about to one or more of them:

> *Busting Loose from The Money Game* www.busting-loose-from-the-money-game.com
>
> *Busting Loose from The Emotions Game* www.masteryofemotions.com
>
> *A Path to True Joy* www.pathtotruejoy.com
>
> *Journey to the Infinite* www.journeytotheinfinite.com

Other Home Transformational Systems may be released from time to time. To stay in the loop, visit this site: www.bustingloose.com/resources.html.

By the way, I mentioned how radically different my marketing is in Phase 2 as I play The New Business Game—how I simply create multimedia invitations for the projects I feel moved to share. The sites just listed will give you examples of that, what I call my "T.O.T. Model."

Live Events

You also may be interested in attending or referring someone to one of the multimedia live events I conduct to support or supplement what you've gained from this book. To get details and schedules for these events (I don't do many), and others that may be announced from time to time throughout the world, visit this page on my web site: www.robertscheinfeld.com/cms/events.

Mailing Lists

If you'd like to join my Phase 2 Player Mailing List or my General Mailing List to stay in touch and receive e-mail notification of opportunities within my sphere of influence, visit: www.robert scheinfeld.com/cms/email-list-signup.

Twitter

If you feel so moved, follow me on Twitter and receive a stream of highly supportive "tweets" on playing the Phase 2 game in your personal and business worlds: www.twitter.com/phase2player.

Facebook

I created a Facebook page for Phase 2 Players where we can gather, socialize, connect, network, and support each other. You can find that page here: www.rasd1.com/fbf.

People, Resources, and Tools

I use the tools offered in this book to play the Phase 2 game. However, within the context of living my life and playing The New Business Game in Phase 2, to make things more fun and interesting, I create support by networking with specific other aspects of myself, and use a variety of tools—hardware, software, Internet, and more. For a list of the people, resources, and tools I play with, and also the people who offered amazing support with the launch of this book, visit: www.bustingloose.com/resources-and-tools.html.

Expressions of Appreciation

The Human Game and The Business Game are team sports. In the end, it's just you playing in various disguises, but in the way it appears, you create other aspects of your Consciousness to play with you.

Along those lines, I created many aspects of myself to support me in creating the illusion of this book, and I'd like to express my appreciation for those aspects of myself here. I'm expressing my appreciation purely as a stream of Consciousness, with no importance placed on the order in which they appear.

The illustrations in the book were created beautifully and brilliantly by my graphic designer friend Dale Novak, of Novak Creative Services (www.novakcreative.net). I appreciate you and your work immensely, Dale. I love the feeling I get when I look at the illustrations and am reminded that we partnered once again on this project!

Brian Bevirt partnered with me, for the third time, on initial editing and the technical aspects of preparing the manuscript for my publisher. I appreciate so much how easy that made the process of creating the book for me. My hat's off to you, Brian, as the old saying goes. I appreciate you and your contributions very much.

In the story line, this book would not be appearing in my hologram if it weren't for the ongoing enthusiasm and support for me and my work I've created to flow through Richard Narramore, my editor at John Wiley & Sons. Richard, my appreciation for you and your continued support of my work is off the charts!

The first puzzle pieces I received on my journey toward busting loose came from my grandfather, Aaron Scheinfeld. In the story line, he did not live long enough for a scene to play out in which I expressed my appreciation for him and his support in person. Therefore, I'm doing it now: Gramps, you got me started on a most incredible journey, and the appreciation I feel for you and that journey cannot be described in words.

I created what I call a "soul dog" named Peri to support me on my journey. She's an American Eskimo. As I wrote this book, as I've created all my Phase 2 materials, and for the past 14 years, she's been at my side as my co-pilot. In my Human Experience, I created Peri to be a shining light and an amazing embodiment of True Joy and unconditional love, devotion, and loyalty, which are subsets of that state. At the time of this writing, I am creating her to be in the process of exiting my hologram stage left through the illusions called "old age" and "death." Peri, your shining light, example, and embodiment of True Joy meant more to me than I can ever express in any way—and kept me going through what appeared to be so many tough times in Phase 1—and in Phase 2.

I'd like to express my appreciation to John Assaraf for writing the Foreword. In the story line, that form of support took courage and a form of friendship and commitment to sharing The Truth I rarely experienced until I started playing the Phase 2 game. Cheers, John!

I would not be where I am today as a Phase 2 Player if it were not for the support I created being provided in the disguise of Arnold Patent, especially on two separate occasions when I created the illusion of really struggling as I played the Phase 2 game. As much as anyone can feel the appreciation I feel for this, I know you do, Arnold, but I wanted to express it in words here anyway.

When I was in Phase 1 and at my most neurotic and unhappy (to use a couple of judgmental terms), when the cloud cover was its most dense, I created the belief that I did not want to get married or be a father. At the time, I felt I would fail miserably at both and did not want to inflict that kind of pain on anyone. Despite that, when I created meeting my wife Cecily ("Beauty," as I call her), I felt moved to marry her, which I did. When we got married, I still did not want to have kids, but knew Cecily wanted to and that I was committing myself to having kids anyway. I still felt I'd be a terrible father! But then we co-created two extraordinary children, Ali and Aidan; and every day that passes, the appreciation I feel for them, and for the family I never thought I'd have, grows, and just when I thought it couldn't get any bigger, it does! They have also been of such *huge* support to me as I've played the Phase 2 game, made the discoveries I share with you in this book, and created the radical transformations I have in playing The Human Game and The New Business Game.

I'd like to express my appreciation for you, the reader of this book, as well as the readers of my other books, attendees of my live events, members of the Phase 2 Players Community, buyers of my multimedia Home Transformational Systems, followers on Twitter, fans of the Phase 2 Player Facebook page, and all others who have been created to support me in playing The Writing Game and The Teaching Game in Phase 2. Without you, I would not be able to play these games I enjoy so much, and my appreciation for you, too, can never be adequately expressed with words (but I'm trying anyway)!

Last but not least, I must also express my most expanded form of appreciation, once again, for "B.W.," a mentor of mine (*mentor* isn't really the correct word, but no word exists for the role he played on my journey and the support he gave me), who prefers to remain anonymous and in the background for now.

INDEX